A Book Of

BASICS OF COST ACCOUNTING

B.B.A. Semester - II
(Bachelor of Business Administration)
As Per Revised Syllabus

Dr. Suhas Mahajan
B.A., M.Com., Ph.D. (Finance)
Research Guide, Univeristy of Pune and YCMOU,
Nashik.

Dr. Mahesh Kulkarni
M.Com., M. Phil., L.L.B., D.T.L., Ph.D. (Management)
Research Guide, Univeristy of Pune and YCMOU,
Nashik.

N2914

Basics of Cost Accounting (BBA Semester I) ISBN 978-93-83750-35-1

Third Edition : January 2016
© : Authors

The text of this publication, or any part thereof, should not be reproduced or transmitted in any form or stored in any computer storage system or device for distribution including photocopy, recording, taping or information retrieval system or reproduced on any disc, tape, perforated media or other information storage device etc., without the written permission of Authors with whom the rights are reserved. Breach of this condition is liable for legal action.

Every effort has been made to avoid errors or omissions in this publication. In spite of this, errors may have crept in. Any mistake, error or discrepancy so noted and shall be brought to our notice shall be taken care of in the next edition. It is notified that neither the publisher nor the authors or seller shall be responsible for any damage or loss of action to any one, of any kind, in any manner, therefrom.

Published By :
NIRALI PRAKASHAN
Abhyudaya Pragati, 1312, Shivaji Nagar,
Off J.M. Road, PUNE – 411005
Tel - (020) 25512336/37/39, Fax - (020) 25511379
Email : niralipune@pragationline.com

Printed By :
Repro Knowledgecast Limited,
Thane

☞ DISTRIBUTION CENTRES

PUNE
Nirali Prakashan : 119, Budhwar Peth, Jogeshwari Mandir Lane, Pune 411002, Maharashtra
Tel : (020) 2445 2044, 66022708, Fax : (020) 2445 1538
Email : bookorder@pragationline.com, niralilocal@pragationline.com

Nirali Prakashan : S. No. 28/27, Dhyari, Near Pari Company, Pune 411041
Tel : (020) 24690204 Fax : (020) 24690316
Email : dhyari@pragationline.com, bookorder@pragationline.com

MUMBAI
Nirali Prakashan : 385, S.V.P. Road, Rasdhara Co-op. Hsg. Society Ltd.,
Girgaum, Mumbai 400004, Maharashtra
Tel : (022) 2385 6339 / 2386 9976, Fax : (022) 2386 9976
Email : niralimumbai@pragationline.com

☞ DISTRIBUTION BRANCHES

JALGAON
Nirali Prakashan : 34, V. V. Golani Market, Navi Peth, Jalgaon 425001,
Maharashtra, Tel : (0257) 222 0395, Mob : 94234 91860

KOLHAPUR
Nirali Prakashan : New Mahadvar Road, Kedar Plaza, 1st Floor Opp. IDBI Bank
Kolhapur 416 012, Maharashtra. Mob : 9850046155

NAGPUR
Pratibha Book Distributors : Above Maratha Mandir, Shop No. 3, First Floor,
Rani Jhanshi Square, Sitabuldi, Nagpur 440012, Maharashtra
Tel : (0712) 254 7129

DELHI
Nirali Prakashan : 4593/21, Basement, Aggarwal Lane 15, Ansari Road, Daryaganj
Near Times of India Building, New Delhi 110002
Mob : 08505972553

BENGALURU
Pragati Book House : House No. 1, Sanjeevappa Lane, Avenue Road Cross,
Opp. Rice Church, Bengaluru – 560002.
Tel : (080) 64513344, 64513355,Mob : 9880582331, 9845021552
Email:bharatsavla@yahoo.com

CHENNAI
Pragati Books : 9/1, Montieth Road, Behind Taas Mahal, Egmore,
Chennai 600008 Tamil Nadu, Tel : (044) 6518 3535,
Mob : 94440 01782 / 98450 21552 / 98805 82331,
Email : bharatsavla@yahoo.com

niralipune@pragationline.com | www.pragationline.com
Also find us on www.facebook.com/niralibooks

Preface ...

There are a number of books on the subject of 'Basics of Cost Accounting' available in the learner's market, but they do not meet the basic requirements of B.B.A. (Bachelor of Business Administration) Semester – II. This book is written as per the syllabus for B.B.A., Semester – II, students from June, 2013. We do hope that this book will definitely help to meet the growing requirements of students of B.B.A., from the faculty of commerce. This book adopts a modern and novel approach towards the study of Cost Accounting in view with the specific requirements of the readers and practitioners of this subject.

All the topics included in the syllabus are explained in simple, but apt language so that the students coming from different faculties can also understand them very easily. Besides the language, care is also taken to solve the problems at the end of each unit with the help of appropriate illustrations, wherever necessary. This will help the students in understanding the different topics properly. We have taken tabular representation of classified cost statements. Proper emphasis is also given on charts and graphs to simplify the cost accounting theories and practices. This book has been designed to serve as a self sufficient text for B.B.A. students. It will definitely add to our satisfaction if this book would be more useful as a reference for practicing accountants, professional managers, dynamic entrepreneurs and enthusiastic teachers of the subject concern. This book is also useful for M.Com., D.B.M., M.B.A., M.C.M., Diploma in Hotel Management and Diploma in Hospital Management and many other professional courses.

We are very thankful to Shri. Dineshbhai Furia, Shri. Jignesh Furia, Malik Shaikh, Prasad Chintakindi and the entire staff of Nirali Prakashan, Pune, for their earnest help in bringing out this book with vigour and accuracy. We have put in maximum efforts to make the text error free. Nevertheless, we do not rule out the possibility of certain shortcomings or misprints still remaining. We will be grateful to the readers, if such errors are being pointed out from time to time.

We must concede that this book would never have been written without the support, encouragement and inspiration of our family members, many, many thanks to them.

Any criticism or valuable suggestion for further improvement of this book will be greatfully acknowledged and highly appreciated.

Sankashti Chaturthi
21st November, 2013
Pune 411021

Dr. Mahesh Kulkarni
Dr. Suhas Mahajan

University of Pune
BBA (Semester - II)

Basics of Cost Accounting
Course Code 204

Syllabus and Contents ...

Unit 1 - Introduction   1.1 - 1.22
  1.1 Concept of Cost, Costing, Cost Accounting and Cost Accountancy
  1.2 Limitations of Financial Accounting
  1.3 Origin, Objectives and Features of Cost Accounting
  1.4 Advantages and Limitations of Cost Accounting
  1.5 Difference between Financial and Cost Accounting
  1.6 Conceptual Analysis of Cost Unit and Cost Centre   **(8L)**

Unit 2 - Elements of Cost and Cost Sheet   2.1 - 2.58
  2.1 Material, Labour and Other Expenses
  2.2 Classification of Cost and Types of Costs
  2.3 Preparation of Cost Sheet   **(10L)**

Unit 3 - Overheads   3.1 - 3.42
  3.1 Meaning and Definitions
  3.2 Classification of Overheads
  3.3 Collection, Allocation, Apportionment and Reapportionment of Overheads
  3.4 Under and Over absorption - Definition and Reasons   **(8L)**

Unit 4 - Methods of Costing   4.1 - 4.96
  4.1 Contract Costing - Meaning and Features of Contract Costing, Works Certified and Uncertified, Escalation Clause, Cost Plus Contract, Work in progress, Profit on Incomplete Contract.
  4.2 Process Costing - Meaning, Features of Process Costing, Preparation of Process Accounts including Normal and Abnormal Loss/Gains
  4.3 Service Costing - Meaning, Features and Application, Cost Unit - Simple and Composite, Preparation of Cost Sheet for Transport Service   **(16L)**

Unit 5 - Cost Audit   5.1 - 5.14
  5.1 Meaning, Definition, Objectives and Scope
  5.2 Advantages of Cost Audit
  5.3 Difference between Financial and Cost Audit
  5.4 Types of Cost Audit   **(6L)**
  (48 L)

- **AT A GLANCE**
  - Glossary   G.1 - G.6
  - Objective Questions
    - True / False Statements   T.1 - T.4
    - Fill in the Blanks   F.1 - F.7
  - Bibliography   B.1 - B.1
- **University Question Paper: October 2014, April 2015**   P.1 - P.6

***

List of Figures, Graphs and Charts ...

1.	Cost Concepts	1.2
2.	Limitations of Financial Accounting	1.6
3.	Objectives of Cost Accounting	1.10
4.	Advantages of Cost Accounting	1.13
5.	Types of Cost Centres	1.20
6.	Elements of Cost	2.2
7.	Division of Cost	2.8
8.	Need of Cost Classification	2.9
9.	Classification of Cost	2.10
10.	Classification of Cost on basis of Traceability, Elements and Functions	2.13
11.	Behaviour of Fixed Cost	2.14
12.	Behaviour of Variable Cost	2.14
13.	Behaviour of Semi-variable Cost	2.15
14.	Behaviour of Fixed, Variable and Semi-variable Cost	2.15
15.	Types of Costs	2.18
16.	Composition of Conversion Cost	2.19
17.	Proforma of Cost Sheet	2.23
18.	Composition of Overheads	3.4
19.	Classification of Overheads	3.5
20.	Features of Fixed Overheads	3.8
21.	Features of Variable Overheads	3.9
22.	Features of Semi-variable Overheads	3.10
23.	Steps involved in Overheads Accounting i.e. Panchasutri of Overheads Accounting	3.14
24.	Methods of Re-apportionment of Service Department Overhead Costs	3.29
25.	Accounting Treatment for Disposal of Under or Over-absorbed Overheads	3.37
26.	Various Methods of Costing	4.4
27.	Process Cost Flow	4.50
28.	Objectives of Cost Audit	5.3
29.	Advantages of Cost Audit	5.8

***

Unit ... 1

INTRODUCTION

1.1 Concept of Cost, Costing, Cost Accounting and Cost Accountancy
1.2 Limitations of Financial Accounting
1.3 Origin, Objectives and Features of Cost Accounting
1.4 Advantages and Limitations of Cost Accounting
1.5 Difference between Financial Accounting and Cost Accounting
1.6 Conceptual Analysis of Cost Unit and Cost Centre
* Questions for Self-Study

In today's competitive environment, the nature and functioning of business organisations have become very complicated. Various parties viz., owners, creditors, employees, government agencies, tax authorities, investors, management of the business etc. are interested in the functioning of the business. Accounting provides substantial information to all these parties. In order to satisfy their needs, a sound organisation of accounting system is essential. The needs of the majority of the users of accounting information can be satisfied by Financial Accounting. Financial Accounting is mainly concerned with preparation of two important statements, viz. Profit and Loss Account and Balance Sheet. This information serves the needs of all those who are not directly associated with the management of business. To carry out the functions of planning, decision-making and control more efficiently, the management require more analytical information relating to cost. The Financial Accounting system fails to some extent to provide all these required information to management and hence a new system of accounting necessitates, which fulfils all the needs of management. Thus, **Cost Accounting** is developed to offset the limitations of **Financial Accounting**. Broadly speaking, there are three branches of accounting viz., Financial Accounting, Cost Accounting and Management Accounting which are concerned with presenting business data to the users.

The following example clearly indicates the need and importance of Cost Accounting as a separate branch of accounting, which has emerged mainly because of the limitations of Financial Accounting.

EXAMPLE

Godrej Ltd.; Gorakhpur a leading soap manufacturer runs three separate divisions viz. Hamam, Rexona and Liril. Their books of accounts for the year 2012-13 discloses the annual results as follows : Actual Turnover ₹ 3,00,000, Expenses incurred ₹ 2,00,000.

Evaluate their business performances.

ANSWER

A) Evaluation of Business Performance by Finance Department.

In the books of Godrej Ltd., Gorakhpur
Profitability Statement for the year ended 31st March, 2013

Particulars		₹
Sales		3,00,000
Less: Expenses	(−)	2,00,000
∴ Profit		1,00,000
Percentage of Profit to Sales		33 1/3%

Comments:

During the year 2012-13, the overall company's financial performance is good as the profits are 33 1/3% of sales.

B) Evaluation of Business Performance by Cost Accounting Department.

In the books of Godrej Ltd., Gorakhpur
Profitability Statement for the year ended 31st March, 2013

Particulars		Divisions			Total
		Hamam ₹	Rexona ₹	Liril ₹	₹
Sales		1,50,000	1,00,000	50,000	3,00,000
Less: Costs	(−)	90,000	70,000	40,000	2,00,000
∴ Profit		60,000	30,000	10,000	1,00,000
Percentage of Profit to Sales		40%	30%	20%	33 1/3%

Comments:

During the year 2012-13, all divisions are working satisfactorily as the overall performance shows a substantial profit of 33 1/3% of actual turnover. Hamam division is earning more profits as compared to Rexona and Liril. As well Rexona division is more profitable as compared to Liril division. It is advisable to exercise additional efforts to control the costs and increase the turnover of particularly Liril division to increase the profit margins substantially.

1.1 CONCEPT OF COST, COSTING, COST ACCOUNTING AND COST ACCOUNTANCY

It is necessary to understand some of the important Cost Concepts used very often in the business world, which are shown in Figure 1.1 as follows.

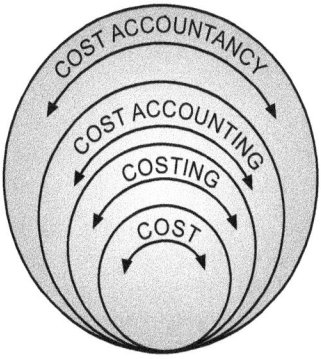

Fig. 1.1 : Cost Concepts

Cost

Meaning and Definitions:

The term "**Cost**" may be defined as a noun or a verb as follows:

1. **As a noun:**

    The amount of expenditure (actual or notional) incurred on or attributable to specified thing or activity.

2. **As a verb:**

    To ascertain the cost of specified thing or activity.

    The term 'Cost' is defined, in different ways by various authorities as follows:

i) *I.C.M.A., London:*

"Cost is the amount of expenditure (actual or notional) incurred on or attributable to a specified thing or activity".

ii) *Crowningshield:*

"It is an expenditure made to secure an economic benefit, generally resources that promise to produce revenue. The resources may have tangible substance (material or machinery) or they may take the form of services (wages, rent, power)".

iii) *Shillinglaw:*

"Cost represents the resources that must be sacrificed to attain a particular objective".

iv) *The Committee on Cost Concepts and Standards of the American Accounting Association:*

"It is the foregoing, in monetary terms incurred or potentially to be incurred to achieve a specific objective".

v) *Anthony and Welsh:*

"Cost is a measurement in monetary terms, of the amount of resources used for some purposes".

vi) *A. I. C. P. A. Committee on terminology:*

"It is the amount measured in money or cash expended or other property transferred, capital stock issued, services performed, or a liability incurred in consideration of goods or services received or to be received".

vii) *W. M. Harper:*

"It is the value of economic resources used as a result of producing or doing the thing costed".

viii) *Oxford Dictionary:*

"Cost is the price paid for something".

Again, the general concept of **Cost** which is most widely used is the "money cost" of production. Another concept of cost is the real cost according to Marshall. Again "Opportunity Cost" concept is there which means the sacrifice made for not utilising the other alternatives.

From the above definitions, we can conclude that **Cost** is the total of all expenses incurred, whether paid or outstanding, in the manufacturing and sale of product or those incurred in giving a service. **Costs** are calculated from the point of view of management which expects costs to perform three functions i.e. cost computation, cost control and cost analysis. Thus, the concept of **Cost** depends upon the purpose for which it is used, the conditions under which it is employed and the people who intend to use this concept. From the management point of view, the cost may be direct, indirect, prime, conversion, joint product, period, controllable, out of pocket, imputed, differential, marginal, standard etc. In short, **Cost** is a sacrifice made to achieve something and measured in terms of money and has always been used with some specific objective. It depends upon many factors and it changes with the changes in factors.

Costing

Meaning and Definitions :

Costing is simply 'cost finding'. It is the process, technique and procedure of ascertaining the costs. It includes all the principles, rules and regulations of calculating the costs.

The term **'Costing'** is defined in different ways by various authorities as follows :

i) *I.C.M.A., London :*

"It is the technique and process of ascertaining costs".

ii) *Wheldon :*

"Costing is the classifying, recording and appropriate allocation of expenditure for the determination of the costs of products or services and for the presentation of suitably arranged data for the purposes of control and guidance of the management. It includes the ascertainment of the cost of every order, job, contract, process, service or unit as may be appropriate. It deals with the cost of production, selling and distribution".

iii) *Harold James :*

"Costing is the proper allocation of expenditure, whereby, reliable cost may be ascertained and suitably presented to afford guidance to the producers in control of their business".

From the above definitions we can summarise that, **Costing** is a technique of ascertaining the cost. This technique is however, dynamic and changes with the changes in time. **Costing** can be carried out by the process of arithmetic, memorandum, statements etc. The costs may be either ascertained from the historical records i.e. after they have been incurred or by the pre-determined standards and analysis of variances between the standard and the actuals or by using the marginal costing method i.e. by differentiating the fixed and variable costs.

Cost Accounting

Meaning and Definitions:

Cost Accounting is the process of accounting for costs. It begins with the recording of income and expenditure and ends with the preparation of periodical statements. The term **'Cost Accounting'** is defined in different ways by various authorities as follows :

i) *Kohler :*

"It is that branch of accounting dealing with the classification, recording, allocation, summarisation and reporting of current and prospective costs".

ii) *Wheldon :*

"It is the classifying, recording and appropriate allocation of expenditure for the determination of the costs of products or services, the relation of these costs to sales values and the ascertainment of profitability".

iii) *Van Sickle :*

"Cost Accounting is the science of recording and presenting business transactions pertaining to the production of goods and services, whereby these records become a method of measurement and means of control".

iv) *Shillinglow* :

"Cost Accounting as a body of concepts, methods and procedures used to measure, analyse or estimate the costs, profitability and performance of individual products, departments and other sequences of a company's operations, for either internal or external use or both and to report on these questions to the interested parties".

v) *I.C.M.A., London* :

"It is the process of accounting for cost from the point at which expenditure is incurred or committed to the establishment of its ultimate relationship with cost centres and cost units". In its widest usage, it embraces the preparation of statistical data, the application of cost control methods and the ascertainment of the profitability of activities carried out or planned.

An analysis of the above comprehensive definitions reveals some of the important functions of **Cost Accounting**. **Cost Accounting** refers to the formal mechanism or a systematic procedure by means of which costs of products and services are computed. This is one of the important aspects which distinguishes **Cost Accounting** from **Costing**.

Cost Accountancy

Meaning and Definition :

It is the application of Costing and Cost Accounting principles, methods and techniques. It is also the science, art and practice of controlling the costs and ascertainment of profitability. **Cost Accountancy** is mainly concerned with the presentation of costing data to the management in a precise form, so that vital decisions can be taken by the management.

- It is a *science* because there are certain definite principles which are followed in cost accountancy.
- It is an *art* because it is the ability and skill of the cost accountant to apply the principles of cost accountancy to solve the intricate and complex problems of the management.
- It is a *practice* because a cost accountant has to keep himself abreast of the latest developments. He has to present the data to the management in a most up-to-date manner with latest techniques and methods for taking various decisions.

The term **'Cost Accountancy'** is defined as follows :

i) *I.C.M.A. London* :

"It is the application of costing and cost accounting principles, methods and techniques to the science, art and practice of cost control and the ascertainment of profitability. It includes the presentation of information derived therefrom, for the purpose of managerial decision-making".

Thus, Cost Accountancy is a comprehensive term and includes the various aspects such as costing, cost accounting, cost control and cost audit and budgetary control.

The Difference between Costing, Cost Accounting and Cost Accountancy can be shown as follows:

Points of Distinction	Costing	Cost Accounting	Cost Accountancy
i) Scope	It is broader in its scope	It is narrow in its scope	It is broadest in its scope
ii) Function	It is concerned with the ascertainment of costs	It is concerned with recording of cost	It is concerned with the formulation of costing principles, methods and techniques to be adopted by a business
iii) Periodicity of functioning	It begins where cost accountancy ends	It begins, where costing ends	It is a starting point
iv) Persons involved	The person involved is cost accountant	The persons involved are cost clerks	The persons involved are experts in the field of cost accountancy such as management accountant.

1.2 LIMITATIONS OF FINANCIAL ACCOUNTING

Financial Accounting is mainly concerned with recording business transactions in the books of accounts for the purpose of presenting final accounts to the Board of Directors, shareholders and tax authorities etc. The objective of Financial Accounting is to present a true and fair view of the company's income, financial position and funds at regular intervals.

In the modern business world, business concerns need some methods and ways by which they can measure their performance. Financial Accounting cannot serve this purpose at all. The indications given by Profit and Loss Account and Balance Sheet are generally inadequate. It is just like thermometer which only indicates the temperature of human body. Only judgements can be made on the basis of such thermometer and a good doctor will have to conduct a number of other checks in order to see what the patient is suffering from. The profit shown by Profit and Loss Account should not be taken as a sign of success because there may be a loss on certain items which might have been compensated by the profit of certain other items. Information regarding wastages and losses is very difficult to be obtained from financial accounts and it is only Cost Accounts which makes such information available to the management. So Cost Accounting, has emerged mainly because of certain **Limitations of Financial Accounting** which are shown in Figure 1.2 as follows.

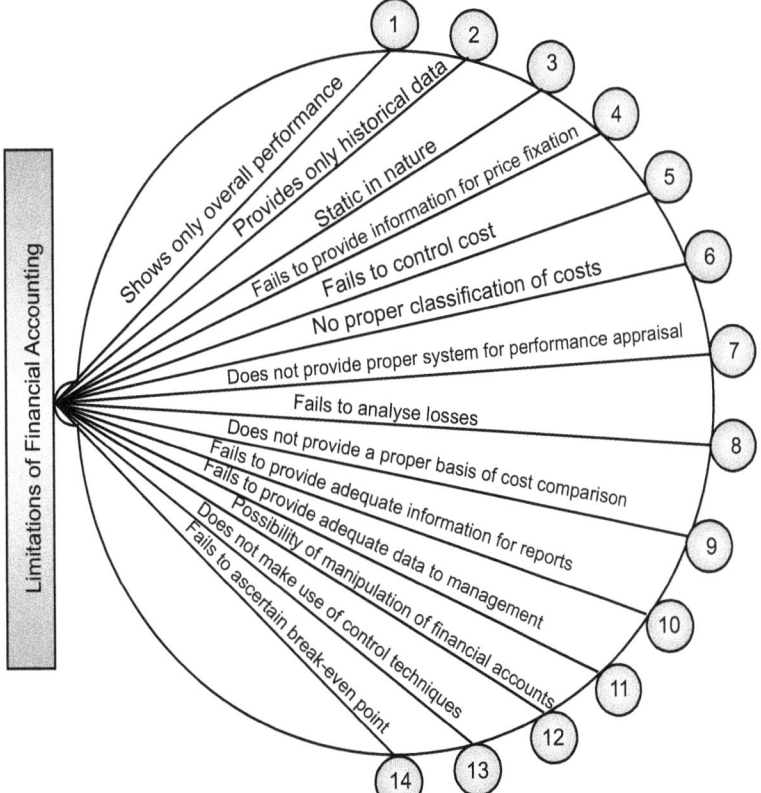

Fig. 1.2 : Limitations of Financial Accounting

i) It shows only Overall Performance :

Financial Accounting provides information about profit, loss, cost etc. of the collective activities of the business as a whole. It does not provide data for each and every product, process, department or operation separately.

ii) It provides only Historical Data :

Financial Accounting is historical in nature and it provides data of past activities. It does not provide current data which management requires for making effective plans for future. So it is rightly said that financial accounts provide only a post-mortem analysis of past activities. It does not help in fixation of selling price.

iii) It is Static in Nature :

Modern business is dynamic and not static. Financial Accounts does not incorporate the changes that takes place within the business.

iv) It fails to provide information for Price Fixation :

In Financial Accounting, costs are not available by division, products, process etc. So, price fixation becomes difficult and estimates cannot be prepared.

v) It fails to Control Cost :

Financial Accounts fail to exercise control over materials, labour and other expenses incurred in a business enterprise. As a result, avoidable wastages and losses remains as it is under this system.

vi) No proper Classification of Costs :

In Financial Accounting, expenses are not classified into direct and indirect, fixed and variable and controllable and uncontrollable. These classifications have utility of their own.

vii) It does not provide proper System for Performance Appraisal :

In Financial Accounting there is no system of developing norms and standards to appraise the efficiency in the use of materials, labour and other costs by comparing the actual performance with what should have been accomplished during a given period of time.

viii) It fails to Analyse Losses :

Financial Accounting does not fully analyse the losses due to idle time, idle plant capacities, inefficient labour, sub-standard materials etc.

ix) It does not provide a Basis of Cost Comparison :

Financial Accounting does not provide cost data regarding operations of the enterprise for the purpose of comparing such data with other periods of operations or other concerns in the industry.

x) It fails to provide Adequate Information for Reports :

It does not provide adequate information for reports to outside agencies like banks, government, insurance companies and trade associations.

xi) It fails to provide adequate Data to Management :

Financial Accounting fails to supply useful data to management for taking various decisions like replacement of labour by machines, introduction of new products, make or buy decisions, selection of the most profitable product mix etc.

xii) Possibility of Manipulation of Financial Accounts:

Very often Financial Accounts are manipulated at the *whim* and *fancies* of the management so as to project a better image in the minds of prospective investors. Financial Accounts may be manipulated by making under or overvaluation of machinery, excessive or inadequate provisions for depreciation, creation of secret reserves etc.

xiii) It does not make use of Control Techniques:

Financial Accounts fail to make use of certain important cost control techniques, such as Budgetary Control, Standard Costing, and so on. Thus, financial accounts do not facilitate in measuring the efficiency of the business with the help of control techniques.

xiv) It fails to ascertain Break-Even Point:

Financial Accounting does not help in ascertaining the break-even point. i.e. the sale or output where the revenue equals the cost. Hence, the point of no profit-no loss cannot be found out under financial accounts.

1.3 ORIGIN, OBJECTIVES AND FEATURES OF COST ACCOUNTING

Origin of Cost Accounting

The science of **Cost Accounting** is of recent origin. The idea of Cost Accounting started in the early years of the 20th century, when the concept of large scale production in the factories started growing. It made the traditional accounting system bulky. The new problems in accounting faced by the factories were numerous. With the increase in the production, different types of costs were found to have different rules on the cost structures of the products. Thus, the variety of expenditures increased and many new items of costs entered the calculations and became vital for taking important decisions by the management.

Costing is a branch of accounting, which has developed because of the limitations of Financial Accounts. It was developed because of certain needs of management which financial account could not meet. The modern industrial requirements were different and to fulfil these requirements some new methods and principles of accounting became necessary over the old traditional method of financial accounting system. This resulted into the outcome of the "Cost Accounting systems". The requirements of management may be summarised as follows:

i) Measurement of performance and efficiency:

To face severe competition in the business world, a management always needs to maintain their customers. Therefore, to evaluate the present product and market it, it is necessary to measure the performance and business efficiency. Financial accounts cannot serve this purpose at all. In normal times, we can say that profit or loss shown by Profit and Loss account is an indicator of overall efficiency or inefficiency. But in the periods of inflation or depression this may not be true. So the management, would be well advised to ascertain the profit or loss of each product separately. Besides this, management must also try to see that in producing each unit of product there is no unnecessary wastage or loss as regards materials, labour and other expenses. This information is available to the management only under Cost Accounting System. Again a management can know the exact reason of profit or loss by making proper cost analysis which is possible only in cost accounts.

ii) Pricing:

For fixing prices of products or services, it is necessary to have information regarding each product or unit of service rather than total expenditure. Only, Cost Accounting system can provide this information to the management.

iii) Control:

To maximise profits by minimising costs, it is necessary to set up standards and then compare actual costs with these standards. The reason for the discrepancy may be ascertained and then only possible action can be taken to rectify the situation. Such action is possible only in Cost Accounting.

iv) Forecasting:

For planning in future, preparation of budgets are necessary. Budgets are prepared on the basis of forecasts of future costs and revenue. In this field also, Cost Accounting is more capable of helping management than Financial Accounting.

v) Day-to-Day decisions:

Besides price fixing decisions, various other decisions have to be taken continuously such as make or buy, whether an old machine should be replaced by a new one, when operational activities be stopped or started, whether an order at concessional rate should be accepted or not etc. Cost accounting is able to provide the necessary information for such decisions.

Thus, the need for Cost Accounting arises because of the management's requirement to know the cost of various activities in various circumstances. Costing has a vital role to play in almost any activity which involves expenditure of money, whether it is a business house or a charitable concern or whether it is a Government Department.

Development of Cost Accounting Phenomenon:

The growth of **Cost Accounting** could be seen during the First World War i.e. 1914-1919 which was rapid, due to the control on the prices imposed by the Government. The Government entered into the "Cost-Plus" contract systems. Cost plus contract provides for the payment by the customers or the contractee of the actual cost of manufacture or of rendering service plus a stipulated profit. This necessitated the maintenance of cost records, ascertainment of cost and cost control for a job or service rendered. Due to increase in competition and rapid growth in the international trade, industries became more cost conscious. In 1929, there was a great depression in the economy during which survival of most of the industries became a problem. Hence, cost reduction techniques had to be adopted for survival.

In today's world of competition, cost consciousness is the key factor for determining the growth of the industrial economy. Ours is a developing country, where we have mixed economy and hence we are having mixed problems. We are facing acute inflation problem, depression in the industries and stagnation in the economy. Hence, cost reduction has become the need of the hour. Therefore, the industrialists must have a perfect knowledge of costs, so that they can take various decisions regarding planning, pricing, budgeting, policy making of the company regarding fixation of wages etc. Thus, the study of **Cost Accounting** is of utmost importance in our country because unless we reduce the costs, we cannot survive in the competitive world and have progress of our economy.

Cost Accounting in Indian Context:

The application of **Cost Accounting** methods in Indian industries was felt from the beginning of the 20th century. The following factors have accelerated the system of Cost Accounting in our country.

i) Increased awareness of cost consciousness by Indian industrialists with a view to ascertain costs more accurately for each product or job.

ii) Growing competition among manufacturers led to fixation of prices at a lower level, so as to attract more customers.

iii) Government economic policy emphasising on planned economy.

iv) Increased Government control over pricing led the Indian manufacturers to give more importance to the installation of cost accounts.

v) The establishment of National Productivity Council in 1958 and a statutory body viz. Institute of Cost and Works Accountants of India.

By realising importance of Cost Accounting techniques, benefits available to the industries, Government of India has made compulsory the maintenance of cost accounts to most of the industries in the corporate sector. For development of cost accounting profession in India, Government passed an Act viz. **"Cost and Works Accountants Act, 1959**, and established a statutory institute styled as **"Institute of Cost and Work Accountant of India"**. The Companies Act, 1956 has been amended and provision has been made to make it obligatory to industries to maintain the Cost Accounting records. Besides this, Government made 'Cost Audit' compulsory to these industries.

During the last 50 years, Cost Accounting emerged as an important tool to the management for improving efficiency and the profitability of the organisation, with increasing complexities in business for efficient management, costing data became important and hence the importance of Cost Accounting is increasing day-by-day.

Objectives of Cost Accounting

The important **Objectives of Cost Accounting** are indicated in Figure 1.3 as follows:

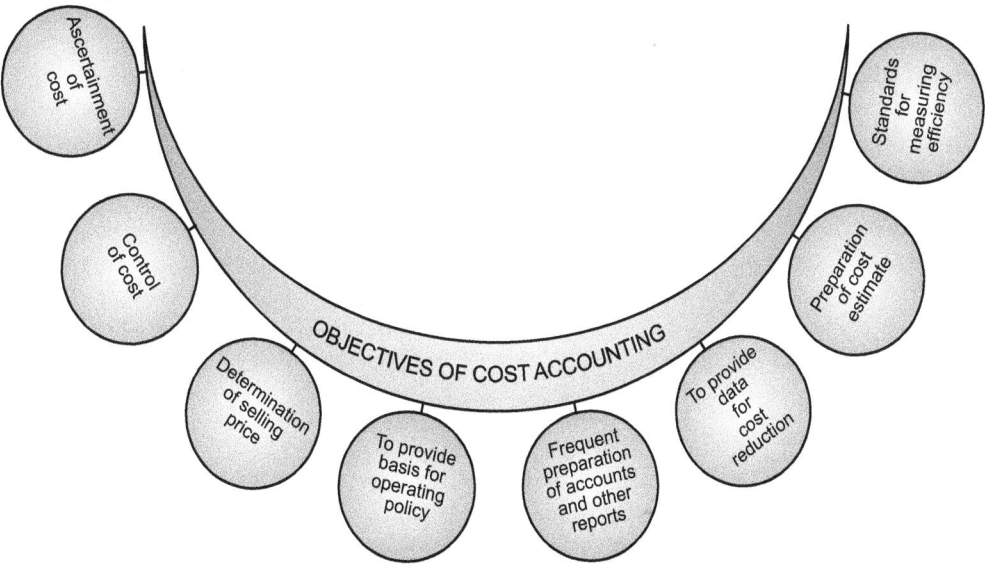

Fig. 1.3 : Objectives of Cost Accounting

i) Ascertainment of Cost:

This is the primary objective of Cost Accounting. For the purpose of ascertaining the cost of a product, process or operation, it is necessary to record the expenses incurred, classify them properly and then allocate or apportion it amongst the respective products, processes or departments for calculating total cost of each of these. If there is only one product, cost per unit can be found out by dividing the total expenditure by the total number of units produced. But if there are many products manufactured, then the cost is to be split up between the various products. For this purpose various techniques may be used.

ii) Control of Cost:

Cost control aims at improving efficiency by controlling and reducing cost. Cost control is exercised at different stages in a factory, viz., acquisition of materials, recruiting and deployment of labour force, during production process and so on. As such, we have material cost control, labour cost control, production control, quality control and so on. Control over cost is exercised through the techniques of budgetary control and standard costing. In these techniques, cost is controlled by comparing actual cost with predetermined cost. Cost control is becoming more and more important because of growing competition.

iii) Determination of Selling Price:

Cost accounting provides information on the basis of which selling prices of products or services may be fixed. Total cost of production constitutes the basis on which selling price is fixed by adding a margin of profit. Cost accounting furnishes both the total cost of production as well as cost incurred at each and every stage of production. In fixation of selling price other factors are also important such as market conditions, the area of distribution, volume of sales etc. But no doubt, cost plays the dominating role in price fixation.

iv) To provide a basis for Operating Policy:

Cost data to a great extent helps the management in formulating the policies of a business and in decision-making. Hence, availability of cost data is a must for all levels of management. Some of the decisions which are based on cost data are make or buy decision, manufacturing by mechanisation or automation, whether to close or continue operations, inspite of losses, selling below cost decision, introduction of new products etc.

v) Frequent Preparation of Accounts and Other Reports:

Every concern rely upon the reports on cost data to know the level of efficiency regarding purchase, production, sales and operation results. Financial accounts provide information only at the end of the year because value of closing stock is available at the end of the year. But cost accounts provide the value of closing stock at frequent intervals by adopting, "continuous stock verification" system. Using the value of closing stock it is possible to prepare final accounts and to know the operating results of the business.

vi) To provide Data for Cost Reduction:

For survival in the world of competition, it is necessary to keep the prices of products or services as low as possible. It is only possible when cost of production is less. So the management has to make continuous efforts to reduce the cost. To provide data for cost reduction is one of the important objectives of Cost Accounting. It helps the management in finding out new and improved methods to reduce costs.

vii) Preparation of Cost Estimates :

Many times, it is required to take new jobs by the manufacturing concern or introduce new product as per customer's requirements. Before manufacturing, cost estimates are to be made. Under cost accounting system, preparation of cost estimates is possible. So the preparation of cost estimates is also one of the important objective of Cost Accounting.

viii) Standards for measuring efficiency :

For measuring the performance of various business activities, management requires some base for evaluating the performance. Standard Cost is one of the means for evaluating the performance. So the development of Standard Cost is also an important objective of Cost Accounting.

Features of Cost Accounting

Cost Accounting is the science of recording and presenting business transactions pertaining to the production of goods and services, whereby these records become a method of measurement and means of control. Thus, it is nothing but the application of cost accounting principles, methods and techniques to the science, art and practice of **control the costs** of operating the business, **ascertainment of costs** for fixing selling prices of the products and **presentation of costs** in the form of statements, reports, with appropriate analysis to the different levels of management as and when they require. The important **features of Cost Accounting** can be summarised as follows :

i) Cost Ascertainment :

The basic feature of any method of cost accounting is to ascertain the cost of each unit, job, process or department, not only the actual costs incurred but also the predetermined. The timely and reliable cost information about the cost of output is to be ascertained appropriately by using various methods of costing viz. job costing and process costing. Such analytical information about the cost of products is provided to the management which becomes the actual basis of the managerial decisions such as pricing, planning and control.

ii) Cost Control :

The basic feature of any technique of cost accounting is to utilise the detailed cost information to controlling the costs at different stages by using different techniques of cost control to keep the costs at the minimum possible extent, to survive in the competitive market. Cost accounting ultimately aims at improving the overall profitability by controlling the cost more strictly by using various techniques like standard costing, budgetary control, marginal costing etc.

iii) Cost Presentation :

The data collected and re-classified systematically is presented scientifically by the Cost Accounting department in the form of cost statements and cost reports to the different levels of management as and when it is required. The analytical cost reports are basically used by the management internally at various levels for performance appraisal and planning, control and decision-making functions.

1.4 ADVANTAGES AND LIMITATIONS OF COST ACCOUNTING

Cost Accounting is a tool with the management for making decisions as regards sales, purchases, production, finance, inventory control etc. If the costing system is sound, it provides the following benefits to the management.

Advantages of Cost Accounting

The Figure 1.4 shows the graphical presentation of **Advantages of Cost Accounting** as follows :

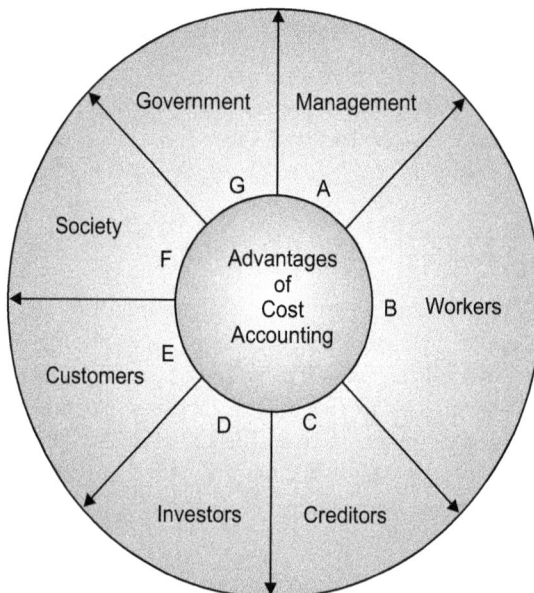

Fig. 1.4 : Advantages of Cost Accounting

A) Advantages to the Management :

i) **Helps in Decision-Making :**

Decision-making is concerned with choosing between alternative courses of action. An important factor involved in the choice is the financial implication of the available alternatives. Cost Accounting is a decision-making tool. It provides suitable cost data and other related information to enable management to evaluate alternative courses of action.

ii) **Supplies detailed Cost Information :**

Cost Accounting classifies cost and revenue by every possible division of the business and supplies management with detailed and regular cost information. Such information is useful for ascertaining the cost of product, process, department, division or unit of service.

iii) **Guides in Price Fixation :**

Cost is one of the most important factor to be considered while fixing prices. It assists the management in fixation of selling price both in normal conditions and during the period of depression. With the help of costing, it is possible to prepare estimates, tenders and quotations.

iv) **It reveals Operating Efficiency :**

Cost information reveals, profitable and unprofitable activities, so that steps may be taken to reduce or eliminate wastages and inefficiencies occurring in any form such as idle time, under-utilisation of plant capacity, spoilage of materials etc.

v) **It Facilitates Planning :**

It enables the management to know the future costs, so that appropriate plans and decisions can be made.

vi) **It reveals Idle Capacity:**

A concern may not be working to full capacity due to reasons such as shortage of demand, machine breakdown or other bottlenecks in production. A Cost Accounting system can easily find out the cost of idle capacity so that the management may take immediate steps to improve the position.

vii) **Helps in Inventory Control:**

Perpetual inventory system which is an integral part of cost accounting, helps in the preparation of interim profit and loss account. Other inventory control techniques like ABC Analysis, Level setting etc., are also used in Cost Accounting.

viii) **Helps in Cost Control:**

Cost Accounting helps in controlling costs with special techniques like standard costing and budgetary control.

ix) **Helps in Cost Reduction:**

It helps in the introduction of cost reduction programme and finding out new and improved ways to reduce costs.

x) **Checks the Accuracy of Financial Accounts:**

Cost Accounting provides a reliable check on the accuracy of financial accounts with the help of reconciliation between the two at the end of the accounting period.

xi) **It Facilitates Cost Comparison:**

Cost Accounting enables management to make cost comparison of jobs, products, departments, sales territories etc. within the same concern. It provides inter-firm cost comparison also.

xii) **It Prevents Frauds and Manipulation:**

It helps in preventing manipulation and frauds through cost audit system. Thus, reliable cost data can be furnished to management and others.

B) **Advantages to the Workers:**

From the cost records, we can find out the efficiency of the workers. Thus, the efficient workers are rewarded and the slow workers are given more incentives to come up to a certain level of efficiency. A sound costing system, therefore, increases the profitability and the workers get more wages. Workers are benefited by the introduction of incentive plans which is an integral part of a cost system.

C) **Advantages to the Creditors:**

The creditors feel secured, where there is a good system of costing in a concern because they can verify the creditworthiness of the concern. Thus, the creditors extent credit facilities on a longer term which is beneficial to the business.

D) **Advantages to the Investors:**

The investors also feel secured if there is prosperity in a business as they feel that their money remains secured. Hence, more and more people are attracted to invest in the concern which further increases the prosperity of the business.

E) **Advantages to the Customers:**

The customers always feel that the products which they are buying are the cheapest in the market but at the same time best in quality. Hence, when the prices are quoted in the products to the nearest paisa the customer feel that there is much accuracy in fixing the selling price.

F) **Advantages to the Society:**

As costing removes all the types of wastages, scraps the general public, gets the products at lower prices. Again when a unit grows in size its requirements also grow. For example, more man-power is needed, more raw material requirements arise, more sales are made etc. Hence, it leads to more employment of the local people, more suppliers of raw materials enter the markets etc. When the sales are more, there can be large scale production and hence the advantages of economies of scale can be achieved, which in turn reduces the prices. Due to reduction in costs, inflation in the economy can be controlled. This is because people will have to pay less price for the products and hence, can save their income.

G) Advantages to the Government :

A cost system provides ready figures to use for Government, wage tribunals, trade unions etc. for use in problems relating to price fixing, wage level fixation, settlement of industrial unions disputes etc. The Government can plan its policies based on the techniques and procedures of cost accounting. Cost accounting, therefore, promotes economic development. To reduce cost of production and sales price, the Government has introduced cost audit in most of the industries for e.g., the industries which are engaged in production, processing, manufacturing and mining activities. Such companies are now required to keep certain costing records and have to submit certain statutory returns to the Government periodically. By doing all these, the advantage to the Government is that there can be price stability in the economy.

Limitations of Cost Accounting

Besides the various advantages of Cost Accounting system, it suffers from certain **limitations** which are as follows :

i) **Expensive :**

Highly paid cost accountants and the organisation of costing system involve additional expenditure. However, before installing it, care must be taken to ensure that the benefits derived are more than the investment made on this system of accounting.

ii) **More Complex :**

Cost accounting system involves a number of steps in ascertaining cost such as collection and classification of expenses, allocation and apportionment of expenses etc. These steps are considered as complicated and requires several forms and documents in preparing the reports. This will lead to delay in the preparation of accounts.

iii) **Limited Applicability :**

All business enterprises cannot make use of a single method and technique of costing. It all depends upon the nature of the business and type of product manufactured by it. If a wrong technique and method is used, it misleads the results of the business.

iv) **Not applicable to Small Concerns :**

A cost accounting system is applicable only to large sized business and not suitable for small sized business because it is more expensive.

v) **Lack of Uniformity :**

This is the greatest limitation of cost accounting system. It fails to confirm to any uniform procedure. It is possible that two equally competent cost accountants may arrive at different results from the same information. So it is said that all cost accounting results are mere estimates and not reliable.

vi) **Lack of Accuracy :**

Accuracy in Cost Accounting is relative. Certain assumptions are always made while ascertaining cost to suit a particular situation.

vii) **Confusion regarding Non-cost Items :**

There may be confusion regarding non-cost items for e.g., interest in capital, cash discount etc. should be included or to be excluded from cost accounts.

viii) Not useful for Handling Futuristic Situations :

The contribution of Cost Accounting for handling futuristic situations has not been much. For example, Cost Accounting has not evolved any tool so far, for handling inflationary situation.

ix) Failure in many Cases :

It is argued that the adoption of costing system failed to produce the desired results in many cases and so it was not effective.

x) It fails in considering Social Obligations :

Cost Accounting fails to take into account the social obligations of the business. In other words, social accounting is outside the purview of the cost accounts.

Thus, Cost Accounting cannot be termed as an exact science like physics, or mathematics but it is a subjective art which is practised based on the accounting theories, reasoning and most important the common sense. Hence, all the decisions of the management are based upon the best judgement of the cost accountants who take into account the various factors while preparing the cost statements, which may not be the same with other cost accountants.

But apart from the above limitations, Cost Accounting helps the management to take vital decisions with valuable cost figures without which management today, cannot solve the complex business problems.

1.5 DIFFERENCE BETWEEN FINANCIAL ACCOUNTING AND COST ACCOUNTING

Financial Accounting refers to recording of all money transactions on double entry principles in a set of books with an object to prepare final accounts of the business. **Cost Accounting** refers to accumulation, classification, analysis and presentation of costs for managerial control. Both the systems of accounting makes use of the same items of expenditure but in different ways, to serve their own purposes. Due to the complexities of large scale production in the modern business activities, the financial accounting falls short of meeting these challenges. Hence, cost accounting has come into existence to solve all the managerial problems.

The following are the differences between Financial Accounting and Cost Accounting.

	Points of Distinction	Financial Accounting	Cost Accounting
i)	Coverage	It covers accounts of whole business relating to all commercial transactions.	It covers the transactions relating to certain specific activities only for e.g., production, sales, services etc.
ii)	Purpose	Its purpose is external reporting mainly to owners, creditors, tax authorities, Government and prospective investors.	Its purpose is the internal reporting i.e. to the management of every business.
iii)	Statutory Requirement	These accounts have to be prepared according to the legal requirements of the Companies Act and Income Tax Act.	These Accounts are generally prepared to meet the requirements of the management. But now it has been made obligatory to keep cost records under the Companies Act.
iv)	Recording of transactions	It records, classifies and analyses the transactions in a subjective manner i.e. according to the nature of expenditure.	It records the expenditure in an objective manner i.e. according to the purposes for which cost are incurred.

Points of Distinction	Financial Accounting	Cost Accounting
v) Nature of costs	It records only historical costs.	Cost Accounts records both historical and estimated costs.
vi) Nature of expenses incurred	In **Financial Accounts** expenses are recorded in totals.	In **Cost Accounts**, cost are expressed by proper analysis and classification in order to find out cost per unit.
vii) Analysis of cost and profit	It disclose profits for the entire business as a whole. It does not show the figures of cost and profit for individual products, departments and processes etc.	It show the profitability or otherwise of each product, process or operation, so as to reveal the areas of profitability.
viii) Duration of Reporting	The reports are prepared periodically, usually on an annual basis.	It is a continuous process and may be prepared daily, weekly, monthly etc.
ix) Control aspect	It does not make use of any control techniques. It does not control material and labour cost.	It makes use of some important control techniques such as Standard costing, Marginal costing, Budgetary costing etc. It exercises control over material cost by ABC Analysis, level setting, EOQ etc. and over labour cost by minimising idle time, overtime etc.
x) Types of Statements prepared	It prepares general purpose statements like Profit and Loss A/c and Balance Sheet.	It generates special purpose statements and reports like Report of Loss of Materials, Idle Time Reports, Variance Report etc.
xi) Pricing	It fails to guide the formulation of pricing policy.	It provides adequate data for formulating pricing policy.
xii) Valuation of Stock	Stock is valued at cost price or market price, whichever is less.	Stock is always valued at cost price.
xiii) Evaluation of Efficiency	The information provided by the Accounts is not sufficient to evaluate the efficiency of the business.	The cost data helps in evaluating the efficiency of the business.
xiv) Break-up of costs	Costs are not broken up, according to their nature and functions.	The costs are analysed according to their nature and functions for further analysis and control.
xv) Inter/Intra Firm comparison	Under **Financial Accounting**, Inter-firm or Intra-firm comparison cannot be made.	Under **Cost Accounting** it is possible to make Inter-firm and Intra-firm comparison.
xvi) Classification of Costs	There is no system of classification of costs into fixed and variable or controllable and uncontrollable.	Since, there is classification of costs into controllable and uncontrollable costs, the management can reduce the controllable costs. The distinction between fixed costs and variable costs also helps the management to take vital decisions.
xvii) Reference	In **Financial Accounting** reference can be made in case of difficulty to the company law, case decisions and to business ethics.	In **Cost Accounting** no such reference is possible. Guidance can be had only from a body of conventions followed by cost accountants.
xviii) Dealing of Transactions	It deals with only monetary transactions and it deals only with actual facts and figures.	It deals with monetary as well as non-monetary transactions and it deals partly with the facts and figures and partly with estimates.

1.6 CONCEPTUAL ANALYSIS OF COST UNIT AND COST CENTRE

The entire accounting process of ascertaining the costs accurately and controlling the costs strictly becomes a very simple task only after analysing the important concepts of cost unit and cost centre scientifically and more logically as follows :

Cost Unit

Meaning :

Cost Unit is a quantitative unit of product or service or time in relation to which costs are ascertained or expressed. Cost Units differ from industry to industry. The cost unit selected should be the most natural to the business and accepted by all concerned. Therefore, utmost care should be taken while selecting cost units. It should be neither too small nor too large. If unit is too large, significant cost trends may pass unnoticed, due to averaging of cost. If the unit is too small, it may necessitate detailed and expensive clerical work.

Definition :

C.I.M.A., London has defined Cost Unit as, "a unit of product of service in relation to which costs are ascertained".

Costing means measuring the costs in relation to a unit. Hence, the unit of measurement must be clearly defined and selected. This should be done before ascertainment of costs. For example in a cement factory, the cost per tonne of cement is found out, in a cloth mill, the cost per meter is ascertained, in case of machine, the cost per machine hour is found out and so on. Thus here, tonne, metre and machine hour become the cost units. Hence, we can say that a cost unit is nothing, but a unit of measurement of cost.

In case of a service unit, it is difficult to find out and decide a suitable cost unit, for example, in case of a transport undertaking, the costs may be either related to the distance travelled in kilometer, or the weight carried i.e. tonnes. While selecting proper cost unit for the transport both factors i.e. distance and weight should be considered. Hence, tonne kilometer or passenger kilometer will be a proper unit.

Types of Cost Units :

i) **Single Cost Unit :**

It is a cost unit in which only one characteristics is used in measurement of cost e.g. per kilometre, per litre, per passenger, and so on.

ii) **Composite Cost Unit :**

It is a cost unit in which two characteristics are used simultaneously in measurement of cost e.g. per tonne-kilometre, per passenger-kilometre, per kilowatt-hour, per patient-bed, and so on.

Each industry has a different cost units, some of which are given below :

Industry/Product	Cost Unit
Automobile	Number
Bricks	Thousand
Cotton/Jute	Bale
Chemicals	Litre, Gallon, K.G. Tonne
Electricity	KWH
Furniture	Number
Gas	Cubic metre
Hotel or Hospital	Room per day or per bed
Mines	Tonne
Steel	Tonne
Shoes	Pair
Transport	Tonne km/Passenger km
Utensils	KG/Tonne
Cement	Tonne
Cable	Metre or km
Fertiliser	Tonne
TV or Radio or VCR	Set
Building	Sq. ft. or Sq. mtr.
Nuts and Bolts	Gross
Sugar and Flour Mills	Quintal
Timber	Cubic foot
Water Supply	Thousand litres/Gallon

Hence, an appropriate cost unit selected should be :

i) same as being followed throughout the industry.

ii) very simple and easy to understand.

iii) neither to big nor too small.

iv) uniformally maintained over a period of time.

v) most natural to the business.

vi) more suitable to that business.

Cost Centre

Meaning:

For the purposes of administrative control, the entire organisation is divided into a number of sub-units which may be in the form of departments, branches, processes etc., for ascertaining and controlling costs. Because, the costs incurred will be charged initially to these sub-units which are known as **Cost Centres**. A cost centre is therefore, a sub-unit of the organisation for which costs may be collected separately and used for cost ascertainment and control.

Definition:

C.I.M.A., England has therefore defined cost centre as **"a location, person or item of equipment (or group of these) for which costs may be ascertained and used for the purposes of control"**. An analysis of this definition reveals that a Cost Centre may be in the form of: a) a location, (such as a department, division, section or process) or b) an item of equipment (like machine) or c) a person (e.g. salesman), or a group of these. However, costs incurred are identified with the cost centres initially (for distribution later amongst cost units). It helps to ascertain the cost centre-wise costs. Divisionalisation of an organisation into a number of cost centres, therefore, assumes importance. The number and size of cost centres differ from one organisation to another depending upon the nature of production activities, size of the organisation, management's informational needs, etc. The Figure 1.5 shows the various **Types of Cost Centres** as follows:

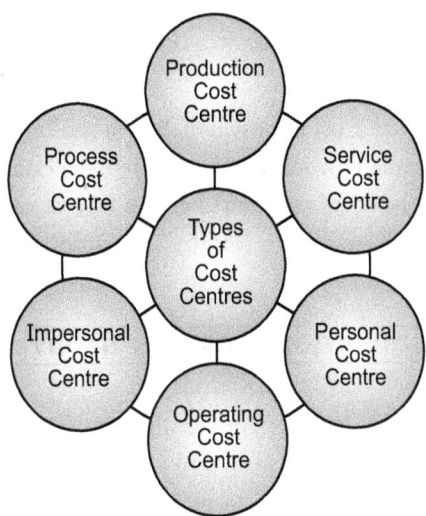

Fig. 1.5 : Types of Cost Centres

Types of Cost Centres:

i) **Production Cost Centre:**

It is a cost centre connected with production i.e. machine shop, welding shop, assembly shop etc. The manufacturing and non-manufacturing costs are charged to product cost centres.

ii) Service Cost Centre :

A Service Cost Centre is one which provides services to the other cost centres. Only non-manufacturing costs are charged to service cost centre. Examples of service cost centre are canteen, machinery maintenance, office service etc.

iii) Personal Cost Centre :

Personal Cost Centre consists of a person or group of persons. Personal Cost Centre follows the organisational structure of a factory. Under this type of cost centre, the costs are analysed and accumulated by Works Manager, Sales Manager, Store-keeper, Foreman etc.

iv) Impersonal Cost Centre :

It consists of a location or item of equipment. A cost centre relating to location may represent a region of sales, a warehouse, or store-room. Cost centre relating to location may represent a region of sales, a warehouse or storeroom. Cost centre relating to an item of equipment could be a machine or group of machines.

v) Operation Cost Centre :

It is a cost centre which consists of machines or persons carrying out similar operations i.e. machines and operations engaged in welding, turning or matching.

vi) Process Cost Centre :

It is a cost centre which consists of a specific process or continuous sequence of operations.

Whatever may be the type of Cost Centre, it is determined by taking into consideration, the following factors viz. the volume of work to be performed, the extent of cost control that can be exercised, responsibilities to be identified and the uses of cost centres to the cost accounting department.

QUESTIONS FOR SELF-STUDY

I. Theory Questions :

i) Explain the concept 'Cost'.

ii) Define the terms :

a) Cost, b) Costing, c) Cost Accounting, d) Cost Accountancy.

iii) "Cost Accounting begins where Financial Accounting ends". Discuss.

iv) What is Financial Accounting ? Explain the limitations of Financial Accounting.

v) "Cost Accounting has been developed out of the limitations of Financial Accounting". Comment.

vi) Define 'Cost Accounting'. State the advantages and limitations of Cost Accounting.

vii) "The scope of the subject of Cost Accounting is not only confined to the ascertainment, but it can be enlarged, so as to cover cost control and cost presentations". Elaborate.

viii) Differentiate between Cost Accounting and Financial Accounting.

ix) "Cost Accounting has become an essential tool of management". Elaborate.

x) What is the difference between Cost Accounting and Cost Accountancy.

xi) What is 'Cost Unit'? State the unit of cost in various industries.

xii) Define the term 'Cost Unit'. State the various types of cost unit giving suitable examples.

xiii) What is 'Cost Centre'? Explain the various types of Cost Centres.

xiv) Write short notes on :

a) Cost, b) Costing, c) Cost Accounting, d) Cost Accountancy, e) Limitations of Financial Accounting, f) Advantages of Cost Accounting, g) Limitations of Cost Accounting, h) Cost Unit, i) Cost Centre.

xv) Differentiate between :

a) Cost Accounting and Financial Accounting

b) Single Cost Unit and Composite Cost Unit

c) Production Cost Centre and Service Cost Centre

Unit ... 2

ELEMENTS OF COST AND COST SHEET

2.1 Material, Labour and Other Expenses
2.2 Classification of Cost and Types of Costs
2.3 Preparation of Cost Sheet
* Illustrations
* Questions for Self-Study

The constituent elements which build up the cost of a unit are materials, labour, energy and equipments. These elements are broadly divided into three major groups of **Materials, Labour and Other Expenses**. These three elements of cost or cost factors could then be further classified into direct and indirect categories. The term **'Materials'** refers to all commodities supplied to an undertaking. **Labour** is an essential factor of production. It is a human resource and participates in the process of production. Labour cost is a significant element of cost of a product or service. All costs other than material costs and labour costs are termed as **'Expenses'**. Direct expenditure is one which is identifiable as belonging exclusively to a particular process, product, unit or service. Indirect expenditure is one which, while still being part of the cost of production, is not incurred exclusively for a particular part of the job and must, therefore, be spread over the whole.

2.1 MATERIAL, LABOUR AND OTHER EXPENSES

On the basis of the nature or elements of costs, costs may be classified into three broad categories as **Material Cost, Labour Cost and Other Expenses**. **Material Cost** denotes the cost of raw materials consumed in the process of manufacturing and marketing a commodity. **Labour Cost** represents the wages, salaries, and so on, payable to the employees of a corporate entity. **Expenses** refer to the costs other than material and labour costs (but including notional costs of the use of owned assets) of other services provided and used in manufacturing and marketing the goods and services of the company. Elementwise classification is important for the purpose of ascertaining the costs of different elements of total cost of a product manufactured or services generated. Further, it also helps to ascertain the relative share and importance of each of the elements of total cost of goods and services.

For the management, it is not just sufficient to have knowledge of total cost control, but for effective control and decision-making the management must know further sub-analysis and classification of costs. Hence, the total cost is analysed according to the elements of cost. There are basically three elements of cost viz. **material, labour and other expenses**. Again they are further analysed into different elements i.e. direct and indirect material, direct and indirect labour and direct and indirect expenses. **Indirect expenses** are termed as **Overheads** or on cost. The Overheads are Factory Overheads, Office and Administrative Overheads and Selling and Distribution Overheads.

The Figure 2.1 indicates the different **Elements of Cost** as follows :

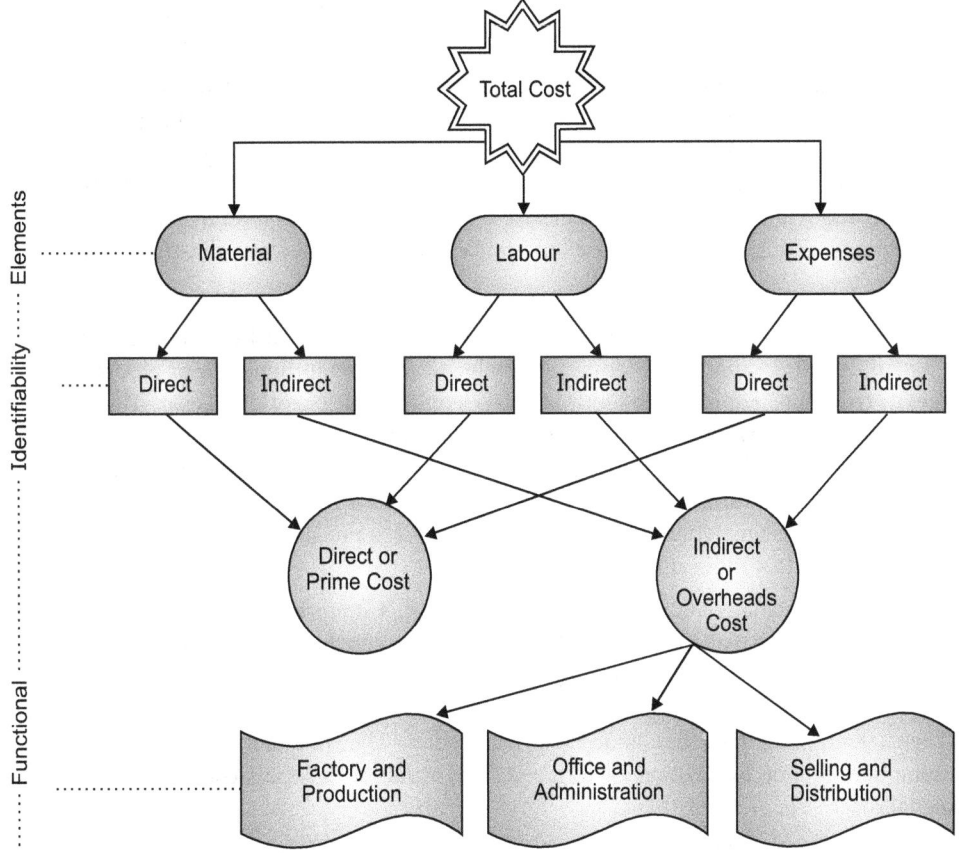

Fig. 2.1 : Elements of Cost

Thus, **Elements of Cost** are the different items or components of cost which are added to get the total cost of any product or service.

According to I.C.M.A., London, Elements of Cost means, "the primary classification of costs according to the factors upon which expenditure is incurred viz. material cost, labour cost and expenses".

Analysis and classification of costs facilitates cost ascertainments, renders it possible to make valid comparisons of the operating efficiency of various departments and assists in locating the responsibility for off-standard performance.

The total cost of a product consists of various elements of cost. These elements are described in detail as under.

Material

According to *I.C.M.A., London-Material Cost* is, "the cost of commodities supplied to an undertaking". Material Cost is further divided into Direct Materials and Indirect Materials as follows :

1) **Direct Materials :**

Direct Materials are those which can be identified in the product and can be measured. They can also be charged to the product directly. Thus, direct materials enter the product and form a part of finished product. For example, cotton used in a textile mill, timber used in furniture making, pig-iron in foundry etc., are treated as direct materials. The cost of direct material is termed as the 'direct material cost'.

But sometimes, even if some materials go directly into the production, they are not treated as direct materials. For example, thread in dress making, nails in shoe making, glue in binding etc. The reason for this is that the value of these materials is very less and the quantity used is also negligible. Hence, attempt is not made to analyse their costs which will otherwise be time consuming and will add to extra cost because of spending more time on them, with their value being negligible. Thus, such materials should conveniently be treated as indirect materials.

2) Indirect Materials :

Indirect Materials are those which do not form a part of the finished products. It is defined as, "materials which cannot be allocated, but which can be apportioned to or absorbed by cost centres or cost units. For example lubricants, oils, cotton wastes, small tools etc.. Thus, materials which cannot be conveniently identified with individual cost units are termed as indirect materials. These are minor in importance. But sometimes, the cost of small items which have less value like the nails in furniture, thread in the dress manufacturing, paper used in polishing, etc. are treated as indirect materials though they go directly into production. The cost of these indirect materials is termed as 'indirect material cost'.

Generally, the materials are purchased from market or directly from manufacturers. The materials purchased have to be brought to the factory for converting them into finished product. So all the expenses which will be incurred for bringing the materials to the place of production will have to be considered for ascertaining the cost of materials. Materials purchased are stored in godowns, therefrom, they are issued for production. The valuation of material issued for consumption is done by Costing Department. This value of materials consumed is charged as 'Material cost'.

Following are the points of differences between Direct Materials and Indirect Materials :

	Direct Materials		Indirect Materials
i)	They can be conveniently identified with and allocated to cost units.	i)	These are certain materials which cannot be conveniently identified with individual cost units.
ii)	They generally form a part of the finished product. e.g., cotton used in a textile mill, clay in bricks, leather in shoes, timber in furniture, etc.	ii)	These are minor in importance, such as a) small and relatively, inexpensive items which may become a part of finished product e.g., pins, screws, nuts and bolts, thread, etc. b) those items which do not physically become a part of the finished products e.g., coal, lubrication oil and greece, sand paper, etc.
iii)	They directly enter the product and form a part of the finished product.	iii)	The costs which relate to the factory form a part of the factory overhead.

Labour

According to *I.C.M.A., London*, **Labour Cost** is defined as, "the cost of remuneration (wages, salaries, commissions, bonus etc.) of the employees of an undertaking". Generally worker's efforts are necessary for producing any particular thing or giving any service. In spite of computerisation and automation, the importance of labour force in manufacturing a product or giving service is increasing day-by-day. The expenses incurred for obtaining the services of human being are known as labour cost of a Job. Labour Cost is further divided into the following :

1) Direct Labour :

All the workers who are directly engaged in a manufacturing activity such as operating machines, doing assembly work etc., are known as direct workers and wages paid to them are known as '**Direct Labour Cost**'. These wages can be conveniently identified with a particular product, job or process. For ascertaining direct labour cost, it is necessary to know how much and what work has been done by an individual worker. For this purpose, various records should be maintained by the management. Wages of skilled and unskilled labour may be included in this item. Examples of direct labour are : Baker, Shoe-maker, Carpenter, Weaver, Tailor, Bus Drivers and Conductors etc.

2) Indirect Labour :

It is of a general character and cannot be conveniently identified with a particular cost unit. In other words, indirect labour is not directly engaged in the production operations, but only to assist or help in production operations. Thus, the wages which cannot be allocated but which can be apportioned or absorbed by cost centres or cost unit is known as **Indirect Labour**. Examples of indirect labour are : salaries and wages paid to foreman, supervisors, chargeman, inspectors, clerical staff etc., working in production department, overtime and night shift allowance paid and any other benefits paid to them.

Following are the points of differences between Direct Labour and Indirect Labour.

Direct Labour	Indirect Labour
i) It consists of wages paid to workers directly engaged in converting raw materials into finished products.	i) They are not directly engaged in the production operations but only assist or help in production operations.
ii) These wages can be conveniently identified with a particular product, job or process.	ii) They are of a general character and cannot be conveniently identified with a particular cost unit.
iii) Wages paid to Baker, Shoe-maker, Carpenter, Weaver and Tailor are examples of Direct Labour.	iii) Wages paid to Supervisor, Inspector, Cleaner, Clerk, Peon, Watchman are examples of Indirect Labour.
iv) 'All labour expended in altering the construction, composition, confirmation or condition of the product' is known as Direct Labour.	iv) The wages which cannot be allocated, but which can be apportioned to or absorbed by cost centres or cost units is known as Indirect Labour.

Other Expenses

All costs, other than material and labour are termed as **Other Expenses**. According to *I.C.M.A., London*, Expense is defined as, "the cost of services provided to an undertaking and the notional cost of the use of owned assets". Expenses are further divided into the following :

1) **Direct Expenses :**

Direct Expenses include all types of expenses other than direct materials and direct labour which are incurred specifically for a particular product or process. It is defined as "expenses which can be identified with and allocated to cost centres and cost units". Direct expenses are also known as 'chargeable expenses'. Direct expenses form a part of the Prime Cost for e.g. chargeable expenses, Hire of special plant, Royalties, Cost of patents and patterns, Engineers Fees, Cost of special drawings, Designs and layouts, Architect's fees, Direct expenses payable, Surveyor's fees, Productive expenses outstanding, Consultants fees, Process expenses due, but not paid, Prime cost expenses etc.

2) **Indirect Expenses :**

All indirect costs other than indirect material and indirect labour costs are termed as **Indirect Expenses**. These expenses are not charged directly to production. Indirect expenses cannot be allocated, but they can be apportioned to or absorbed by cost centres or cost units. Examples of indirect expenses are : rent, rates and taxes, salary of general manager, staff welfare expenses, canteen expenses, telephone expenses, lighting, power, fuel, depreciation, insurance, bank charges and interest paid, etc.

The aggregate of direct material cost, direct labour cost and direct expenses is termed as "**Prime Cost**" while the aggregate of indirect material cost, indirect labour cost and indirect expenses is termed as "**Overheads**".

Following are the points of differences between Direct Expenses and Indirect Expenses.

	Direct Expenses		Indirect Expenses
i)	"Expenses which can be identified with and allocated to cost centres and cost unit" is known as Direct Expenses.	i)	"All indirect costs other than indirect materials and indirect labour costs, are termed as Indirect Expenses.
ii)	These are those expenses which are specifically incurred in connection with a particular job or cost unit.	ii)	These cannot be directly identified with a particular job, proces or work order and are common to cost units and cost centres.
iii)	These are also known as "chargeable" expenses.	iii)	These are also known as non-chargeable expenses or on costs or overheads.
iv)	These form a part of the Prime Cost.	iv)	They form a part of the Overheads.
v)	Cost of Drawings and Patterns, Royalty paid, Excise Duty, Architect Fees are the examples of Direct Expenses.	v)	Rent and Rates, Depreciation, Light and Power, Advertising, Insurance, Carriage Outward are the examples of Indirect Expenses.

Overheads

Overhead Costs are the operating costs of a business enterprise which cannot be identified with a particular unit of output. Overheads consists of all expenses incurred for in connection with the general organisation of the entire concern or a part of it, i.e. cost of operating supplies and services used by the undertaking. It also include maintenance of capital assets. There are four main types of overheads which are as follows :

1) **Factory or Production or Works or Manufacturing Overheads :**

These are the overheads which are concerned with the production function. It includes indirect materials, indirect wages and indirect expenses in producing goods or services. Thus, overhead covers all types of indirect expenses incurred by a concern right from the receipt of an order to the final delivery of goods to the customer or for storing the finished goods in the godowns. Examples of factory overheads are : depreciation of plant and machinery, depreciation of factory buildings, insurance charges and repairs on plant and machinery and factory building, power consumption, coal and other fuel charges, wages of indirect workers, welfare services etc.

2) **Office or Administration or Establishment or Management Overheads :**

These are the indirect expenditure incurred in general administrative function i.e. in formulating policies, planning and controlling the function, directing and motivating the personnel of an organisation in the attainment of its objectives. Examples of office and administration overheads are : Office rent, rates and taxes, salaries of office staff, postage, telegrams and telephone, printing and stationery, office lighting, repairs and depreciation of office building and equipments, legal expenses, audit fees, director's fees, bank charges and interest paid, etc.

3) **Selling Overheads :**

It is the cost of promoting sales and retaining customers. It is the skill of any business to attract new customers by offering extra facilities and services by giving them free samples etc., so that they get attracted to the company. Similarly, the existing customer should be retained by providing the best services for which certain expenses are incurred. Thus, if a concern wants to expand its business it must incur selling expenses which cannot be avoided. Examples of selling overheads are : salaries of the sales manager and sales staff, commission paid to salesman and selling agents, advertising charges, packing charges, free catalogues, pamphlets and price lists, mail order house expenses, showroom expenses, bad debts, after sales service expenses, travelling expenses etc.

4) **Distribution Overheads :**

These are the expenses incurred in moving the goods from the company's godowns to the customers premises. It means that distribution overhead starts with all indirect material, indirect wages and indirect expenses incurred upto the point of packing the product, for making available for despatch and ends with making the re-conditioned returned empty packages and tins available for reuse. The actual definition of distribution expenses is "the cost of the sequence of operations, which begins with making the packed product available for despatch and ends with making the re-conditioned returned empty package, if any available for reuse". Examples of distribution overheads are : warehouse rent and insurance, salary of warehouse keeper and other cost of transportation of goods, insurance of goods in transit, cost of maintenance of vehicles, loading expenses, carriage outward, special packing expenses, cost of repairing and re-conditioning of empty packages etc.

Items to be excluded from Cost or Non-cost Items :

There are certain items of expenses which are purely of financial nature and hence they are simply excluded, while recording the business transactions into the books of cost accounts. The following is the summarised list of financial items which are to be excluded from the computation of Total Cost.

1) **Financial Incomes :**
   Capital Profits, Dividend Received, Brokerage and Commision Received, Share Transfer Fees Received, Interest on Investments, Interest on Bank Deposits, Rent Received, Bad Debts Recovery, Interest on Loan given, Discount Received etc.

2) **Financial Charges :**
   Capital Losses, Cash Discount, Trade Discount, Penalties and Fines, Share Transfer Fees Paid, Interest on Bank Loan, Interest on Debentures, Preliminary Expenses, Underwriting Commission, Discount on Issue of Shares and Debentures, Loss on Investments, Capital Expenses, Interest on Capital, Salary or Commission paid to Partners, Income Tax, Wealth Tax, Interest on Debentures, Reconstruction Expenses, Development Expenses, Reorganisation Expenses etc.

3) **Appropriations :**
   Bad Debts Reserve, Dividends or Bonus Paid, Charitable Donations, Transfer to Reserves, General Reserves, Sinking Fund, Debenture Redemption Fund, Machinery Replacement Fund, Investment Fluctuation Fund, etc.

4) **Abnormals :**
   Abnormal Wastage, Abnormal Idle Time, Loss by fire, Loss by Theft, Loss of Stock, etc.

Division of Costs :

The division of costs are obtained with the help of Elements of Cost. The following are the various divisions of costs of an article or a product.

1) **Prime Cost :**
   This is the total of Direct material, Direct labour and Direct expenses.
   Prime Cost = Direct Material + Direct Wages + Direct Expenses.

2) **Works Cost :**
   This consists of Prime cost plus Works overheads.
   Works Cost = Prime Cost + Works Overheads

3) **Cost of Production :**
   This is made up of Works Cost plus Office and Administrative Overheads. Cost of production is termed as "Gross Cost".
   Cost of Production = Works Cost + Office and Administration Overheads.

4) **Total Cost or Cost of Sales :**
   This is the cost of production plus selling and distribution overheads. In other words, it is the total expenditure incidental to production, administration, selling and distribution of commodities manufactured. Total Cost is termed as "Net Cost".
   Total Cost / Cost of Sales = Cost of Production + Selling and Distribution Overheads.

5) **Selling Price =**
   Total Cost / Cost of Sales + Profit (or – Loss).

The **Division of Costs** may be shown in the following chart indicated in Figure 2.2.

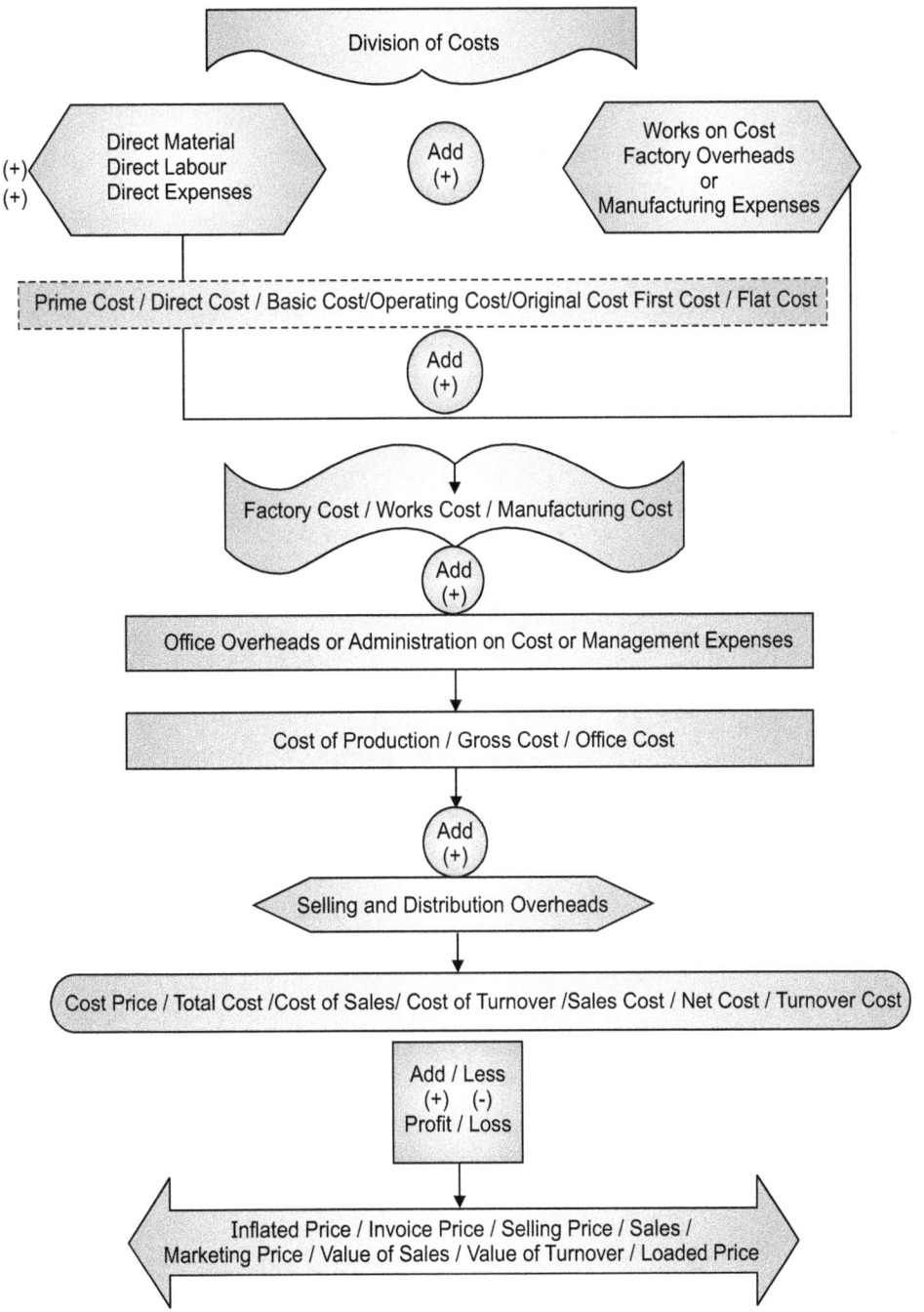

Fig. 2.2 : Division of Costs

2.2 CLASSIFICATION OF COST AND TYPES OF COSTS

Classification of Cost

Meaning and Definition :

Cost Classification means grouping of costs according to their common characteristics. It is the process of grouping the items together which are alike.

According to *Dickey*, "Classification is the process of grouping like facts under a common designation on the basis of similarities of nature, attributes or relations".

The *Committee on National Association of Accountants defines Classification* as, "The identification of each item and the systematic placement of like items together according to their common features".

Items grouped together under common heads are further defined according to their fundamental differences. Suitable classification of costs is of utmost important, so that these costs can be identified with the cost centres or cost units.

Need of Cost Classification :

The need for classification arises having to use cost data for a variety of purposes. For different purposes different kinds of cost informations are required. Therefore, costs must be arranged and classified in such a manner that they can be combined in different ways to serve different purposes. Generally, **Cost Classification** is required for the attainment of the following **purposes** shown in Figure 2.3.

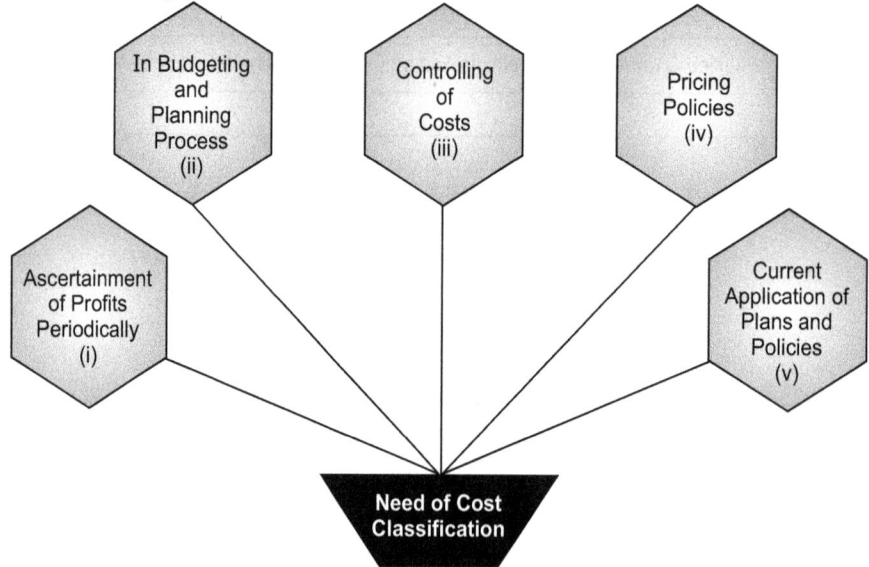

Fig. 2.3 : Need of Cost Classification

Methods of Classification :

Costs are classified in different ways according to their elements i.e. material, labour and expenses. Other basis of cost classification are function, variability, controllability, normality, period, investment etc. The costs may be the same, but the classification of costs are made in different ways depending upon the **specific requirement and the purpose** to be achieved in a particular organisation. The Figure 2.4 shows the graphical presentation of **Classification of Costs** as follows.

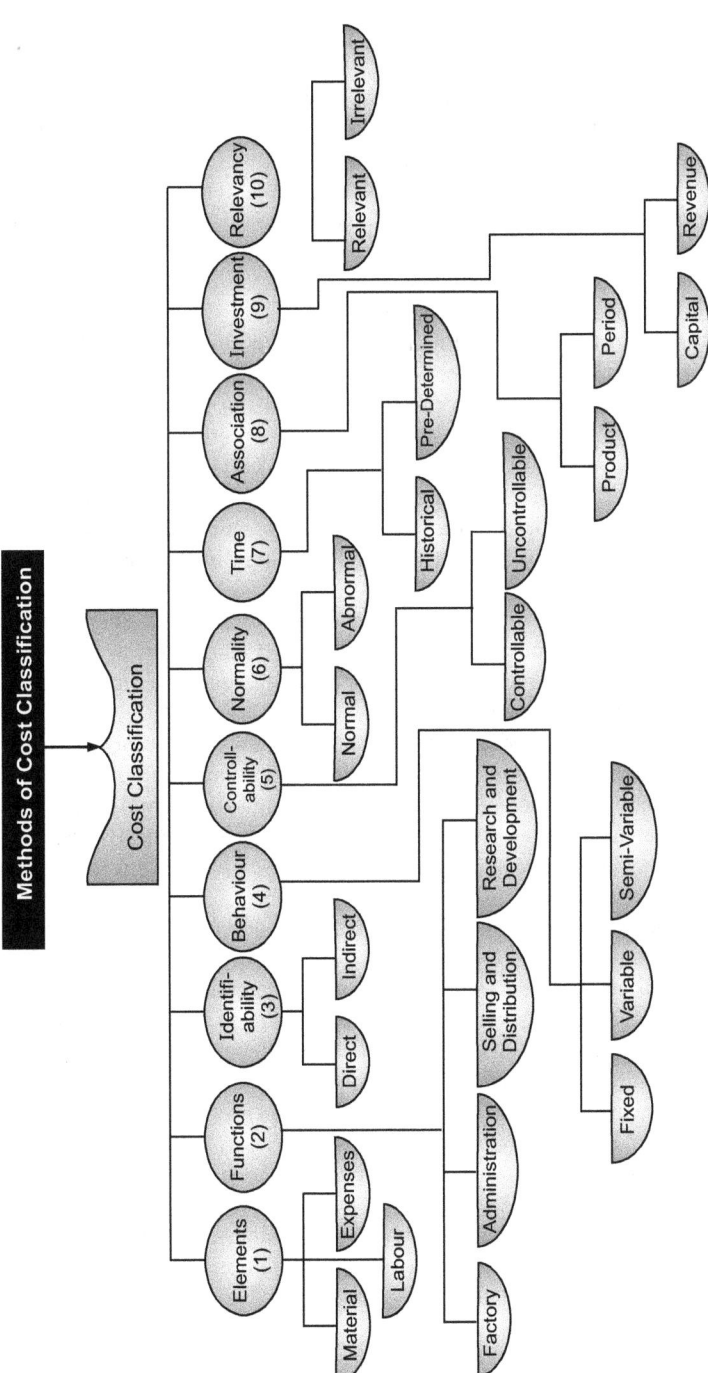

Fig. 2.4 : Classification of Cost

1) Elements :

The **cost elements** of a product are Material, Labour and Expenses.

i) Materials :

The ***I.C.M.A., London*** defines material cost as, "the cost of commodities, other than fixed assets, introduced into products or consumed in the operation of an organisation. Material cost may be either direct material cost or indirect material cost.

Direct material cost is defined as "the cost of materials entering into and becoming constituent element of a product or saleable service". Thus, materials which can be identified with the production of a product or which can be traced to the finished product are known as direct materials. Examples of direct materials are cotton in cotton textile, timber in furniture making industries, leather in shoe making industries etc.

Indirect material cost has been defined as, "material cost other than direct material cost". In other words, material cost which cannot be identified with a product, job or process or traceable to the same, is known as indirect material cost. Examples of indirect materials are consumable stores such as oil, cotton waste, small tools, works stationery etc.

But in some cases, even direct materials which can be traced to the product concerned may be treated as indirect materials because of time and labour involved in ascertaining their cost for the purposes of a direct charge. For example, thread, buttons, nails, gum, metal strips etc. which are used in production are treated as indirect, although they are direct in nature.

ii) Labour :

Labour is the physical or mental effort expended in production. The remuneration for such efforts is known as wages. Labour cost may be either direct labour cost or indirect labour cost.

Direct labour cost is defined as, "the cost of remuneration for employee's efforts and skills applied directly to a product or saleable service".

Indirect labour cost is defined as, "labour cost other than direct labour cost". Thus, indirect labour is not directly engaged in the production operations, but only to assist or help in production operations. Examples of indirect labour are : salaries and wages paid to foreman, supervisors, chargeman, inspectors, maintenance workers, clerical staff etc. working in production department, overtime and night shift allowance paid and any other benefit paid.

iii) Expenses :

The term 'Expenses' denotes the cost of services provided to an undertaking. Expenses may be direct or indirect.

ICMA, defines direct expenses as "Costs other than materials or wages which are incurred for a specific product or a saleable service". Direct expenses form a part of Prime Cost. Examples of direct expenses are : Cost of drawings and patterns, Repairs and maintenance of plant and equipment taken on hire, Architect's fees, Research expenditure, Excise duty, Royalty etc.

Indirect expenses are "expenses other than direct expenses". These expenses are not charged directly to production. Examples of indirect expenses : Rent and rates, Salary of General Manager, Staff welfare expenses, Canteen expenses, Lighting, Telephone expenses etc.

2) Functions :

Costs may be classified on the **basis of business functions** like manufacturing, administration, selling and distribution, research and development etc. Ascertainment of costs for all these functions is necessary and hence they are classified as follows :

i) Factory Costs :

This is the cost which is incurred for a series of operations i.e. right from the supply of materials, labour and expenses incurred, till the completion of production. Thus, materials, labour and expenses, both direct and indirect, constitute production cost. Examples of manufacturing cost are : material, labour, factory rent rates and taxes, depreciation on factory building and plant and machinery, factory lighting and power, store keeping expenses, insurance of factory building etc.

ii) Administration Costs :

This is the cost of running a concern i.e. for framing the policies, directing and controlling all the activities of the organisation other than manufacturing and selling and distribution expenses. According to *I.C.M.A.*, it defines as, "the sum of these costs of general and management and of secretarial, accounting and administrative services which cannot be directly related to production, marketing, research and development function of the enterprise". Examples of administration cost are : Director's fees and allowances, Salaries of office staff, Audit fees, Legal expenses, Office rent and taxes, Office lighting, Expenses of secretarial and accounting department, Postage and telegram, Printing and stationery etc.

iii) Selling and Distribution Costs :

Selling costs are those costs which are incurred for attracting the potential customers and retaining the existing customers. Thus, demand is created in the market through advertisement and publicity, so that new orders can be secured.

Selling costs include : Advertisement, Hoarding / Neon signs etc. Salaries and commission to salesman and sales staff, Costs of free samples / brochures etc. Showroom expenses, Travelling expenses of salesman etc.

Distribution expenses are incurred for despatching the products which are ready after packing. These expenses include : Carriage outward, Warehouse expenses, Packing costs, Running and maintenance cost of delivery van, Salary of the godown staff etc.

iv) Research and Development Costs :

Research Cost is defined as, "the cost of seeking new or improved products, applications of material or methods". **Development Cost** is defined as, "the cost of process which begins with the implementation of the decision to produce a new or improve methods and ends with the commencement of formal production of that product or by that method.

3) Identifiability :

According to the identifiability with the cost units, jobs or processes the costs are classified into direct and indirect. In costing, Direct and Indirect costs have much significance.

- i) **Direct Costs :**

  All the costs which can be conveniently allocated to cost unit or cost centre is known as direct cost. For example, the cost of cotton in case of textile industries, the cost of timber in furniture industries etc.

- ii) **Indirect Costs :** It is a cost which is of a general character and which cannot be identified with a particular unit of cost. These cost cannot be allocated, but can be apportioned to cost unit or cost centre. The terms 'direct' and 'indirect' relate to the methods of allocating them because it depends upon whether the same cost should be treated as direct or indirect. Thus, same item may be treated as a direct cost in one case and indirect cost in another case. This bifurcation depends upon the nature of business and also cost unit decided by the management. For example, we can treat depreciation as a direct cost, if there is only one machine or cost centre, but if there are many cost units it becomes difficult to allocate the cost accurately. In this case, it is treated as an indirect cost, for e.g. in cost of construction sites, the depreciation of machinery etc. is taken as direct cost, while in case of a factory where there are many departments which use the same machine, it is treated as an indirect cost.

Identifiability classification is important because,
- it facilitates accurate ascertainment of cost.
- it facilitates controlling of costs.
- it enables in fixing the responsibility to the executives.

Direct Costs are those costs which are incurred for and may easily and conveniently be identified with a particular cost unit or cost centre. Direct costs include direct material cost, direct labout cost and other direct expenses. **Indirect Costs**, on the other hand, represent the costs which are of general nature and which cannot easily and conveniently be identified with a particular cost unit or cost centre. They include indirect material cost, indirect labour cost and other indirect expenses. The indirect costs are therefore called **Overhead Expenses.** These indirect or overhead expenses can further be divided into three sub-categories as factory overhead expenses, administration overhead expenses, and selling and distribution overhead expenses (on the basis of the functions). The Classification of Costs on the basis of Traceability Elements and Functions is shown in Figure 2.5.

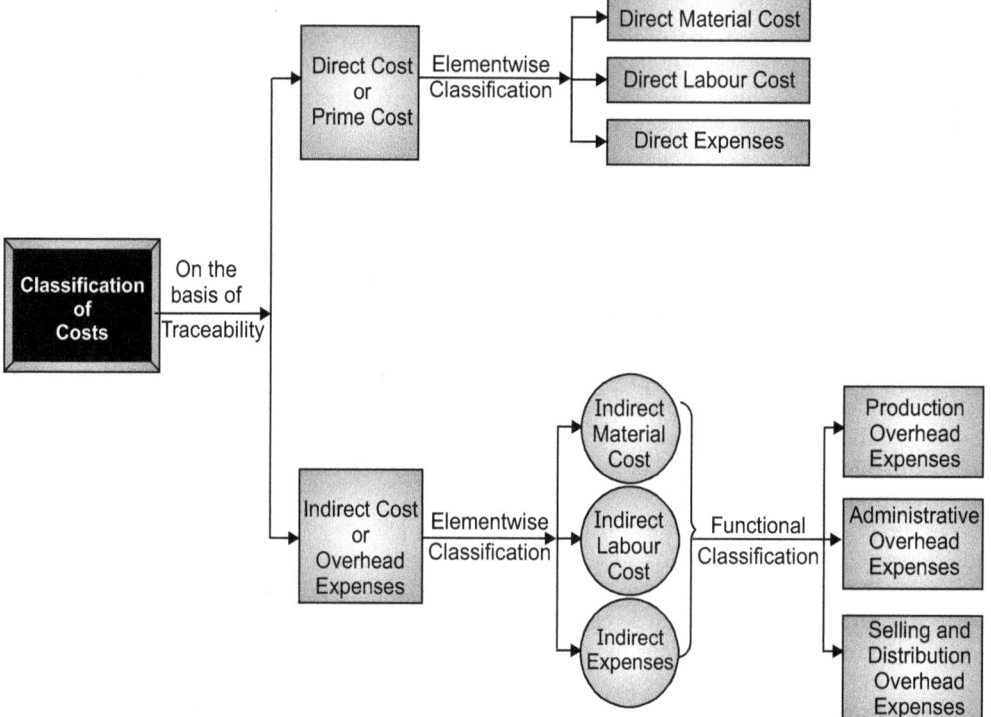

Fig. 2.5 : Classification of Cost on the basis of Traceability, Elements and Functions

4) **Behaviour :**

On the basis of this characteristic, costs are classified **according to their nature or behaviour** in relation to changes in the level of activity or volume of production. On the basis of variability, costs are classified as under :

i) **Fixed Costs :**

According to *I.C.M.A., London* Fixed Cost is defined as, "a cost which accrues in relation to the passage of time and which within certain output or turnover limits tends to be unaffected by fluctuations in volume of output or turnover".

In other words, fixed costs remain fixed in total amount and do not increase or decrease with volume of production. But the fixed cost per unit increases when volume of production decreases, and decreases when the volume of production increases. Thus, fixed costs are constant in total amount, but fluctuate per unit as production changes. The characteristics of fixed cost are :

- fixed total amount within a relevant output range.
- increase or decrease in per unit fixed cost, when volume of production changes.
- fixed costs are apportioned to departments on some equitable basis.
- fixed cost can be controlled mostly by the top level management.

Examples of fixed cost are Rent, Rates, Taxes, Insurance of factory building, Manager's salary, Office staff salaries, Municipal taxes etc.

The following is the graph indicating the Behaviour of Fixed Cost in Figure 2.6.

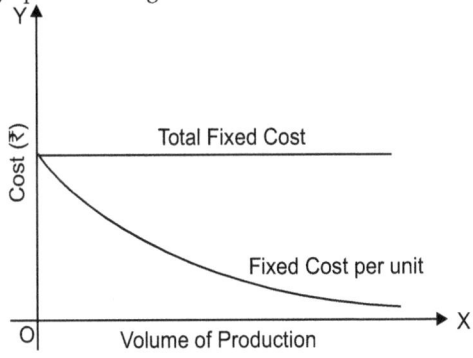

Fig. 2.6 : Behaviour of Fixed Cost

ii) Variable Costs :

I.C.M.A., London defines Variable Cost as, "a cost which in aggregate tends to vary in direct proportions to changes in the volume of output or turnover". In other words, when volume of output increases, total variable cost also increases and vice-versa, when volume of output decreases, total variable cost also decreases. But the variable cost per unit remains fixed.

Example of variable costs are : direct material cost, direct labour cost, direct expenses, power, repairs, royalties, commission of salesman, normal spoilage etc.

The following is the graph indicating the Behaviour of Variable Cost in Figure 2.7.

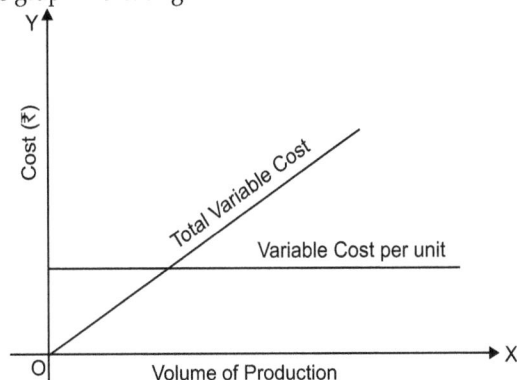

Fig. 2.7 : Behaviour of Variable Cost

Thus, variable costs, in general, indicate the following characteristics:
- they vary in direct proportion to volume of output or turnover.
- the variable cost per unit of product remains constant.
- it is easy for allocation and apportionment to departments.
- such costs can be controlled by departmental heads.

iii) Semi-Variable or Semi-Fixed Costs :

I.C.M.A., London defines **Semi-Variable Cost** as, "a cost containing both fixed and variable elements, which is therefore partly affected by fluctuations in the volume of output or turnover". Thus, these costs are partly fixed and partly variable. A semi-variable cost has often a fixed element below which it will not fall in any level of output. The variable element in semi-variable costs changes either at a constant rate or in lump-sum. For example, if there is additional shift in the factory, it will require additional supervisors and certain costs will increase in lump-sum. In case of telephone charges, there is a minimum rent and after a specified number of calls, the charges are according to the number of calls made. Thus, there is no fixed pattern of behaviour of semi-variable costs. The following is the graph indicating the Behaviour of Semi-Variable Cost in Figure 2.8.

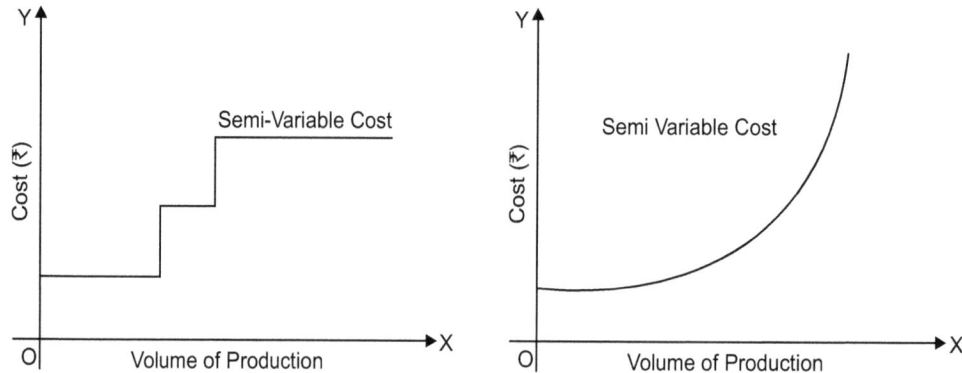

Fig. 2.8 : Behaviour of Semi-Variable Cost

Following is the graph indicating the Behaviour of Fixed, Variable and Semi-Variable Cost in Figure 2.9.

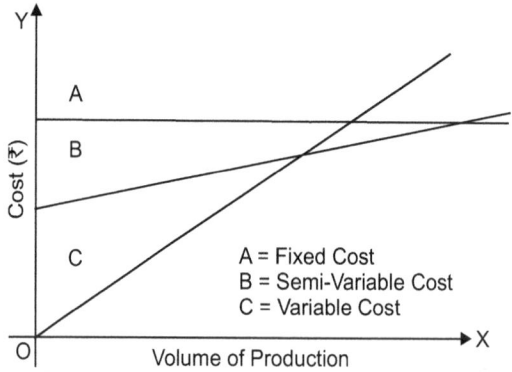

Fig. 2.9 : Behaviour of Fixed, Variable and Semi-Variable Cost

Examples of semi-variable costs are Telephone charges, depreciation, repairs and maintenance of plant and machinery, building, supervision, compensation for accidents, light and power etc.

5) Controllability :

On this basis, costs are classified into two types which are as follows :

i) Controllable Costs :

I.C.M.A., London defines Controllable Costs as, "a cost chargeable to a cost centre, which can be influenced by the actions of the person in whom control of the centre is vested". In other words, these are the costs which may be directly regulated at a given level of management authority. Variable costs are generally controlled by department heads. Practically, all variable costs are controllable cost.

ii) Uncontrollable Costs :

I.C.M.A., London defines Uncontrollable Cost as, "a cost chargeable to a cost centre, which cannot be influenced by the actions of the person in whom, control of the centre is vested". In other words, these are those costs which cannot be influenced by the action of the specified member of an enterprise. It means, these costs are not within the control of management. Practically, all fixed costs are uncontrollable.

6) Normality :

Under this method, costs are classified according to whether these costs are normally incurred at a given level of output in the condition in which that level of activity is normally attained. On this basis, costs are classified into two types which are as follows :

i) Normal Cost :

Normal Cost is defined as, "the cost which is normally incurred to a given level of output in the condition in which that level of output is normally attained". It is a part of the cost of production.

ii) Abnormal Cost :

It is defined as, "a cost which is not normally incurred at a given level of output in the condition in which that level of output is normally attained". It is not a part of cost of production and charged to *Costing Profit and Loss Account*.

7) Time :

On this basis, costs are classified into two types which are as follows :

i) Historical Costs :

It is defined as, "the costs which are ascertained after these have been incurred". Thus, such costs are available only when the production of a particular thing has already been done. Such costs are only of historical value and not useful for cost control purposes. The characteristics of such costs are :
- they are based on recorded facts.
- these costs may be verified with the help of supported documents.
- these are objective in nature because they relate to the past events.

ii) Pre-determined Costs :

It is defined as, "the costs which are ascertained in advance of production on the basis of a specification of all factors affecting cost". These costs are set up from analysis and forecast made before the event and thus, represent not what has happened, but what is expected to happen. Pre-determined cost determined on scientific basis becomes standard cost. Such costs when compared with actual costs determines the reasons of variance. Thus, by these costs, management can fix the responsibility and can take remedial action to avoid its recurrence in future. Pre-determined costs may be in various forms like budgeted cost, estimated cost, standard cost and so on.

8) Association :

On this basis, costs are classified into two types which are as follows :

i) Product Costs :

It is described as the costs which are directly associated with the product. Thus, unit product is sold, these costs provide no benefit. When the products are sold, the total product costs are recovered as an expense. This expense is called the cost of goods sold. Examples of product costs are : Direct material, Direct labour and Factory overheads.

ii) Period Costs :

It is described as the costs which are associated with a particular accounting period. These are not related with the products delivered to the customers. Such costs are charged to Profit and Loss Account of the period. Examples of period costs are : Rent, salaries of office staff, travelling expenses etc. These costs are inventoried i.e. these are not included in the value of closing stocks.

This classification is important for ascertainment of profit. Product cost can be carried forward to the next accounting period as a part of unsold finished stock, whereas period cost is written off in the accounting period in which it is incurred.

9) Investment :

On this basis, costs are classified into two types which are as follows :

i) Capital Costs :

It is defined as, "a cost which is intended to benefit in future period". Capital cost is treated as purchase of an asset. Examples of capital cost are purchase of premises, plant and machinery, furniture etc.

ii) Revenue Costs :

It is defined as, "a cost which is incurred to benefit the current period". Revenue cost is treated as an expense. Examples of revenue costs are : salaries, postage, printing and stationery, rent, rates and taxes, insurance etc.

10) Relevancy :

On the basis of whether the cost items are relevant or irrelevant to the decisions under the consideration of the management, costs may broadly be classified into two types which are as follows :

i) Relevant Costs :

Relevant costs are those costs which have a bearing, or which have an effect on the decisions under the consideration of the management. That means, they are the most pertinent costs and therefore their effects are to be reckoned before taking a decision.

ii) Irrelevant Costs :

Irrelevant costs represent the costs which have no effect on the decisions under the consideration of the management. For instance, marginal cost is an example to relevant costs. It may be noted here that the marginal costs represents the extra cost for an additional unit. On the other hand, sunk cost is a good example to irrelevant costs. Because, sunk cost represents the costs incurred in the past. They are therefore called **past costs.** Since they represent the costs which have already been incurred, no present or future decision is able to alter them. Hence, they are irrelevant.

Types of Costs

These costs are not used for recording purposes, but mostly used for decision-making. From this point of view, Types of Costs may be classified as indicated in Figure 2.10 as follows.

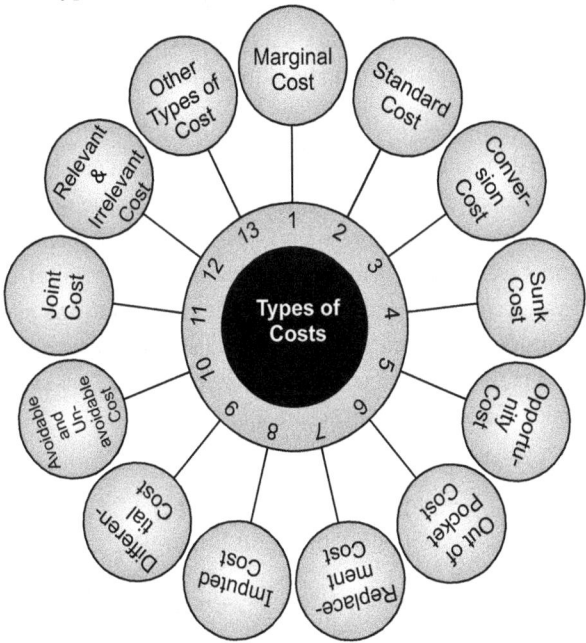

Fig. 2.10 : Types of Costs

1) Marginal Cost :

Marginal Costs are the sum total of variable costs. *I.C.M.A., London* defines it as, "the variable cost of one unit of product or a service i.e. a cost which would be avoided if the unit was not produced or provided". It consists of all direct costs and variable overheads. It is based on the distinction between fixed and variable costs. Fixed costs are ignored and only variable costs are taken into consideration for determining the cost of products and value of work in progress and finished goods. Thus, marginal cost is the additional cost of producing additional units. It remains the same per unit irrespective of the volume of output.

For example, if the cost of producing 50 T.V. sets is given as follows :

			₹
	Variable Costs		1,00,000
Add :	Fixed Costs		(+) 25,000
∴	**Total Costs**		**1,25,000**

If the output is increased by 10 units of T.V. sets, the cost will be as follows :

			₹
	Variable Cost		1,20,000
	(60 T.V. set × ₹ 2,000)		
Add :	Fixed Cost		(+) 25,000
∴	**Total Cost**		**1,45,000**

Thus, the additional costs of producing 10 units of T.V. sets is ₹ 20,000 which is known as the 'Marginal cost or Variable cost'.

2) Standard Cost :

This is a pre-determined estimated cost which an organisation tries to attain under standard normal conditions. Thus, estimates of costs are made before incurring them and then the actual results are compared with the standards to find out the efficiency of a business.

3) Conversion Cost :

It is the term used to denote the sum total of Direct Labour, Direct Expenses and Overhead Costs in the production of a certain product where Material Cost is negligible as in the case of Brick Manufacturing Business. Hence, 'Conversion Cost' is the total of Direct Labour Cost, Direct Expenses and Overhead Costs incurred to convert raw materials – input into finished goods – output. As it includes only the conversion of raw materials from one stage of production to another, it does not consider the negligible Direct Material Cost. Under these circumstances, Labour Cost becomes the major part of Prime Cost as well as Total Cost i.e. Conversion Cost. The composition of Conversion Cost is shown in Figure 2.11 as follows :

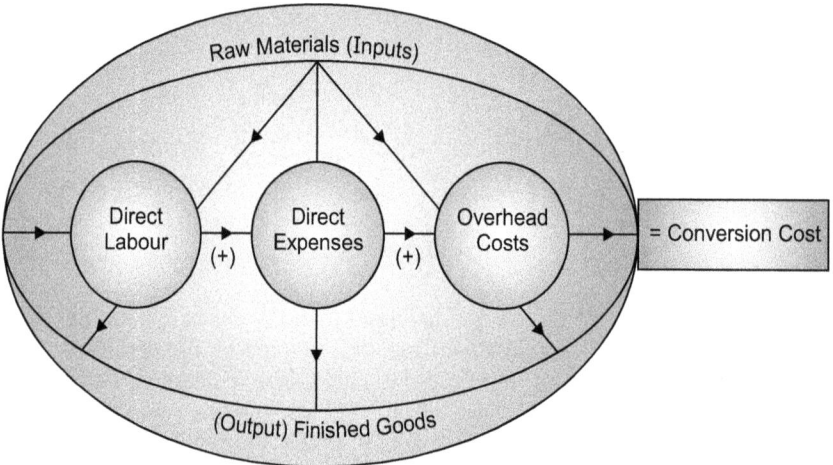

Fig. 2.11 : Composition of Conversion Cost

4) Sunk Cost :

The **National Association of Accountants**, defines a sunk cost as, "an expenditure for equipment or productive resources which has no economic relevance to the present decision-making process". As the name implies it is historical in nature. It is a cost which has been created by a decision that was made in the past which cannot be changed by any decision that will be made in the future. These costs are not relevant for decision-making about the future. Thus, the book value of an asset currently being used is not relevant in making the decision to replace it.

5) Opportunity Cost :

I.C.M.A., London defines it as, "the value of benefit sacrificed in favour of an alternative course of action". *Edward Hermanson and Salmonson* defines it as "the benefit lost by rejecting the best competing alternatives to the one chosen". Thus, Opportunity cost is the sacrifice involved in accepting the alternative under consideration. This concept is used in the problems of alternative choices. Opportunity cost is a pure decision-making cost and is not entered in the books of account. Suppose a company owns a building which is proposed to be used for a special project, the likely rent of the building is the Opportunity Costs, which should be taken into consideration that evaluates the profitability of the project.

6) Out of Pocket Cost :

These are the costs which require cash payments to be made (such as wages, rent etc.) whereas many costs do not require cash outlay (such as depreciation). Out-of-pocket costs are those costs that involve cash outlays or require the utilisation of current resources. Out-of-pocket cost may be either fixed (such as manager's salary) or variable (such as raw material, direct wages etc.) This cost is frequently used as an aid in make or buy decisions, price fixation during recession and many other vital decisions.

7) Replacement Cost :

It is the current market price of replacing an existing asset. The present market price is always considered for taking any decision for buying a machine and not the original cost at which it was bought.

8) Imputed Cost :

I.C.M.A., London defines it as, "a hypothetical cost taken into account to represent a benefit enjoyed by the undertaking in respect of which no actual expense is incurred". They are computed for decision-making purposes. These are the built-up costs which are imaginary. These are the non-cash items. Examples of imputed costs are : rent of owned land, salary of owner, interest on owned capital etc.

9) Differential Cost :

It is the increase or decrease in the total cost which results from taking alternative decisions by the management from amongst the various choices. Thus, the difference between two alternative course of action is known as 'Differential Cost'.

10) Avoidable and Unavoidable Cost :

Avoidable costs are those which can be eliminated if a particular product or department with which they are directly related, is discontinued. For example, salary of the clerks employed can be eliminated if a particular department in which they are employed is decided to discontinue. Unavoidable costs are those costs which cannot be eliminated with the discontinuation of a particular product or department. Such costs are merely allocated if the product or department is discontinued. For example, salary of factory manager or factory rent cannot be eliminated even if a product is eliminated.

11) Joint Cost :

When two or more products are produced from the use of a single raw material, we get either two main products from it, or one may be a main product and the other a by-product. But the cost to produce these are the combined costs. Then the management can take decisions whether to take up manufacture of joint products or to go in for processing of the by-products further, so that the total costs can be reduced.

12) Relevant and Irrelevant Cost:

Relevant costs are those costs that would be changed by the decision. Irrelevant costs are those costs that would not be affected by the decision. It means a relevant cost is a cost whose magnitude will be affected by a decision being made. Management is concerned only with those things which it can affect. For example, management cannot change the cost of equipment purchased in 1980. It can change future costs by its current decisions. Hence, relevant costs are future costs that will differ depending on the action of the management. For each decision the management must decide which costs are relevant. For example, when a manufacturer decides to close a certain unit, the wages associated with the maintenance of such unit is relevant cost as wage payment cease if the unit is closed. But rent which was already paid under lease agreement which cannot be recovered is irrelevant cost.

13) Other Types of Cost:

Other types of costs are described as under:

i) Discretionary Cost:

These are also called managed costs or programmed costs and consist of fixed costs that arise from periodic appropriation decisions that directly reflect top management policies.

ii) Engineered Cost:

These are costs which vary directly with the level of production. These are opposed to managed or discretionary costs.

iii) Shut Down Cost:

A cost which is still incurred although a plant is shut down temporarily, for e.g., rent, rates, depreciation, maintenance of plant, etc.

iv) Traceable Cost:

These are cost which can be easily identified with cost unit or cost centres. The term is used to distinguish it from joint or common costs.

2.3 PREPARATION OF COST SHEET

Meaning

A **Cost Sheet** is an important document prepared by the costing department which shows the analysis for the different elements of cost of the job or a product. The cost data incorporated in Cost Sheet are collected from various statements of accounts which have been recorded in cost accounts, either on day-to-day basis or regular basis. It analyses and classifies the various expenses on different items for a particular period in a tabular form. It may be prepared for a day, a week, a month or so on, as per the specific requirement for a particular period.

Definitions

The term 'Cost-sheet' is defined by various authorities as follows:

i) **C.I.M.A., London** defines Cost-Sheet as, *"a document which provides for the assembly of the estimated detailed cost in respect of a cost centre or a cost unit"*.

ii) W. W. Bigg :

"*the expenditure which has been incurred upon production for a particular period is extracted from the financial books and stores records and set out in a memorandum statement. If the statement is confined to the disclosure of the cost of the units produced during the period, it is termed as 'Cost-Sheet' but where the statement records cost, sales and profit, it is usually known as 'Production Statement'.*

But nowadays, the practice is to prepare the 'Cost-Sheet to show the profit and sales also, hence it is termed as Statement of 'Cost and Profit'.

Thus, **Cost Sheet** is a statement usually prepared to present the analytical cost of total production during a particular period. There is no fixed form for preparation of cost sheet but, in order to make the cost sheet more useful, it is generally presented in columnar form. A Cost Sheet may include as many columns as is desired to show in detail e.g. cost per unit of product, total cost for all the units produced, total cost and per unit cost for the previous year, estimated cost for the future period and so on. A **Cost Sheet** not only shows the total cost but also the various components of total cost. Thus, a cost sheet is a statement prepared to show the detailed analysis of the total cost of production and cost of sales.

Purposes

A Cost Sheet serves the following **purposes** :

i) It discloses the cost per unit as well as the total cost of output.

ii) It discloses the various elements of cost.

iii) It is useful for calculation of tender price as selling price may be fixed in advance.

iv) It helps the management to find out the causes of variations and take steps to eliminate the factors which are responsible for increasing total cost. It is possible by making comparative study of the current cost with the past results and standard costs.

v) It enables a manufacturer to keep a close watch and control over the cost of production.

vi) It helps the management in formulating a definite useful production policy.

Thus, a Cost Sheet is a statement prepared by showing the items of cost of production and services which are analysed by their nature, elements, functions and behaviour. It should also be noted that the non-cost items like the dividends and income-tax paid should not be included in the cost sheets, because they are the appropriations of profits.

A Cost Sheet, including sale, and profit is also known as **Production Account**. Like expanded form of Cost Sheet, the product account consists of two parts. The first part shows the cost of production in total and break-up of costs and the second part known as the 'Statement of Profit' shows sales and profit. Thus, a Cost Sheet is a statement which shows the break-up and built-up of costs. It is a basic document that provides for the assembly of the detailed cost centre or a cost unit.

Proforma of Cost Sheet

(A) Simple Cost Sheet

In the books of a Company

Cost Sheet for the period ended ......

Name of the Product .... Units Produced .... Units Sold ....

	Particulars		Total Cost ₹	Unit Cost ₹
	Direct Materials		–	–
Add :	Direct Labour	(+)	–	–
Add :	Direct Expenses	(+)	–	–
∴	**Prime Cost**	i)	–	–
Add :	Factory Overheads	(+)	–	–
∴	**Factory Cost / Works Cost**	ii)	–	–
Add :	Office Overheads	(+)	–	–
∴	**Cost of Production / Office Cost**	iii)	–	–
Add :	Selling and Distribution Overheads	(+)	–	–
∴	**Total Cost / Cost of Sales**	iv)	–	–
Add :	Profit /	v) (+)	–	–
Less :	Loss	(–)		
	Sales		–	–

(B) Cost Sheet with Stock Adjustments

In the books of a Company

Cost Sheet for the period ended ......

Name of the Product ...... Units Produced ...... Units Sold ......

	Particulars		Total Cost ₹	Unit Cost ₹
	Opening Stock of Raw Materials		–	–
Add :	Purchases of Raw Materials	(+)	–	–
Add :	Expenses on Purchases of Raw Materials	(+)	–	–
			–	–
Less :	Closing Stock of Raw Materials	(–)	–	–
Less :	Purchases Returns	(–)	–	–
Less :	Sale of Scrap or Defectives of Raw Materials	(–)	–	–

	Particulars		Total Cost ₹	Unit Cost ₹
∴	Cost of Materials Consumed	i)	–	–
Add :	Direct Labour	(+)	–	–
Add :	Direct Expenses	(+)	–	–
∴	**Prime Cost**	ii)	–	–
Add :	Factory Overheads	(+)	–	–
Add :	Opening Stock of Work-in-Progress	(+)	–	–
			–	–
Less :	Closing Stock of Work-in-Progress	(–)	–	–
Less :	Sale of Scrap or Defectives of Work-in-progress	(–)	–	–
∴	**Factory Cost / Works Cost**	iii)	–	–
Add :	Office Overheads	(+)	–	–
∴	**Cost of Production / Office Cost**	iv)	–	–
Add :	Opening Stock of Finished Goods	(+)	–	–
			–	–
Less :	Closing Stock of Finished Goods	(–)	–	–
∴	**Cost of Goods Sold**	v)	–	–
Add :	Selling and Distribution Overheads	(+)	–	–
∴	**Total Cost / Cost of Sales**	vi)	–	–
∴	Add Profit or	vii) (+)	–	–
	Less Loss	(–)	–	–
	Sales		–	–

In present day practice, a 'Cost-Sheet' is prepared in columnar form to show the actual cost details for current period, historical costs for previous period and cost estimations for future period with total cost and unit cost calculations shown separately. The comparative analysis of the cost helps the management to make use of such analytical cost sheet as an instrument of cost planning and cost control. The Proforma of such Analytical Cost Sheet is as follows :

(C) Analytical Cost Sheet

In the books of a Company
Cost-Sheet for the period ended ......

Name of the Product .... Units Produced .... Units Sold ....

Previous Period		Particulars	Current Period		Future Period		Remarks
Historical Costs			Actual Costs		Estimated Costs		
Total Cost ₹	Unit Cost ₹		Total Cost ₹	Unit Cost ₹	Total Cost ₹	Unit Cost ₹	
		Direct Materials Add : Direct Labour Add : Direct Expenses ∴ **Prime Cost** i) Add : Works Overheads ∴ **Works Cost** ii) Add : Office Overheads ∴ **Cost of Production** iii) Add : Selling and Distribution Overheads ∴ **Cost of Sales** iv) Add : Profit or v) Less : Loss ∴ **Sales**					

Thus, **Cost Sheet** is an analytical statement of cost prepared periodically to show the details of cost incurred during a particular period, on production of a specific unit of cost. It gives cost details regarding total cost, various components of total cost and unit cost. The actual cost built up and the details of cost components are as follows :

i) **Cost of Materials Consumed :**

    = Opening Stock of Raw Materials (+) Purchases of Raw Materials (+) Expenses for Purchases of Raw Materials (–) Closing Stock of Raw Materials (–) Purchases Returns (–) Sale of Scrap of Raw Materials.

ii) **Prime Cost :**

    = Direct Materials (+) Direct Labour (+) Direct Expenses.

iii) **Works Cost :**

    = Prime Cost (+) Factory Overheads (+) Opening Stock of Work-in-Progress (–) Closing Stock of Work-in-Progress

iv) Cost of Production :

= Works Cost (+) Office Overheads

v) Cost of Goods Sold :

= Cost of Production (+) Opening Stock of Finished Goods (–) Closing Stock of Finished Goods

vi) Cost of Sales :

= Cost of Goods sold (+) Selling and Distribution Overheads

vii) Sales :

= Cost of Sales (+) Profit or Loss

Summary List

Following is the summary list of various items of cost included in the major group of cost and the synonymous terms used for the same in the simplified preparation of a Cost Sheet, Tender, Quotation and Estimates.

(DM) Direct Materials :

Viz. Direct Materials Cost, Prime Cost Materials, Cost of Materials Consumed, Process Materials, Cost of Materials Purchased, Operating Materials, Value of Raw Materials Used, Basic Materials, Productive Materials Cost.

e.g. **Opening Stock of Raw Materials**

Add : Purchases of Materials

Add : Primary Packing Charges

Add : Expenses for Purchases of Raw Materials, e.g. Carriage Inward, Freight Inward, Carriage and Cartage, Octroi Duty and Customs, Excise Duty, Dock Charges, Clearing Charges, Forwarding Charges, Loading and Unloading, Transportation Charges etc.

Less : Closing Stock of Raw Materials

Less : Sale of Scrap or Defectives of Raw Materials

Less : Returns Outward or Purchases Returns or Returns to Suppliers or Defective Materials Returned to Creditors.

(DL) Direct Labour :

Viz. Direct Labour Cost, Prime Cost Labour, Direct Wages, Process Labour, Operating Labour, Basic Labour, Productive Labour.

e.g. Productive Wages, Wages paid to direct Workers, Outstanding Wages etc.

(DE) Direct Expenses :

Viz. Chargeable Expenses, Prime Cost Expenses, Productive Expenses, Basic Expenses.

e.g. Royalty, Hire of Special Plant, Cost of Patterns, Layout, Designs or Drawings, Architects Fees, Engineers Fees, Surveyors Fees, Licence Fees, Outstanding Direct Expenses etc.

(PC) **Prime Cost :**

viz. Direct Cost, Basic Cost, Operating Cost, First Cost, Productive Cost, Flat Cost.

(F) **Factory Overheads :**

viz. Works on Cost, Manufacturing Expenses, Factory Burden.

e.g. Indirect Materials, Factory Lighting Expense, Materials, Motive Power, On Cost Materials, Factory Rent, Rates, Taxes and Insurance, Indirect Labour, Property Tax on Factory Premises, On Cost Wages, Electric Power, Indirect Expenses, Rent of Raw Material Stores, On Cost Expenses, Workshop Rent, Heating and Lighting, Coal and Coke, Steam, Gas and Water, Power and Fuel, Wages to Indirect Labourers i.e. Shop Floor Helpers, Supervisors, Cleaners, Oilers etc. Remunerations to Watch and Ward Staff, Instructors, Factory Clerical Staff, Works Manager, Production Engineer, etc., Technical Directors Fees, Labour Welfare and Amenities to Production Staff, Expenses on Workers Canteen, Entertainment Room, Creches etc., Consumable Stores, Cotton, Oil and Wastes, Haulage, Lubricants, Expenses of Testing Labs., Laboratory Expenses, Drawing Office Salaries, Repairs, Maintenance, Renewals and Depreciation on Plant and Machinery, Tools and Equipments, Fixtures and Patterns, Factory Buildings etc. Cost of Factory Supervision, General Works Overheads, Sundry Factory Expenses, Other Manufacturing on Cost, Factory Cleaning Charges, Storekeeping Expenses, Upkeep of Raw Materials Stores, Time-keeping Expenses, Time Office Expenses, Normal Wastage and Spoilage, Miscellaneous Production Expenses, Works Stationery, Idle Time Wages, Subscription of Technical Journals and Magazines, Works Office Expenses, Internal Transport, Materials Handling Charges, Unproductive Wages, Wages and Salaries, Power and Lighting etc.

(FC) **Factory Cost :**

Viz. Works Cost, Manufacturing Cost, Production Cost.

(O) **Office Overheads :**

Viz. Administration Expenses, Management on Cost, Establishment Overheads.

e.g. Indirect Materials, Indirect Labour and Indirect Expenses of Administrative Office, Office Rent, Rates, Taxes, Insurance, Lighting Expenses , Petrol and Maintenance on Vehicles etc. Property Tax on Office Premises, Office Salaries, Salaries and Wages, Directors Fees, General Managers Salaries and Allowances, Counting House Salaries, Directors Travelling Expenses, General Office Overheads, Electric Lighting, Electricity and Lighting Charges, General on Cost, Sundry Expenses, Other Adminstrative Charges, Miscellaneous Office Expenses, Expenses of Management, Branch Office Expenses, Office Cleaning Charges, Repairs, Maintenance, Renewals and Depreciation on Office Furniture, Office Buildings, Office Equipments, Office Appliances, etc. Renovation of Administrative Office, Lighting and Power, Salaries and Wages, Printing and Stationery, Postage and Telegrams, Telephone Charges, Legal Fees, Audit Fees, Accountancy Charges, Office Conveyance, General Fees, Air-conditioning to Administrative Office, Office Supplies and Expenses, Bank Charges, General Establishment Charges, Office Lighting, Subscription of Trade Journals, Public Relation Expenses, Petrol and Maintenance of Office Vehicles etc.

(COP) Cost of Production :

Viz. Gross Cost, Office Cost.

(S) Selling and Distribution Overheads :

viz. Selling Expenses, Distribution on Cost, Marketing Overheads.

e.g. Indirect Materials, Indirect Labour and Indirect Expenses of Sales Office, Salaries and Allowances to Sales Manager, Marketing Executive, Publicity Officer, Travelling Salesmen, Sales Office Staff, etc.; Travelling Salesmen Salaries and Commission, Selling Agents Salaries and Commission, Carriage on Sales, Commission on Sales, Travelling Expenses, Carriage and Cartage Outward, Freight Outward, Loading and Unloading of Finished Goods, Recurring Expenses of Delivery Vans, Show-room Expenses, Sales Branches and Sales Depat Expenses, Packing Charges, Secondary Packing Charges, Advertisement, Publicity Charges, Cost of Special Advertisement, After Sales Service Expenses, Distribution of Free Samples and Gifts, Diaries and Calendars, Gift Articles and Folders, etc., Bad Debts, Debts Collection Charges, Cash Discount Allowed, Catalogue Expenses, Tendering Expenses, Repairs, Maintenance, Renewals and Depreciation on Delivery Vans, Sales Depats, Show-rooms, Sales Premises etc., Delivery Van Running Expenses, Upkeep of Delivery Vans, Warehouse Expenses, Sales Promotion Expenses, Rent, Rates, Taxes, Insurance and Lighting of Sales Office, Selling on Cost, Warehouse Labour Charges, Other Expenses for Handling of Finished Goods in Stores, Sales Printing and Stationery, Market Research Expenses, Estimating Expenses, Demonstration Expenses, Loading and Unloading of Finished Goods, Price List, Catalogue, Banners, Hand Bills, Posters, etc. Export Duty, Drivers, Conductors, Cleaners Salaries and Wages, Cost of Mailing Literature, Sales Promotion Expenses etc.

(TC) Total Cost :

Viz. Cost of Sales, Cost Price, Cost of Turnover, Sales Cost, Turnover Cost, Net Cost.

(P) Profit :

Viz. Net Margin

(L) Loss :

(S) Sales :

Viz. Selling Price, Value of Sales, Market Price, Value of Turnover, Invoice Price, Inflated Price, Loaded Price.

(NCI) Non Cost Items :

Viz. Items to be excluded from Cost.

e.g.

  (1) Financial Incomes :

  Capital Profits, Dividend Received, Brokerage and Commission Received, Share Transfer Fees Received, Interest on Investments, Interest on Bank Deposits, Rent Received, Bad Debts Recovery, Interest on Loan given, Discount Received etc.

(2) **Financial Charges:**

Capital Losses, Cash Discount, Trade Discount, Penalties and Fines, Share Transfer Fees Paid, Interest on Bank Loan, Interest on Debentures, Preliminary Expenses, Underwriting Commission, Discount on Issue of Shares and Debentures, Loss on Investments, Capital Expenses, Interest on Capitals, Salary or Commission paid to Partners, Income Tax, Wealth Tax, Interest on Debentures, Reconstruction Expenses, Development Expenses, Reorganisation Expenses etc.

(3) **Appropriations:**

Bad Debts Reserve, Dividends Paid, Charitable Donations, Transfer to Reserves, Sinking Fund, Debenture Redemption Fund, Machinery Replacement Fund, Investment Fluctuation Fund, etc.

(4) **Abnormals:**

Abnormal Wastage, Abnormal Idle Time, Loss by fire, Loss by Theft, Loss of Stock, etc.

EXAMPLE

Prepare a Statement of Cost from the following information relating to Mumbai Traders, Mumbai for the year ended 31st March, 2015.

	₹
Cost of Direct Materials	2,00,000
Sales	4,00,000
Direct Wages	1,00,000
Office Indirect Materials	5,000
Cost of special patterns	40,000
Postage and Telegrams	2,000
Factory Rent and Insurance	5,000
Outstanding Chargeable Expenses	2,000
Carriage Outward	2,500
Interest on Loan	2,150
Printing and Stationery	500
Factory Indirect wages	3,000
Selling on cost	4,000
Travelling salesman's salary	4,000
Factory Indirect Material	1,000
Royalties	8,000
General Works Overheads	2,000
Bad debts written-off	1,000

Also calculate the percentage of profits earned to sales.

ANSWER

In the books of Mumbai Traders, Mumbai
Statement of Cost for the year ended 31st March, 2015

Particulars			Amount ₹	Amount ₹
	Cost of Direct Materials		2,00,000	
Add :	Direct Wages	(+)	1,00,000	
Add :	Direct Expenses :			
a)	Cost of Special Patterns		40,000	
b)	Outstanding Chargeable Expenses		2,000	
c)	Royalties	(+)	8,000	
	Prime Cost	i)	3,50,000	3,50,000
Add :	Factory Expenses :			
a)	Factory Rent and Insurance		5,000	
b)	Factory Indirect Wages		3,000	
c)	Factory Indirect Material		1,000	
d)	General Works Overheads	(+)	2,000	
	Factory Cost	ii)	3,61,000	3,61,000
Add :	Office Expenses :			
a)	Office Indirect Materials		5,000	
b)	Postage and Telegrams		2,000	
c)	Printing and Stationery	(+)	500	
	Cost of Production	iii)	3,68,500	3,68,500
Add :	Selling and Distribution Expenses :			
a)	Carriage Outward		2,500	
b)	Selling on Cost		4,000	
c)	Travelling Salesman's Salary		4,000	
d)	Bad Debts written-off	(+)	1,000	
	Total Cost	iv)	3,80,000	3,80,000
Add :	**Profit for the year**	v) (+)	20,000	20,000
	Sales		4,00,000	4,00,000

Working Notes :

i) Calculation of percentage of profits earned to sales :

For ₹ 4,00,000 Sales = ₹ 20,000 Profits.

∴ 100 = ?

$$= \frac{100 \times ₹\, 20,000}{₹\, 4,00,000}$$

$$= 5\%$$

ii) Interest on Loan is an item of financial nature hence it should be excluded from cost.

ILLUSTRATIONS

ILLUSTRATION 1

From the following particulars relating to M/s Rajchand Rayon Manufacturers, Chinchwad, prepare a Simple Cost-Sheet showing a) Prime Cost, b) Works Cost, c) Cost of Production, d) Cost of Sales, e) Profit or Loss for the period, for six months ended 31st March, 2015.

	₹
Cost of Materials Consumed	40,000
Oil and Waste	100
Operating Labour	9,000
Wages of Foreman	1,000
Direct Expenses	2,000
Store keepers Wages	500
Sales – Cash and Credit	1,00,000
Commission paid to the partner, Mr. Chandmal	350
Electric Power	200
Salary paid to the partner, Mr. Rajmal	650
Consumable Stores	1,000
Direct Wages Payable	1,000
Lighting :	
• Factory Plant	500
• Office Establishment	200
Carriage Outward	150
Rent :	
• Administrative Office	1,000
• Workshop	2,000
Warehouse Charges	200
Repairs and Renewals :	
• Factory Plant	500
• Machinery	1,000
• Office Premises	200
• Warehouse	100
Interest on Bank Overdraft	340
Advertising	400
Depreciation :	
• Office Buildings	500
• Machinery	200
Travelling Expenses	200
Office Manager's Salary	2,250
Salesmen's Commission and Salaries	500
Director's Fees	500
Printing and Stationery	200
Telephone Charges	50
Postage	100
Bad Debts	450

SOLUTION

In the books of M/s Rajchand Rayon Manufacturers, Chinchwad
Cost-Sheet for the six months ended 31st March, 2015

	Particulars		Amount ₹	Amount ₹
	Cost of Materials Consumed		40,000	
Add :	Direct Labour :		10,000	
	a) Operating Labour	9,000		
	b) Direct Wages Payable	(+) 1,000		
Add :	Direct Expenses	(+)	2,000	
∴	**Prime Cost**	i)	52,000	52,000
Add :	Factory Overheads :		7,000	
	a) Oil and Waste	100		
	b) Wages of Foreman	1,000		
	c) Storekeepers Wages	500		
	d) Electric Power	200		
	e) Consumable Stores	1,000		
	f) Lighting – Factory Plant	500		
	g) Rent – Workshop	2,000		
	h) Repairs and Renewals - Factory Plant	500		
	i) Repairs and Renewals - Machinery	1,000		
	j) Depreciation - Machinery	(+) 200		
		(+)		
∴	**Works Cost**	ii)	59,000	59,000
Add :	Office Overheads :		5,000	
	a) Lighting – Office Establishment	200		
	b) Rent – Administrative Office	1,000		
	c) Repairs and Renewals – Office Premises	200		
	d) Depreciation – Office Buildings	500		
	e) Office Manager's Salary	2,250		
	f) Director's Fees	500		
	g) Printing and Stationery	200		
	h) Telephone Charges	50		
	i) Postage	(+) 100		
		(+)		
∴	**Cost of Production**	iii)	64,000	64,000
Add :	Selling and Distribution Overheads :		2,000	
	a) Carriage Outward	150		
	b) Warehouse Charges	200		
	c) Repairs and Renewals – Warehouse	100		
	d) Advertising	400		
	e) Travelling Expenses	200		
	f) Salesmen's Commission and Salaries	500		
	g) Bad Debts	(+) 450		
		(+)		
∴	**Cost of Sales**	iv)	66,000	66,000
Add :	Profit for the period	v) (+)	34,000	34,000
	Sales – Cash and Credit		1,00,000	1,00,000

Basics of Cost Accounting — Elements of Cost and Cost Sheet

Working Notes :

i) Commission paid to the partner Mr. Chandmal, salary paid to the partner Mr. Rajmal and Interest on Bank Overdraft are the items to be excluded from cost.

ILLUSTRATION 2

The Cost of Sale of product 'Butnol' is made up as follows :

	₹
Royalties	1,000
Materials used in Production – Direct	12,000
Carriage on Sales	1,250
Materials used in Primary Packing	9,000
Carriage on Purchases	5,000
Materials used in Secondary Packing	1,500
Bad Debts	3,250
Materials used in Factory Workshop	750
Coal and Coke	1,750
Materials used in Administrative Office	1,250
Administration on Cost	750
Labour required in Manufacturing – Direct	9,500
General Overheads	1,000
Purchases of Raw Materials	44,000
Labour required for Works Supervision	2,500
Motive Power	1,000
Productive Wages Payable	500
Chargeable Expenses	4,000

Assuming that all products manufactured in Peterson Chemicals Ltd., Bhosari are sold, what should be the Invoice Price to obtain a profit of 20% on Selling Price ?

SOLUTION

In the books of Peterson Chemicals Ltd., Bhosari
Cost Sheet for the period ended ……   Product : Butnol

Particulars			Amount ₹	Amount ₹
Direct Materials :				
a) Materials used in Production – Direct		12,000		
b) Materials used in Primary Packing		9,000		
c) Purchases of Raw Materials		44,000		
d) Carriage on Purchases	(+)	5,000	70,000	
Add : Direct Labour :				
a) Labour required in Manufacturing – Direct		9,500		
b) Productive Wages Payable	(+)	500	10,000	
Add : Direct Expenses :				
a) Royalties		1,000		
b) Chargeable Expenses	(+)	4,000	5,000	
∴ **Prime Cost**		i)	85,000	85,000

Particulars		Amount ₹	Amount ₹
Add: Factory Overheads:			
a) Materials used in Factory Workshop	750		
b) Coal and Coke	1,750		
c) Labour required for Works Supervision	2,500		
d) Motive Power	(+) 1,000	6,000	
∴ Factory Cost ii)		91,000	91,000
Add: Office Overheads:			
a) Materials used in Administrative Office	1,250		
b) Administration on Cost	750		
c) General Overheads	+ 1,000	3,000	
∴ Cost of Production iii)		94,000	94,000
Add: Selling and Distribution Overheads:			
a) Carriage on Sales	1,250		
b) Materials used in Secondary Packing	1,500		
c) Bad Debts	(+) 3,250	6,000	
	(+)		
Total Cost iv)		1,00,000	1,00,000
Add: Profit v)		25,000	25,000
(20% on Selling Price)	(+)		
∴ Invoice Price		1,25,000	1,25,000

Working Notes:

i) Calculation of Profit i.e. 20% on Selling Price

Selling Price = Total Cost + Profit
100   80   20

If 80 TC = 20 P

∴ ₹ 1,00,000 TC = ?

$$= \frac{₹\,1,00,000 \times 20}{80}$$

= ₹ 25,000

ILLUSTRATION 3

Prepare a Statement of Cost from the following information relating to Cotton Textiles Ltd., Mumbai, for the year ended 31st March, 2015.

	₹
Cost of Direct Materials	2,00,000
Sales	4,00,000
Direct Wages	1,00,000
Office Indirect Materials	5,000
Cost of Special Patterns	40,000
Postage and Telegram	2,000
Bad Debts Recovered	250
Factory Rent and Insurance	5,000
Outstanding Chargeable Expenses	2,000

Basics of Cost Accounting — Elements of Cost and Cost Sheet

Particulars	Amount ₹
Carriage Outward	2,500
Interest on Loan	2,150
Printing and Stationery	500
Factory Indirect wages	3,000
Selling on Cost	4,000
Travelling Salesman's Salary	4,000
Works Indirect Material	1,000
Royalties	8,000
General Works Overheads	2,000
Bad Debts written-off	1,000

Also calculate the percentage of profits earned to sales.

SOLUTION

In the books of Cotton Textiles Ltd., Mumbai
Statement of Cost for the year ended 31st March, 2015

	Particulars		Amount ₹	Amount ₹
	Cost of Direct Materials		2,00,000	
Add:	Direct Wages	(+)	1,00,000	
Add:	Direct Expenses:		50,000	
	a) Cost of Special Patterns	40,000		
	b) Outstanding Chargeable Expenses	2,000		
	c) Royalties	(+) 8,000		
		(+)		
	∴ **Prime Cost**	i)	3,50,000	3,50,000
Add:	Factory Overheads:		11,000	
	a) Factory Rent and Insurance	5,000		
	b) Factory Indirect Wages	3,000		
	c) Works Indirect Material	1,000		
	d) General Works Overheads	(+) 2,000		
		(+)		
	∴ **Factory Cost**	ii)	3,61,000	3,61,000
Add:	Office Overheads:		7,500	
	a) Office Indirect Materials	5,000		
	b) Postage and Telegram	2,000		
	c) Printing and Stationery	(+) 500		
		(+)		
	∴ **Cost of Production**	iii)	3,68,500	3,68,500
Add:	Selling and Distribution Overheads:		11,500	
	a) Carriage Outward	2,500		
	b) Selling on Cost	4,000		
	c) Travelling Salesman's Salary	4,000		
	d) Bad Debts written-off	(+) 1,000		
		(+)		
	∴ **Total Cost**	iv)	3,80,000	3,80,000
Add:	Profits for the year	v) (+)	20,000	20,000
	Sales		4,00,000	4,00,000

Working Notes :

i) Calculation of percentage of profits earned to sales

If ₹ 4,00,000 Sales = ₹ 20,000 Profit

∴ 100 = ?

$$= \frac{100 \times ₹ 20,000}{₹ 4,00,000}$$

= 5%

ii) Bad Debts recovered and Interest on Loan are the items to be excluded from cost.

ILLUSTRATION 4

Majestic Furnitures Ltd., Manmad, manufactures Cots, Tables, Chairs and Cupboards. The following are the cost details available for the year ended 31st March, 2015.

Particulars	Prime Cost Materials ₹	Process Labour ₹	Productive Expenses ₹	Value of Turnover ₹
Cots	50,000	30,000	16,000	1,50,000
Tables	45,000	20,000	19,000	1,20,000
Chairs	70,000	40,000	18,000	2,00,000
Cupboards (+)	28,000	50,000	2,000	1,30,000
Total	1,93,000	1,40,000	55,000	6,00,000

Additional Information :

- Works on Cost ... 80% of Direct Wages   ₹
- Bad Debts Provision   ...   600
- Administrative Overheads   ...   15,000
- Bad Debts Recovery   ...   250
- Selling and Distribution Expenses ... 12,000
- Book Debts   ...   41,000

Allocate Management on Cost on the basis of Works Cost and Selling and Distribution Overheads on the basis of Actual Sales. You are required to prepare a Simple Cost Statement showing the following in case of each of the product in the columnar form.

a) Direct Cost, b) Factory Cost, c) Cost of Production, d) Cost of Sales and e) Profit or Loss for the year.

SOLUTION

In the books of Majestic Furnitures Ltd., Manmad
Cost Statement for the year ended 31st March, 2015

Particulars		Cots ₹	Tables ₹	Chairs ₹	Cupboards ₹	Total ₹
Prime Cost Materials		50,000	45,000	70,000	28,000	1,93,000
Add : Process Labour		30,000	20,000	40,000	50,000	1,40,000
Add : Productive Expenses (+)		16,000	19,000	18,000	2,000	55,000
∴ Direct Cost	i)	96,000	84,000	1,28,000	80,000	3,88,000
Add : Works on Cost (80% of Direct Wages i.e. Process Labour) (+)		24,000	16,000	32,000	40,000	1,12,000
∴ Factory Cost	ii)	1,20,000	1,00,000	1,60,000	1,20,000	5,00,000
Add : Administrative Overheads (+)		3,600	3,000	4,800	3,600	15,000
∴ Cost of Production	iii)	1,23,600	1,03,000	1,64,800	1,23,600	5,15,000
Add : Selling and Distribution Expenses (+)		3,000	2,400	4,000	2,600	12,000
∴ Cost of Sales	iv)	1,26,600	1,05,400	1,68,800	1,26,200	5,27,000
Add : Profits for the year	v) (+)	23,400	14,600	31,200	3,800	73,000
Value of Turnover		1,50,000	1,20,000	2,00,000	1,30,000	6,00,000

Working Notes :

i) Allocation of Management on Cost (i.e. Administrative Overheads) on the basis of Works Cost (i.e. Factory Cost).

Particulars		Cots	Tables	Chairs	Cupboards
Factory Cost	₹	1,20,000	1,00,000	1,60,000	1,20,000
∴ Ratio		6	5	8	6
Allocation of Administrative Overheads (₹ 15,000 / 6 : 5 : 8 : 6)	₹	3,600	3,000	4,800	3,600

ii) Allocation of Selling and Distribution Overheads (i.e. Selling and Distribution Expenses) on the basis of Actual Sales (i.e. Value of Turnover).

Particulars		Cots	Tables	Chairs	Cupboards
Value of Turnover	₹	1,50,000	1,20,000	2,00,000	1,30,000
∴ Ratio		15	12	20	13
Allocation of Selling and Distribution Expenses (₹ 12,000 / 15 : 12 : 20 : 13)	₹	3,000	2,400	4,000	2,600

iii) Bad Debts Provision, Bad Debts Recovery and Book Debts are the items to be excluded from cost.

ILLUSTRATION 5

Sudarshan Chemicals Ltd., Satana, produces a standard product, the cost data relating to the same for April, 2015 is given below. You are required to prepare a Cost Sheet showing separately
 i) Cost of Materials Consumed, ii) Prime Cost, iii) Works Cost,
 iv) Cost of Production   v) Total Cost, vi) Net Profit and vii) Market Price.

₹

Purchases of Materials – Cash	4,000
Establishment Overheads : 20% of Factory Cost	
Wages Payable	800
Purchases of Materials – Credit	12,000

Works Overheads : 80% of Direct Wages
Cost of Special Designs — 850
Clearing Charges on Purchases — 1,200
Productive Wages — 3,200
Selling on Cost : ₹ 4 per unit sold
Chargeable Expenses Payable — 150
Defective Materials Returned — 400
Distribution Overheads : ₹ 1 per unit despatched
Trade Discount — 785

During the month of April, 2015, units sold and despatched were 1,300 units only. Also find out the market price per unit on the basis that profit mark-up is uniformly made to yield a profit of 4% on Cost of Sales.

SOLUTION

In the books of Sudarshan Chemicals Ltd., Satana

Cost Sheet for the month ended 30th April, 2015

Units Produced – 1,300
Units Sold – 1,300

	Particulars			Amount ₹	Amount ₹
	Purchases of Materials		16,000		
	a) Cash	4,000			
	b) Credit	(+) 12,000			
Add :	Clearing Charges on Purchases		(+) 1,200		
			17,200		
Less :	Defective Materials Returned		(–) 400		
	∴ **Cost of Materials Consumed**	i)		16,800	16,800
Add :	Direct Labour :				
	a) Wages Payable		800		
	b) Productive Wages		(+) 3,200	4,000	
Add :	Direct Expenses :				
	a) Cost of Special Designs		850		
	b) Chargeable Expenses Payable		(+) 150	1,000	
	∴ **Prime Cost**	ii)		21,800	21,800
Add :	Works Overheads :				
	(80% of Direct Wages i.e. ₹ 4,000)			3,200	
	∴ **Works Cost**	iii)		25,000	25,000
Add :	Establishment Overheads :				
	(20% of Factory Cost i.e. ₹ 25,000)			5,000	
	∴ **Cost of Production**	iv)		30,000	30,000
Add :	Selling and Distribution Overheads :				
	a) Selling on Cost			5,200	
	(₹ 4 × Units Sold – 1,300 i.e. ₹ 5,200)				
	b) Distribution Overheads –			1,300	
	(Re. 1 × Units Despatched – 1,300 i.e. ₹ 1,300)				
	∴ **Total Cost**	v)		36,500	36,500
Add :	Net Profit	vi)			
	(4% on Cost of Sales i.e. ₹ 36,500)			1,460	1,460
	∴ **Market Price**	vii)		37,960	37,960

Working Notes:

i) Calculation of Net Profit i.e. 4% on Cost of Sales.
 = 4% of ₹ 36,500 i.e. Cost of Sales
 = ₹ 1,460

ii) Calculation of Market Price per unit.
 = Market Price / Number of Units Sold
 = ₹ 37,960 / Units 1,300
 = ₹ 29.20 per unit.

ILLUSTRATION 6

The accounts of Dorabjee Manufacturers, Deolali for the year ended 31st March, 2015 shows the following.

	₹
Stock of Raw Materials as on 1-4-2015	67,200
Bad Debts written-off	9,100
Raw Materials Purchased	2,59,000
Motive Power	320
Traveller's Commission	10,780
Depreciation on Office Equipments	420
Carriage Inward	720
Interest on Bank Loan	380
Factory Taxes	11,900
Productive Wages	1,76,400
Directors Travelling Expenses	8,400
Coal and Coke	560
General Overheads	4,760
Gas and Water - Factory	1,680
Packing Charges	940
Sales of Finished Goods	6,00,000
Manager's Salary (Factory - $2/3$, Office - $1/3$)	15,000
Delivery Van Expenses	4,060
Depreciation on Factory Buildings	18,200
Publicity Charges	2,000
Repairs to Plant	6,340
Carriage Outward	7,120
Hire Charges of Special Machinery	9,010
Office Rent	2,800
Surveyor's Fees	590
Legal Charges	620
Stock of Raw Materials as on 31-3-2015	87,920

Prepare a Cost Statement giving the following details for the year ended 31st March, 2015.

i) Cost of Material Consumed ii) Prime Cost
iii) Works Cost iv) Cost of Production
v) Total Cost vi) Net Profit for the year.

SOLUTION

In the books of Dorabjee Manufacturers, Deolali
Cost Statement for the year ended 31st March, 2015

Particulars			Amount ₹	Amount ₹
	Stock of Raw Materials as on 1-4-2014	67,200		
Add :	Raw Materials purchased	2,59,000		
Add :	Carriage inward	(+) 720		
		3,26,920		
Less :	Stock of Raw Materials as on 31-3-2015	(−) 87,920		
	∴ Cost of Materials Consumed i)		2,39,000	2,39,000
Add :	Productive Wages	(+)	1,76,400	
Add :	Direct Expenses :			
a)	Hire Charges of Special Machinery	9,010		
b)	Surveyor's Fees	(+) 590	9,600	
	∴ Prime Cost ii)		4,25,000	4,25,000
Add :	Factory Overheads :			
a)	Motive Power	320		
b)	Factory Taxes	11,900		
c)	Coal and Coke	560		
d)	Gas and Water - Factory	1,680		
e)	Manager's Salary – Factory ($2/3 \times ₹15,000$)	10,000		
f)	Depreciation on Factory Buildings	18,200		
g)	Repairs to Plant	(+) 6,340	49,000	
	∴ Works Cost iii)		4,74,000	4,74,000
Add :	Office Overheads :			
a)	Depreciation on Office Equipments	420		
b)	Director's Travelling Expenses	8,400		
c)	General Overheads	4,760		
d)	Manager's Salary – Office ($1/3 \times ₹15,000$)	5,000		
e)	Office Rent	2,800		
f)	Legal Charges	(+) 620	22,000	
	∴ Cost of Production iv)		4,96,000	4,96,000
Add :	Selling and Distribution Overheads :			
a)	Bad Debts written-off	9,100		
b)	Traveller's Commission	10,780		
c)	Packing Charges	940		
d)	Delivery Van Expenses	4,060		
e)	Publicity Charges	2,000		
f)	Carriage Outward	(+) 7,120	34,000	
	∴ Total Cost v)		5,30,000	5,30,000
Add :	Net Profit for the year vi)		70,000	70,000
	Sales of Finished Goods		6,00,000	6,00,000

Working Notes :
i) Interest on Bank Loan is an item to be excluded from cost.

ILLUSTRATION 7

Following details have been obtained from the cost records of Colgate Ltd., Kolkata, for the year ended 31st March, 2015.

	₹
Stock of Operating Materials as on 1-4-2014	30,000
Wages paid to Direct Workers	55,000
Interim Dividend paid	12,000
Purchases of Raw Materials	87,000
Heating and Lighting	6,000
Counting House Salaries	20,000
Carriage and Cartage on Purchases of Raw Materials	3,000
Commission on Sales	5,000
Wages Payable	5,000
Technical Director's Fees	10,000
Stock of Operating Material as on 31-3-2015	40,000
Showroom Expenses	7,000
Establishment on Cost	12,000
Share Transfer Fees	2,000
Expenses of Testing Labs.	4,000
Branch Office Expenses	8,000
After-Sales Service Expenses	8,000
Selling Price	2,50,000

Prepare a Cost-Sheet showing :

i) Cost of Raw Materials Consumed, ii) Prime Cost, iii) Works Cost, iv) Cost of Production, v) Total Cost and vi) Profit or Loss

Also calculate the percentage of :

i) Factory Overheads to Direct Wages, ii) Office on-Cost to Works Cost and iii) Selling and Distribution Expenses to Cost of Production.

SOLUTION

In the books of Colgate Ltd., Kolkata
Cost-Sheet for the year ended 31st March, 2015

Particulars		Amount ₹	Amount ₹
Stock of Operating Material as on 1-4-2014	30,000		
Add : Purchases of Raw Materials	87,000		
Add : Carriage and Cartage on Purchases of Raw Materials	(+) 3,000		
	1,20,000		
Less : Stock of Operating Material as on 31-3-2015	(−) 40,000		
∴ Cost of Raw Materials Consumed i)		80,000	80,000
Add : Direct Labour :			
a) Wages paid to Direct Workers	55,000		
b) Wages Payable	(+) 5,000	60,000	
∴ Prime Cost ii)		1,40,000	1,40,000
Add : Factory Overheads :			
a) Heating and Lighting	6,000		
b) Technical Director's Fees	10,000		
c) Expenses of Testing Labs.	(+) 4,000	20,000	
∴ Works Cost iii)		1,60,000	1,60,000
Add : Office Overheads :			
a) Counting House Salaries	20,000		
b) Establishment on Cost	12,000		
c) Branch Office Expenses	(+) 8,000	40,000	
∴ Cost of Production iv)		2,00,000	2,00,000
Add : Selling and Distribution Overheads :			
a) Commission on Sales	5,000		
b) Show Room Expenses	7,000		
c) After Sales-Service Expenses	(+) 8,000	20,000	
∴ Total Cost v)		2,20,000	2,20,000
Add : Profit vi)		30,000	30,000
Selling Price		2,50,000	2,50,000

Working Notes :

i) Calculation of percentage of Factory Overheads to Direct Wages.

If ₹ 60,000 D.W. = ₹ 20,000 F.O.

∴   100 = ?

$$= \frac{100 \times ₹ 20,000}{₹ 60,000}$$

= 33.33%

ii) Calculation of percentage of Office on Cost to Works Cost.

If ₹ 1,60,000 W.C. = ₹ 40,000 O.O.C.

∴   100 = ?

Basics of Cost Accounting 2.43 Elements of Cost and Cost Sheet

$$= \frac{100 \times ₹40,000}{₹1,60,000}$$

$$= 25\%$$

iii) Calculation of percentage of Selling and Distribution Expenses to Cost of Production.
If ₹ 2,00,000 C.O.P. = ₹ 20,000 S. & D.E.
∴ 100 = ?

$$= \frac{100 \times ₹20,000}{₹2,00,000}$$

$$= 10\%$$

iv) Interim Dividend and Share Transfer Fees etc., are the items to be excluded from cost.

ILLUSTRATION 8

The following is the Trading and Profit and Loss Account of Sarabhai Chemicals Ltd. Surat, for the year ended 31st March, 2015.

Dr.   Trading and Profit and Loss Account   Cr.
for the year ended 31st March, 2015

Particulars	₹		Particulars	₹	
To Stock of Raw Materials 1-4-2014		18,000	By Sales	5,10,000	5,00,000
To Purchases of Raw Materials	2,52,000	2,50,000	Less : Returns Inward (−)	10,000	
Less : Returns Outward (−)	2,000		By Stock of Raw Materials on 31-3-2015		10,000
To Productive Wages		1,02,000	By Sale of Scrap Materials		1,000
To Carriage on Purchases		25,000			
To Royalty		7,200			
To Gas and Water		19,000			
To Customs and Duty		8,000			
To Chargeable Expenses due, but not paid		2,800			
To Wages Outstanding		8,000			
To Heating and Lighting		11,000			
To Gross Profit C/D		60,000			
		5,11,000			5,11,000
To Carriage on Sales		5,000	By Gross Profit B/D		60,000
To Underwriting Commission		4,500	By Interest on Investment		1,000
To Commission on Sales		7,600			
To Sales Depat Expenses		2,400			
To Salaries		16,000			
To Bad Debts Provision		1,500			
To Property Tax on Office Premises		2,000			
To Depreciation on Office Equipments		2,000			
To Net Profit C/D *		20,000			
		61,000			61,000

You are required to prepare a Cost Statement for the year ended 31st March, 2015 showing i) Cost of Materials Consumed, ii) Flat Cost, iii) Manufacturing Cost, iv) Gross Cost, v) Cost of Turnover, vi) Profits for the year.

Also calculate the percentage of profit on sales.

SOLUTION

In the books of Sarabhai Chemicals Ltd., Surat
Cost Statement for the year ended 31st March, 2015

Particulars		Amount ₹	Amount ₹
Stock of Raw Materials on 1-4-2014	18,000		
Add : Purchases of Raw Materials	2,52,000		
Add : Expenses on Purchases of Raw Materials :			
a) Carriage on Purchases	25,000		
b) Customs and Duty	8,000		
	3,03,000		
Less : Stock of Raw Materials on 31-3-2015	10,000		
Less : Returns Outward	2,000		
Less : Sale of Scrap Materials	1,000		
∴ **Cost of Materials Consumed** i)		2,90,000	2,90,000
Add : Direct Labour :			
a) Productive Wages	1,02,000		
b) Wages Outstanding (+)	8,000	1,10,000	
Add : Direct Expenses :			
a) Royalty	7,200		
b) Chargeable Expenses due, but not paid (+)	2,800	10,000	
∴ **Flat Cost** ii)		4,10,000	4,10,000
Add : Factory Overheads :			
a) Gas and Water	19,000		
b) Heating and Lighting (+)	11,000	30,000	
∴ **Manufacturing Cost** iii)		4,40,000	4,40,000
Add : Office Overheads :			
a) Salaries	16,000		
b) Property Tax on Office Premises	2,000		
c) Depreciation on Office Furniture (+)	2,000	20,000	
∴ **Gross Cost** iv)		4,60,000	4,60,000
Add : Selling and Distribution Overheads :			
a) Carriage on Sales	5,000		
b) Commission on Sales	7,600		
c) Sales Depat Expenses (+)	2,400	15,000	
∴ **Cost of Turnover** v)		4,75,000	4,75,000
Add : Profits for the year vi)		25,000	25,000
Sales		5,00,000	5,00,000

Working Notes :

i) Calculation of percentage of Profit on Sales.

If ₹ 5,00,000 Sales = ₹ 25,000 Profit

∴   100 = ?

$$\frac{100 \times ₹\ 25,000}{₹\ 5,00,000} = 5\%$$

ii) Underwriting Commission, Bad Debts Provision, and Interest on Investment are the items to be excluded from cost.

ILLUSTRATION 9

Following information of Finolex Ltd., Faizpur, relates to a commodity for the year ended 31st March, 2015.

	₹
Opening Stock as on 1-4-2014	
• Raw Materials	5,000
• Work-in-Progress	1,200
• Finished Goods (1,000 Tons)	4,000
Closing Stock as on 31-3-2015	
• Raw Materials	3,000
• Work-in-Progress	3,200
• Finished Goods (2,000 Tons)	9,000
Purchases of Raw Materials	35,000
Prime Cost Labour	25,000
Excise Duty on purchases of Raw Materials	2,000
Administration Overheads	8,000
Cost of Factory Supervision	12,000
Income Tax	5,000
Carriage and Cartage	1,000
Management Expenses	1,000
Accountancy Charges	1,000
Preliminary Expenses	3,200
Sale of Finished Goods	1,17,500

Advertising, Bad Debts and Selling on Cost amounted to 50 paise per ton sold. 16,000 tons of commodities were produced during the year 2014-2015.

Prepare a Cost-Sheet showing

i) Cost of Materials Consumed, ii) Prime Cost, iii) Works Cost, iv) Cost of Production, v) Cost of Goods Sold, vi) Cost of Sales, vii) Profits for the period, viii) Profits per ton of commodity sold.

SOLUTION

In the books of Finolex Ltd. Faizpur
Cost-Sheet for the year ended 31st March, 2015

Units Produced – 16,000 Tons
Units Sold – 15,000 Tons

Particulars		Amount ₹	Amount ₹
Opening Stock as on 1-4-2014 of Raw Materials	5,000		
Add : Purchases of Raw Materials	35,000		
Add : Expenses for purchases of Raw Materials :			
a) Excise Duty on Purchases of Raw Materials	2,000		
b) Carriage and Cartage	(+) 1,000		
	43,000		
Less : Closing Stock as on 31-3-2015 Raw Materials	(–) 3,000		
∴ **Cost of Materials Consumed** i)		40,000	40,000

Particulars		Amount ₹	Amount ₹
Add : Prime Cost Labour (+)		25,000	
∴ Prime Cost ii)		65,000	65,000
Add : Cost of Factory Supervision 12,000		13,200	
Add : Opening Stock as on 1-4-2014 Work-in-Progress (+) 1,200			
		78,200	
Less : Closing Stock as on 31-3-2015 Work-in-Progress (−) 3,200		3,200	
∴ Works Cost iii)		75,000	75,000
Add : Office Overheads :			
a) Administration Overheads 8,000			
b) Management Expenses 1,000			
c) Accountancy Charges (+) 1,000		10,000	
∴ Cost of Production iv)		85,000	85,000
Add : Opening Stock as on 1-4-2014 Finished Goods		4,000	
		89,000	
Less : Closing Stock as on 31-3-2015 Finished Goods		9,000	
∴ Cost of Goods Sold v)		80,000	80,000
Add : Advertising, Bad Debts and Selling on Cost			
(50 Ps. × 15,000 Tons)		7,500	
∴ Cost of Sales vi)		87,500	87,500
Add : Profits for the period vii)		30,000	30,000
Sales of Finished Goods		1,17,500	1,17,500

Working Notes :

i) Calculation of Units Sold during the year 2014-2015

	Tons
Opening Stock of Finished Goods as on 1-4-2014	1,000
Add : Production during the year	(+) 16,000
	17,000
Less : Closing Stock of Finished Goods as on 31-3-2015	(−) 2,000
∴ Units Sold	15,000

ii) Calculation of profits per ton of commodity sold –

If 15,000 Tons = Profit ₹ 30,000

∴   1 Ton = ?

$$= \frac{1 \text{ ton} \times ₹\, 30{,}000}{15{,}000 \text{ Tons}}$$

= ₹ 2 per ton

iii) Income Tax, Preliminary Expenses etc. are the items to be excluded from Cost.

Basics of Cost Accounting — Elements of Cost and Cost Sheet

ILLUSTRATION 10

The following information has been obtained from the records of Quality Manufacturing Co. Ltd., Bharatpur, for the year ended 31st March, 2015.

Summary of Stock Position

Type of Stock	As on 1-4-2014 (₹)	As on 31-3-2015 (₹)
Finished Goods-Stock	50,000	75,000
Raw Materials	20,000	25,000
Stock of Work-in-Progress	5,000	7,000

Additional Information	₹
Purchases of Raw Materials	1,30,000
Wages Outstanding	3,000
Indirect Material	12,000
Discount on issue of Debentures	8,000
Freight Inward	15,000
Property Tax on Factory Buildings	8,000
Director's Travelling Expenses	8,000
Carriage on Sales	5,000
Defective Raw Materials Returned	5,000
Direct Chargeable Expenses	2,000
Workshop Rent	7,000
Expenses for participating in Industrial Exhibition	3,000
Value of Sales	3,00,000
Office Cleaning Charges	2,000
Sales Promotion Charges	6,000
Miscellaneous Overheads	7,000
Upkeep of Delivery Vans	1,000
Motive Power	5,000
Productive Wages	60,000
Postage and Telegrams	3,000

Prepare a Statement of Cost showing :

i) Value of Raw Materials Consumed, ii) Direct Cost, iii) Manufacturing Cost, iv) Cost of Production, v) Cost of Goods Sold, vi) Cost of Turnover, vii) Profit.

Also calculate the percentage of Profit on Cost Price and on Selling Price separately.

SOLUTION

In the books of Quality Manufacturing Co. Ltd., Bharatpur
Statement of Cost for the year ended 31ˢᵗ March, 2015

Particulars		Amount ₹	Amount ₹
Raw Materials as on 1-4-2014	20,000		
Add : Purchases of Raw Materials	1,30,000		
Add : Freight Inward	(+) 15,000		
	1,65,000		
Less : Raw Materials as on 31-3-2015	(−) 25,000		
Less : Defective Raw Materials returned	(−) 5,000		
∴ Value of Raw Materials Consumed i)		1,35,000	1,35,000
Add : Direct Labour :		63,000	
a) Productive Wages	60,000		
b) Wages Outstanding	(+) 3,000		
Add : Direct Chargeable Expenses		2,000	
∴ **Direct Cost** ii)		2,00,000	2,00,000
Add : Factory Overheads :			
a) Indirect Material	12,000		
b) Property Tax on Factory Buildings	8,000		
c) Workshop Rent	7,000		
d) Motive Power	(+) 5,000	32,000	
Add : Work-in-Progress as on 1-4-2014		5,000	
		2,37,000	
Less : Work-in-Progress as on 31-3-2015		7,000	
∴ **Manufacturing Cost** iii)		2,30,000	2,30,000
Add : Office Overheads :			
a) Director's Travelling Expenses	8,000		
b) Postage and Telegrams	3,000		
c) Miscellaneous Overheads	7,000		
d) Office Cleaning Charges	(+) 2,000	20,000	
∴ **Cost of Production** iv)		2,50,000	2,50,000
Add : Finished Goods - Stock as on 1-4-2014		50,000	
Less : Finished Goods - Stock as on 31-3-2015		75,000	
∴ **Cost of Goods Sold** v)		2,25,000	2,25,000
Add : Selling and Distribution Overheads :			
a) Carriage on Sales	5,000		
b) Expenses for participating in Industrial Exhibition	3,000		
c) Upkeep of Delivery Vans	1,000		
d) Sales Promotion Charges	(+) 6,000	15,000	
∴ **Cost of Turnover** vi)		2,40,000	2,40,000
Add : Profits vii)		60,000	60,000
Value of Sales		3,00,000	3,00,000

Working Notes:

i) Calculation of percentage of Profit on Cost Price.

If ₹ 2,40,000 CP = ₹ 60,000 P

∴ 100 = ?

$$= \frac{100 \times ₹\,60,000}{₹\,2,40,000}$$

= 25%

ii) Calculation of percentage of Profit on Sales.

If ₹ 3,00,000 SP = ₹ 60,000 P

∴ 100 = ?

$$= \frac{100 \times ₹\,60,000}{₹\,3,00,000}$$

= 20%

iii) Discount on issue of Debentures is an item to be excluded from cost.

ILLUSTRATION 11

Jindal Cables and Conductors Ltd., Jalgaon, provides the following cost data relating to the manufacture of a standard product during the month of May, 2015.

	₹
Carriage and Cartage	200
Units Sold – 900 units @ ₹ 40 per unit	
Raw Materials Stock as on 31st May, 2015	2,850
Monthly Production – 1,000 units	
Sale of Raw Materials Scrap	150
Selling and Distribution on Cost : ₹ 3.60 per unit	
Operating Wages Payable	600
Operation of Machine Hours – 1,600	
Stock of Raw Materials as on 1st May, 2015	1,200
Administration Overheads : 10% of Works Cost	
Hire of Special Machinery	1,500
Machine Hour Rate	2.50
Raw Materials Purchases	14,600
Productive Wages	4,400
Cost of Layout	500

You are required to prepare a Cost-Sheet showing Total Cost Unit and Unit Cost for the month ended 31st May, 2015. Also calculate Profit earned for the month and Profit per unit sold.

SOLUTION

In the books of Jindal Cables and Conductors Ltd., Jalgaon
Cost-Sheet for the month ended 31st May, 2015

Units Produced – 1,000 units
Units Sold – 900 units

Particulars		Total Cost ₹	Unit Cost ₹
Stock of Raw Materials as on 1-5-2015	1,200		
Add : Raw Materials Purchases	14,600		
Add : Carriage and Cartage	(+) 200		
	16,000		
Less : Raw Materials - Stock as on 31-5-2015	(–) 2,850		
Less : Sale of Raw Materials Scrap	(–) 150		
∴ **Cost of Materials Consumed** i)		13,000	13.00
Add : Direct Labour :		5,000	5.00
a) Operating Wages Payable	600		
b) Productive Wages	(+) 4,400		
Add : Direct Expenses :		2,000	2.00
a) Hire of Special Machinery	1,500		
b) Cost of Layout	(+) 500		
	(+)		
∴ **Prime Cost** ii)		20,000	20.00
Add : Factory Overheads :	(+)	4,000	4.00
∴ **Works Cost** iii)		24,000	24.00
Add : Administration Overheads :	(+)	2,400	2.40
∴ **Cost of Production** iv)		26,400	26.40
Add : Stock of Finished Goods on 1-5-2015	(+)	–	
Less : Stock of Finished Goods on 31-5-2015	(–)	2,640	–
∴ **Cost of Goods sold** v)		23,760	26.40
Add : Selling and Distribution on Cost			
(900 Units × ₹ 3.60)	(+)	3,240	3.60
∴ **Total Cost** vi)		27,000	30.00
Add : Profits for the month	vii) (+)	9,000	10.00
Sales (900 Units × ₹ 40)		36,000	40.00

Working Notes :

i) Calculation of Factory Overheads :

   Operation of   Machine Hour   Factory
   Machine Hours × Rate   = Overheads
   1,600 Hrs.   ₹ 2.50   ₹ 4,000

ii) Calculation of Administration Overheads i.e. 10% of Works Cost :

   =   10% of ₹ 24,000

   =   ₹ 2,400.

Basics of Cost Accounting   2.51   Elements of Cost and Cost Sheet

iii) Valuation of Closing Stock of Finished Goods on the basis of Cost of Production :

	Units
Monthly Production	1,000
Less : Units Sold	(–) 900
∴ Closing Stock	100

If 1,000 Units = ₹ 26,400 Cost of Production

∴ 100 Units = ?

$$= \frac{100 \text{ Units} \times ₹ 26,400}{1,000 \text{ Units}}$$

= ₹ 2,640.

Illustration 12 :

Mafatlal Cotton Textiles Ltd., Bhandup, submits the following information for the year ended 31st March, 2015.

                                                                                                      ₹

Inventories as on 31st March, 2014 :
- Raw Materials   12,500
- Work-in-Progress   16,400
- Finished Goods   17,300

Inventories as on 31st March, 2015 :
- Raw Materials   9,300
- Work-in-Progress   6,400
- Finished Goods   5,300

Additional Information :

	₹
Special Trade Discount	275
Annual Turnover :	
a) Cash	45,000
b) Credit	1,55,000
Excise Duty on Purchases	3,200
Defective Materials Returned	1,400
Materials Inventory Purchases	62,700
Prime Cost Labour	29,400
Raw Materials Scrap Sold	200
Hire of Cutting Machinery	10,800
Dock Charges	1,400
Carriage Inward	1,100
Productive Wages Payable	10,600
Preliminary Expenses	1,300
Cost of Patterns	5,200
Productive Expenses	4,000

Factory Overheads – 50% of Basic Wages
Management on Cost – 5% of Sales Value
Selling Expenses – 3% of Invoice Price
Distribution Overheads – 1% of Loaded Price

You are required to prepare a Statement of Cost showing –
i) Cost of Raw Materials Consumed,   ii) Prime Cost,
iii) Works Cost,   iv) Cost of Production,
v) Cost of Goods Sold,   vi) Cost of Sales and   vii) Profits for the year.

SOLUTION

In the books of Mafatlal Cotton Textiles Ltd., Bhandup
Statement of Cost for the year ended 31st March, 2015

Particulars		Amount ₹	Amount ₹
Inventories of Raw Materials as on 1-4-2014	12,500		
Add: Materials Inventories Purchases	62,700		
Add: Expenses for Purchases of Raw Materials			
a) Excise Duty on Purchases	3,200		
b) Dock Charges	1,400		
c) Carriage Inward	(+) 1,100		
	80,900		
Less: Inventories of Raw Materials as on 31-3-2015	9,300		
Less: Defective Materials Returned	1,400		
Less: Raw Materials Scrap Sold	(−) 200		
∴ **Cost of Raw Materials Consumed** i)		70,000	70,000
Add: Direct Labour :			
a) Prime Cost Labour	29,400		
b) Productive Wages Payable	(+) 10,600	40,000	
Add: Direct Expenses :			
a) Hire of Cutting Machinery	10,800		
b) Cost of Patterns	5,200		
c) Productive Expenses	(+) 4,000	20,000	
∴ **Prime Cost** ii)		1,30,000	1,30,000
Add: Factory Overheads		20,000	
(50% of Basic Wages i.e. Direct Labour ₹ 40,000)			
Add: Inventories of Work-in-Progress as on 1-4-2014		16,400	
		1,66,400	
Less: Inventories of Work-in-Progress as on 31-3-2015		6,400	
∴ **Works Cost** iii)		1,60,000	1,60,000
Add: Management on Cost		10,000	
(5% of Sales Value i.e. Annual Turnover ₹ 2,00,000)			
∴ **Cost of Production** iv)		1,70,000	1,70,000
Add: Inventories of Finished Goods as on 1-4-2014		17,300	
		1,87,300	
Less: Inventories of Finished Goods as on 31-3-2015		5,300	
∴ **Cost of Goods sold** v)		1,82,000	1,82,000
Add: Selling and Distribution Overheads :			
(i) Selling Expenses	6,000		
(3% of Invoice Price i.e. Annual Turnover ₹ 2,00,000)			
(ii) Distribution Overheads			
(1% of Loaded Price i.e. Annual Turnover ₹ 2,00,000)	(+) 2,000	8,000	
∴ **Cost of Sales** vi)		1,90,000	1,90,000
Add: Profits for the year vii)		10,000	
Annual Turnover		2,00,000	2,00,000
(Cash ₹ 45,000 + Credit ₹ 1,55,000)			

Working Notes :
i) Special Trade Discount, Preliminary Expenses etc. are the items to be excluded from cost.

QUESTIONS FOR SELF-STUDY

I. Theory Questions:

i) Define the term 'Cost'. Explain the various Elements of Cost.

ii) Define the term Elements of Cost. State the different elements of costs with suitable examples.

iii) What is 'Material Cost'? State the importance of Material Cost in total cost structure.

iv) Explain briefly the various elements of cost. Give suitable examples for the same.

v) What is 'Labour Cost'? State the importance of Labour Cost in total cost structure.

vi) Explain the importance of 'Other Expenses' as the elements of cost.

vii) What do you understand by the term 'Element of Cost'? What is the important basis of such Classification of Cost?

viii) "Direct Costs and Controllable Costs are not necessarily the same". Explain.

ix) What is Cost? How would you classify the cost? Give suitable examples.

x) What is Cost Classification? Explain the need for Cost Classification. State the various methods of Cost Classification with suitable examples.

xi) Distinguish between Fixed Costs and Variable Costs with suitable examples.

xii) "Costing systems are classified according to the nature of operation". Explain.

xiii) "Fixed Costs are Variable per unit while Variable costs are fixed per unit". Comment.

xiv) What is Fixed Cost? Explain the important characteristics of Fixed Cost.

xv) What is Variable Cost? Explain the important characteristics of variable cost.

xvi) What is Semi-variable Cost? Explain the important characteristics of Semi-variable Cost.

xvii) Explain the various costs used in decision-making and their characteristics.

xviii) What is 'Cost-Sheet'? Explain the various purposes for preparing a 'Simple Cost Sheet'.

xix) Why a 'Cost Sheet' is to be prepared? Give the specimen of a 'Simple Cost Sheet'.

xx) Define the terms 'Direct Costs' and 'Indirect Costs'. A particular cost may be a direct cost in one situation and indirect in the other. Illustrate.

xxi) 'Variable Costs may be direct or indirect'. Discuss giving suitable examples.

xxii) 'Variable costs are constant on per unit basis, while fixed costs are constant in total'. Explain.

xxiii) Importance of Fixed Cost lies in decision-making, due to their special characteristics'. Discuss.

xxiv) Explain the importance of Decision-Making Costs.

xxv) Write short notes on:

a) Material Cost, b) Labour Cost, c) Direct Expenses, d) Cost Classification, e) Types of Cost, f) Need for Classification of Cost, g) Semi-fixed Costs, h) Types of Cost, i) Decision-Making Costs, j) Functional Classification of Cost, k) Avoidable Cost, l) Purposes of a Cost Sheet, m) Shut-Down Costs, n) Opportunity Cost, o) Out of Pocket Costs, p) Sunk Costs, q) Fixed Costs.

xxvi) Differentiate between :
   a) Direct Material and Indirect Material
   b) Direct Labour and Indirect Labour
   c) Direct Expenses and Indirect Expenses
   d) Fixed Costs and Variable Costs
   e) Variable Costs and Semi-variable Costs
   f) Controllable Costs and Non-Controllable Costs
   g) Capital Costs and Revenue Costs
   h) Period Costs and Product Costs
   i) Factory Costs and Administration Costs
   j) Normal Costs and Abnormal Costs
   k) Cost Estimation and Cost Ascertainment
   l) Cost of Goods Sold and Cost of Sales
   m) Prime Cost and Factory Cost
   n) Sunk Costs and Out-of-Pocket Costs
   o) Office Cost and Selling Cost
   p) Simple Cost Sheet and Estimated Cost Sheet.

II. Practical Problems :

i) Tata Cement Co., Badalapur, furnishes you with the following cost data. You are required to prepare a Cost Sheet for the year ended 31st March, 2015, showing therein the Prime Cost, Works Cost, Cost of Production and Cost of Sales alongwith cost per unit and the percentage of each element of cost to total cost.

	₹
Units Produced - 10,000	
Material Consumed	10,00,000
Wages paid to Workers	40,000
Power and Fuel (Factory)	20,000
Repairs to Machines	8,000
Depreciation - Machinery	6,000
Depreciation - Office Furniture	1,000
Supervision Expenses (Factory)	2,000
Hire Charges for machines of special purposes	4,000
Wages paid to Maintenance Workers	20,000
Audit Fees	1,500
Director's Fees	7,500
Bad Debts	2,500
Office Expenses	3,500
Salaries	2,000
Rent, Rates and Taxes (Factory)	5,000
Sales	3,00,000
Salesman Salary	8,000
Advertising Expenses	2,000
Delivery Van Expenses	8,000
Warehouse Rent	6,000
Printing and Stationery	1,000
Direct Expenses	8,000

ii) From the following particulars of Goldstar Cement Ltd., Chalisgaon, prepare a Cost Sheet showing : i) Prime Cost, ii) Factory Cost, iii) Total Cost of Production and iv) Cost of Sales for the period ended 31st March, 2015.

	₹
Raw Material Consumed	50,000
Wages paid to Workers	20,000
Direct Expenses incurred for production	2,500
Consumable Stores	500
Supervisor's Wages	2,000
Wages paid to shop floor helper	600
Electric Power (Factory)	800
Electric Power (Office)	500
Rent (Factory)	5,000
Rent (Office)	2,000
Repairs and Renewals Plant and Machinery	5,000
Renovation of Office Buildings	1,000
Depreciation on Plant and Machinery	500
Depreciation on Office Buildings	200
Manager's Salary	3,000
Telephone Charges	200
Printing and Stationery	400
Postage and Telegrams	150
Director's Fees	800
Advertisement	800
Travelling Expenses	300
Salesmen's Salary and Commission	1,000
Warehouse Rent	900
Delivery van Expenses	1,000

iii) Atlas Cycle Co. Ltd., Dombivili, produce auto parts. From the following particulars prepare Cost Sheet for the period ended 31st March, 2015.

	₹
Opening Stock of Raw Materials	20,000
Raw Material purchased	70,000
Closing Stock of Raw Materials	15,000
Direct Labour Cost (20% of Factory on Cost)	
Factory on Cost	30,000
Administrative Overhead (10% of Works Cost)	
Selling and Distribution Expenses	10,000
Details of the Finished Goods are as follows :	
Opening Stock of Finished Goods 2,000 units	25,000
Finished Goods produced during the period	20,000 units
Closing Stock of Finished Goods	4,000 units

You are required to find out the profit made during the year @ 10% on the Selling Price.

Note : i) There was no balance of Opening or Closing Stock of Work-in-Progress.

ii) Show the working of calculating the profit.

iv) The accounts of MRF Ltd., Fatehpur for the year ended 31st March, 2015, shows the following :

	₹
Drawing Office Salaries	6,500
Counting-House Salaries	12,600
Cash-Discount Allowed	2,900
Carriage and Cartage Outwards	4,300
Carriage and Cartage Inwards	7,150
Bad Debts written off	6,500
Repairs of Plant, Machinery and Tools	4,450
Rent, Rates, Taxes and Insurance - Factory	8,500
Rent, Rates, Taxes and Insurance - Office	2,000
Sales	4,61,100
Stock of Materials – 1st April, 2014	62,800
Stock of Materials – 31st March, 2015	48,000
Materials purchased	1,85,000
Travelling Expenses	2,100
Traveller's Salaries and Commission	7,700
Productive Wages	1,26,000
Depreciation – Plant, Machinery and Tools	6,500
Depreciation – Furniture	300
Director's Fees	6,000
Gas and Water – Factory	1,200
– Office	400
Manager's Salary ($\frac{3}{4}$ Factory and $\frac{1}{4}$ Office)	10,000
General Expenses	3,400
Income-Tax	1,000
Dividend	2,000

Prepare a statement giving the following information :
i) Materials Consumed; ii) Prime Cost; iii) Factory on-Cost and the percentage on Wages; iv) Factory Cost; v) General on Cost and percentage on Factory Cost; vi) Total Cost; vii) Net Profit.

v) The following details have been obtained from the cost records of Cement India Ltd., Manmad for April, 2015.

	₹
Stock of Raw Materials on 1st April, 2015	75,000
Stock of Raw Materials on 30th April, 2015	91,500
Direct Wages	52,500
Indirect Wages	2,750
Sales	2,11,000
Work-in-Progress 1st April, 2015	28,000
Work-in-Progress 30th April 2015	35,000
Purchases of Raw Materials	66,000
Factory Rent, Rate, Power	15,000

Depreciation on Plant and Machinery	3,500
Expenses on Purchases	1,500
Carriage Outward	2,500
Advertising	3,500
Office Rent and Taxes	2,500
Travellers Wages and Commission	6,500
Stock of Finished Goods 1st April, 2015	54,000
Stock of Finished Goods 30th April, 2015	31,000

Prepare Cost-Sheet for the month ended 30th April, 2015.

vi) Following information has been obtained from the records of a Caustic Soda Manufacturing Co., Gurgaon.

	1st April, 2014 ₹	31st March, 2015 ₹
Stock of Raw Materials	40,000	50,000
Stock of Finished Goods	1,00,000	1,50,000
Stock of Work-in-Progress	10,000	14,000

Other Particulars:

Indirect Labour	50,000
Lubricants	10,000
Insurance on Plant	3,000
Purchase on Raw Materials	4,00,000
Sales Commission	60,000
Salaries of Salesmen	1,00,000
Administrative Expenses	1,00,000
Carriage Outward	20,000
Power	30,000
Direct Labour	3,00,000
Depreciation on Machinery	50,000
Factory Rent	60,000
Property Tax on Factory Buildings	11,000
Sales	12,00,000

Prepare a statement of cost and profit showing:
i) Value of Raw Materials Consumed   ii) Prime Cost
iii) Factory Cost   iv) Cost of Production
v) Cost of Sales   vi) Profit

vii) The following information is received from the books of ABC Co. Ltd., Hinjewadi, for the year ending 31st March, 2015.

	₹
Stock of Materials 31-3-2015	75,000
Purchases of Material	7,95,000
Stock of Material on 1-4-2014	1,05,000
Travelling Expenses	5,100
Carriage Inward	8,290
Carriage Outward	9,150
Labour Welfare Expenses	14,200
Depreciation on Plant	18,000
Factory Rent	11,200
Office Rent	29,100

	₹
Bad Debts	9,000
Productive Wages	2,27,000
Travellers' Salary and Commission	9,000
Expenses regarding Purchase of Materials	4,500
Director's Fees	8,700
Fuel, Gas and Water	17,900
Manager's Salary	18,000
(He devotes 2/3 of his time to factory)	
Airconditioning Charges of Office	9,000
Outstanding Productive Wages	33,000
Sales	14,29,500

Prepare Cost-Sheet giving
i) Prime Cost, ii) Works Cost, iii) Cost of Production, iv) Total Cost

viii) The following data have been extracted from the books of Birla Tractors Ltd., Pune, for the year 2014-2015.

	₹
Opening Stock of Raw Materials	25,000
Purchase of Raw Materials	85,000
Closing Stock of Raw Materials	40,000
Carriage Inward	5,000
Wages – Direct	75,000
Wages – Indirect	10,000
Other Direct Charges	15,000
Rent and Rates –	
Factory	5,000
Office	500
Indirect Consumption of Material	500
Depreciation –	
Plant and Machinery	1,500
Office Furniture	100
Salary –	
Office	2,500
Salesmen	2,000
Other Factory Expenses	5,700
Other Office Expenses	900
Manager's Remuneration	12,000
Bad Debts written off	1,000
Advertisement Expenses	2,000
Travelling Expenses of Salesmen	1,100
Carriage and Freight Outward	1,000
Sales	2,50,000
Advance Income Tax	15,000
Cash Discount	5,000

The manager has the overall charge of the company and his remuneration is to be allocated ₹ 4,000 to Factory, ₹ 2,000 to Office and ₹ 6,000 to the Selling.

From the above particulars prepare a Cost Statement showing :
i) Prime Cost, ii) Factory Cost, iii) Cost of Production, iv) Cost of Sales, and v) Net Profit.

Unit ... 3

OVERHEADS

3.1 Meaning and Definitions
3.2 Classification of Overheads
3.3 Accounting of Overheads
    3.3.1 Collection of Overheads
    3.3.2 Allocation of Overheads
    3.3.3 Apportionment of Overheads
    3.3.4 Re-apportionment of Overheads
    3.3.5 Absorption of Overheads
        3.3.5.1 Under and Over-Absorption of Overheads
* Questions for Self-Study

On the basis of the identifiability of cost items with the cost centres or units, costs may be classified into **direct and indirect costs. Direct Cost** can be conveniently traced into or identified with the product manufacturers. Direct costs which are also called Prime Costs or Basic Costs which represent the cost which can be easily and directly be identified with the cost centres or the cost units. On the other hand, indirect costs represent the costs which are not directly identifiable with the cost centres or cost units. These indirect costs are called **Overheads.**

The conceptual understanding of an item of cost viz. "**Packing Charges**", and its accounting treatment gives a clear idea about Direct Cost which differs from Indirect Cost.

Packing Charges are certain expenses incurred on wrapping, tying, sealing the bottles, boxes, containers, bags etc. Accounting of packing charges simply depends upon its basic purposes for which it is incurred and its treatment can be classified as follows :

    i) Packing Charges are treated as '**Direct Material Costs**' in case of those products which cannot be sold without the use of packing materials. Such packing is necessary to protect and preserve the quality and convenient handling of the product. e.g. Bottling Mineral Water, Tooth-Paste, Ink-Pot, Medicine, Basic Packing for Biscuits and Bread etc. Primary Packing.

    ii) Packing Charges are treated as '**Factory Overhead Costs**' if packing is done in the factory of a number of products e.g. making one single pack of different chocolates etc. Secondary Packing.

iii) Packing charges are treated as **'Selling Overhead Costs'** if it is incurred for attractive-fancy packing meant to attract customers is an advertisement cost e.g. wrappers of confectionary items and cosmetics etc. (Secondary Packing).
iv) Packing charges are treated as **'Distribution Overhead Costs'** if it is incurred to facilitate transportation of finished product e.g. Packing of TV sets, Refrigerators, Washing Machines etc. (Secondary Packing).
v) Cost of any special packing incurred as per customers request, is directly charged to that job or order separately (Primary Packing).

Thus, a cost is treated as **direct** when it is easily, conveniently and directly be identified with the cost centres or cost units, whereas a cost is treated as **indirect** when it is conveniently be allocated to the cost or cost units. Accounting and control of overhead costs is more complicated than that of direct material costs and direct labour costs.

3.1 MEANING AND DEFINITIONS

Meaning

Overhead is the aggregate of indirect material cost, indirect labour cost and indirect expenses which cannot be conveniently identified with and directly allocated to a particular cost centre or cost object in an economically feasible way. It is also known as indirect cost or burden on cost.

Different terminologies such as overheads, overhead expenses, overhead cost, overhead charges, overhead expenditure, on cost, supplementary costs, non-productive costs, burden, loading etc. are used by different authors to denote the indirect costs incurred over and above the prime costs.

It may be recalled that the total cost is broadly divided into direct cost and indirect cost. The total of all direct costs i.e. direct materials, direct wages and direct expenses, is termed as Prime Cost whereas the total of all indirect costs i.e. indirect materials, indirect wages and indirect expenses is known as **'Overheads'**.

Thus, **Overhead** is the aggregate of indirect material cost, indirect wages and indirect expenses. The word **indirect** is that which cannot be allocated, but which can be apportioned to, or absorbed by cost centres or cost units. All expenses over and above the prime cost are known as 'Overhead' charges. Hence,

Overheads = Indirect Material (+) Indirect Wages (+) Indirect Expenses

Definitions

Following are some of the authoritative definitions of the term **'Overhead'**.

i) *Certified Institute of Management Accountants, London :*
"overhead is an aggregate of indirect materials, indirect wages and indirect expenses".

ii) *Blocker and Weltmer :*
"Overheads are the operating costs of a business enterprise which cannot be traced directly to a particular unit of output".

iii) *Wheldon :*
"Overheads are the cost of indirect materials, indirect labour and such other expenses, including services as cannot conveniently be charged direct to specific cost units. Alternatively, overheads are all expenses other than direct expenses".

iv) *Harper :*
"Overheads are those costs which do not result from the existence of individual cost units".

v) The National Association of Accountants (U.S.A.) :

"Overheads are the costs that have to be incurred although they have no directly measurable, observable relationship to specific activity units, production or cost objectives".

vi) W. W. Bigg :

"All indirect costs are termed as overheads".

Thus, overhead is the total of all indirect material, indirect labour and indirect expenditure. It comprises of those costs which the cost accountant is either unable or unwilling to allocate to particular cost units.

The term **'overheads'** is used interchangeably with such terms as "burden", "supplementary costs", "operating expenses" and 'indirect expenses'. With the help of above definitions the **features of overhead expenses** can be summarised as follows :

i) Overheads are indirect costs,
ii) They are common costs,
iii) Overheads comprise of both cash expenses i.e. rent, taxes, insurance etc. and non-cash expenses i.e. depreciation.
iv) Overheads consist of both production and non-production expenses.
v) Overheads are both variable and fixed and
vi) They include both escapable and inescapable.

> **All Overheads are the costs, but all costs are not the Overheads**

In the United States, the word **'burden'** is used in place of **overhead**. So difficult and confusing are some of the basic problems relating to overhead and its treatment in cost accounts that one may perhaps be pardoned for saying that the cost accountant's "burden" is overhead". Other synonymous terms in use for overheads are 'on-cost', 'supplementary costs', 'non-productive costs', etc. Of all the terms, overhead is the most common and C.I.M.A. London does not recommend the use of the terms 'on-cost' and 'burden'.

In certain manufacturing concern, the actual overhead costs are much higher than direct material cost or direct labour cost and at times even both put together e.g. in beverage manufacturing company overhead cost (i.e. advertisement expenses) is more than its total production cost. Therefore, it will be a very serious mistake to overlook the overhead costs either for the purpose of ascertaining the total cost by the cost accounting department or for controlling the overhead costs by the management people.

> Any increase in overhead costs, without a corresponding improvement in the quality and quantity of output and, without a marginal reduction in direct cost, indicates total inefficiency of the organisation.

Overhead is becoming an increasingly important element of cost in todays competitive environment as a result of several factors such as increased mechanisation, plant automation and use of modern advanced technology. Use of costly plant and machinery result in higher overhead costs because of higher amounts of plant depreciation, repairs and maintenance etc. Use of automatic machines also require less human effort thereby resulting in employment of less number of workers. Thus, the proportion of overhead costs in total cost in modern industry is appreciably high and careful planning and control of overhead costs can result in significant saving in the total cost of production.

Composition of Overheads :

Following Figure 3.1 shows very clearly the Composition of Overheads.

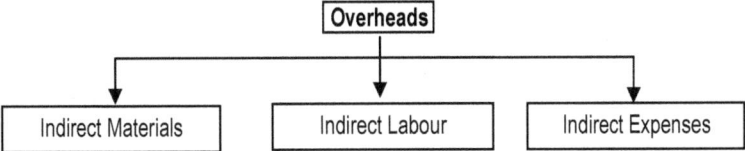

Fig. 3.1 : Composition of Overheads

To understand such composition of overheads mentioned above, the following illustrative chart showing examples of overheads will simplify the concepts well.

Type of Overhead Costs	Department Concerned	Indirect Materials	Indirect Labour	Indirect Expenses
Works	Factory or Works or Production or Manufacturing	Lubricants, Consumable Stores, Cotton Waste, Oil, Dusters, Brooms, Cleaning Materials, Industrial Oil and Grease, Soaps and Detergents etc.	Salary to Foremen, Shop-Supervisor, Technical Directors, Works Manager, Store-keeper, Shop-floor Inspectors etc.	Coal and Coke, Gas and Water, Heating and lighting, Motive Power, Haulage, Time-keeping Expenses etc.
Office	Administration or Office or Management or Establishment	Printing and Stationery etc.	Salary to Office Manager, Cashier, Telephone Operator, Computer Staff, Accountants, Administrative Officer etc.	Public Relation Expenses, Audit Fees, Postage and Telegrams, Accountancy Charges, Branch Office Expenses, Legal Charges, Management Expenses etc.
Selling	Sales or Marketing	Catalogues and Price Lists, Banners and Hand Bills, Free Samples and Gifts, Posters etc.	Salary to Sales Manager, Travelling Salesmen, Sales-Depat Manager, Marketing Staff etc.	Market Research Expenses, Advertisement, Bad Debts, Debt Collection Charges, Travelling Expenses, Publicity Charges, Export Duty etc.
Distribution	Distribution or Delivery	Secondary Packing Materials etc.	Salary to Distribution Staff, Wages of Packers, and Dispatch Clerks, Delivery Van-Drivers and Conductors etc.	Packing Charges, Carriage on Sales, Freight Outward, Delivery Van Running Charges, Repairs and Maintenance of Delivery Vans, Warehousing Charges etc.

3.2 CLASSIFICATION OF OVERHEADS

Classification is the process of grouping like facts under a common designation on the basis of similarities of nature, attributes or relations. **Classification of Overheads** is the process of grouping of indirect costs on the basis of common characteristics and clear objectives. All overhead expenses are grouped together under common heads and are further classified according to their fundamental differences. Suitable classification of overheads is of utmost importance, so that overhead costs can be classified and appropriately used by the management to exercise better control, to plan the future activities in advance and to take important decisions in time.

The basic need for overhead classification arises because of the requirement of different types of cost data for a number of purposes. Hence, overhead costs must be suitably arranged and sub-classified in such a manner that they can be utilised analytically in different ways to serve different purposes. Figure 3.2 shows the graphical presentation of **Classification of Overheads** as follows:

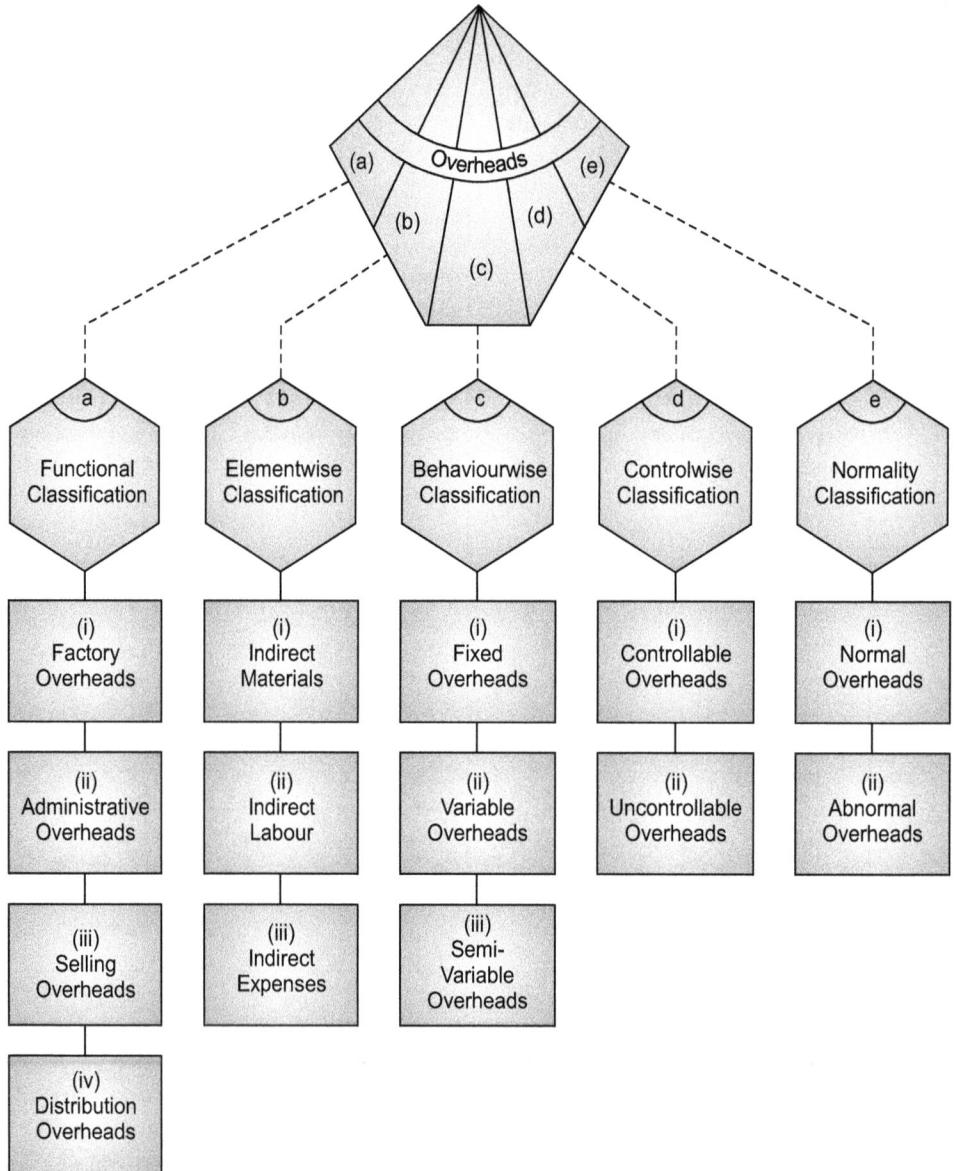

Fig. 3.2 : Classification of Overheads

(a) Functional Classification

The main groups of overheads on the basis of functional classification are as follows:

i) Factory Overheads:

These are the costs associated with manufacturing activities, the sequence of which begins with the procurement of materials and ends with primary packing of the product. **Factory overheads** are also termed as production overheads, works overheads or manufacturing overheads, and so on. It means indirect expenditure incurred in connection with production operations. It is the aggregate of factory indirect material cost, indirect wages and indirect expenses. Unlike direct material and direct labour, production overhead is an invisible part of the finished product. e.g. lubricants, consumable stores, indirect wages, factory power and light, depreciation of plant and machinery, depreciation of factory buildings, insurance of plant and factory building, storekeeper expenses, repairs and maintenance etc.

ii) Administration Overheads:

These are the cost of formulating the policy, directing the organisation and controlling the operations of an undertaking which is not related directly to production, selling, distribution research or development activity. Administration overheads are also termed as office overheads or management overheads or establishment overheads, etc. For example, General Manager's salaries, audit fees, legal charges, postage and telephone, stationery and printing, office rent and rates, office lighting, and salaries of office staff, management expenses, etc.

> Though Cost of Training and Education to administrative staff is accounted as Office Overhead, it is much more beneficial to treat the same as an investment in human assets.

iii) Selling Overheads:

These are the costs of seeking to create and stimulate demand or of securing orders. It is the cost incurred for transferring the ownership of goods to the buyer. These are the expenses incurred for promoting sales and retaining customers. e.g. advertising, salaries and commission of sales personnel, showroom expenses, travelling expenses, bad debts, catalogues and price lists etc.

iv) Distribution Overheads:

It comprises of all expenditure incurred from the time, product is completed in the factory, until it reaches its destination or customer. e.g. packing cost, carriage outward, delivery van costs, warehousing costs etc.

Both selling and distribution costs are incurred after the production work is over and thus taken together, these are known as "After Production Costs".

The distinction between **Selling Overheads and Distribution Overheads** can be shown as follows:

Selling Overheads	Distribution Overheads
i) It includes the costs incurred in selling the product.	i) It includes costs incurred for the distribution of the finished product.
ii) It includes the costs of the selling department and involves primarily the marketing costs.	ii) It also includes all costs incurred for making products available to the customers.
iii) It may also be divided into fixed and variable overheads.	iii) It may also be divided into fixed and variable overheads.

Selling Overheads	Distribution Overheads
iv) Showroom rent, electricity, advertisement, salary and commission to salesman, bad debts, travelling and market research expenses are the examples of Selling Overheads.	iv) Warehouse rent, electricity, salary and wages paid to delivery van driver, warehouse keeper, carriage outwards, packing charges, insurance, depreciation of delivery van are the examples of Distribution Overheads.
v) They are incurred for promoting the product or securing and executing orders.	v) They are incurred in relation to the delivery and despatch of the products from the factory to the warehouse and from warehouse to the customers.

Factory Overheads are the part of manufacturing operations cost, the Selling and Distribution Overheads are the results of policy.

(b) Elementwise Classification

This type of classification is based on the definition of overheads given above. The main classes under this head are; indirect materials, indirect labour, and indirect expenses.

i) **Indirect Materials :**

In the course of manufacturing of a product, indirect materials do not form part of finished product. The indirect materials are consumable items, electrodes, coolants, cotton waste etc. which are required for completion of a finished product. Indirect materials cost is the cost which cannot be allocated, but which can be apportioned to or absorbed by cost centres or cost units.

ii) **Indirect Labour :**

Indirect labour are the actual wages and overtime wages paid for all labour, other than direct labourers, in the factory, viz. helpers in factory, foremen, supervisors, inspection staff and production manager etc. who do not help directly in converting the raw materials into a finished product. It also includes salary paid to office and selling and distribution staff.

iii) **Indirect Expenses :**

Indirect expenses are all expenses of the factory such as rent, rates, taxes and insurance of factory, repairs of factory machinery, power etc. including depreciation of plant, machinery, equipment, loose tools and factory buildings. It also includes indirect expenses incurred for office and selling and distribution.

(c) Behaviourwise Classification

Different overhead costs behave in different ways when volume of production increases or decreases. On the basis of behaviour or variability, overheads may be classified as follows.

i) **Fixed Overheads :**

These overheads remain unaffected or fixed in total amounts by fluctuations in volume of output. e.g. rent and rates, managerial salaries, buildings depreciation, postage, stationery, legal expenses etc.

Fixed Overheads have the following **important characteristics** :
- Total fixed overheads do not vary with the change in the volume of production upto a given range.
- Fixed overheads per unit varies with change in the volume of production i.e. fixed overheads per unit decreases as the production increases and vice-versa.
- Fixed overheads are uncontrollable in nature.
- They are classified into i) Cash fixed overheads e.g. rent and taxes and ii) Non-cash fixed overheads i.e. depreciation on buildings.

Graphically the important **features of fixed overheads** may be shown below in Figure 3.3.

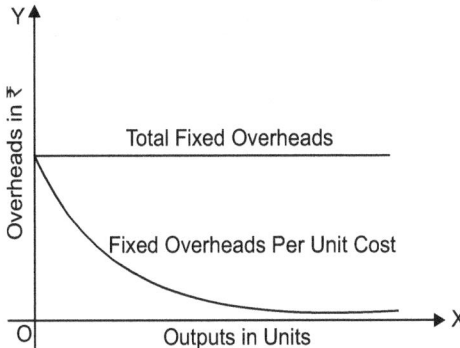

Fig. 3.3 : Features of Fixed Overheads

Example :

Output in units (A)	Total Fixed Overheads in ₹ (B)	Fixed Overheads per unit in ₹ (C = B/A)
0	100	100.
1	100	100.
10	100	10.
100	100	1.
1,000	100	.10

Thus, the above mentioned example clarifies that, Fixed Overheads per unit goes on decreasing as the total number of output increases.

ii) Variable Overheads :

This is the cost which, in aggregate, tends to vary in indirect proportion to changes in the volume of output. Variable overhead per unit remain fixed. e.g. indirect materials, indirect labour, salesman's commission, power, light, fuel etc.

Variable Overheads have the following **important characteristics** :
- Total variable overheads vary in direct proportion to the volume of production i.e. total variable overheads decrease as the production decreases and vice-versa.
- Variable overheads per unit remains fixed.
- Variable overheads are controllable in nature.
- They are classified into: i) Material variable overheads e.g. indirect material and ii) Labour variable overheads e.g. indirect labour.

Graphically, the important features of variable overheads may be shown below in Figure 3.4.

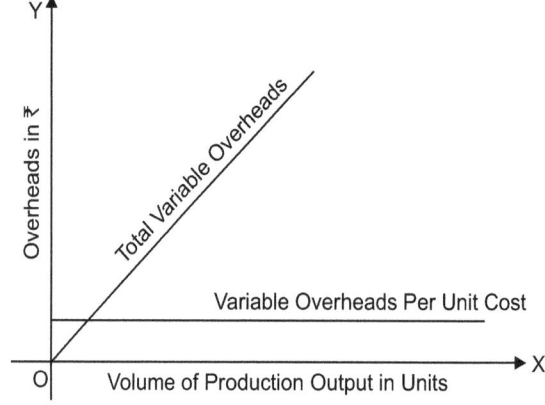

Fig. 3.4 : Features of Variable Overheads

Example :

Output in units (A)	Total Variable Overheads in ₹ (B)	Variable Overheads per unit in ₹ (C = B/A)
0	0	0.
1	100.	100.
10	1,000.	100.
100	10,000.	100.
1,000	1,00,000	100.

Thus, the above mentioned example clarifies that Variable Overheads per unit remains constant as the total number of output increases.

The distinction between **Fixed Overheads** and **Variable Overheads** can be shown as follows.

Fixed Overheads	Variable Overheads
i) They do not change with change in production or activity.	i) They vary in direct proportion with change in level of activity.
ii) The cost per unit decreases with increase in output and vice-versa.	ii) The cost per unit remains unaffected with increase or decrease in volume.
iii) They are related to period hence they are termed as capacity costs.	iii) They are related to product hence they are termed as inventoriable costs.
iv) Rent, insurance, salary to office staff are the examples of fixed overheads.	iv) Power consumption, salesman's commission, indirect materials, heating and lighting are the examples of variable overheads.
v) They does not vary with output.	v) They vary with output.
vi) They are uncontrollable.	vi) They are controllable.

iii) Semi-Variable Overhead :

These overheads are also termed as semi-fixed overheads, mixed overheads or step overheads.

Basics of Cost Accounting 3.10 Overheads

This type of overhead is partly fixed and partly variable. In other words, such costs vary in part with the volume of production and in part they are constant, whatever be the volume of production. e.g. supervisory salaries, depreciation, repairs and maintenance, electricity charges, telephone charges, delivery van expenses, material handling, storage costs etc.

Semi-variable overheads have the following **important characteristics** :

- These overheads stand mid-way between fixed overheads and variable overheads.
- They change by small steps.
- They change in the same direction as change in the level of activity but not in the same proportion.
- They remain fixed in total over a short range of variation in output.
- The per unit semi-variable overheads decline with increase in output, and vice-versa.
- These overheads are controllable in nature.

Graphically, the important features of semi-variable overheads may be shown below in Figure 3.5.

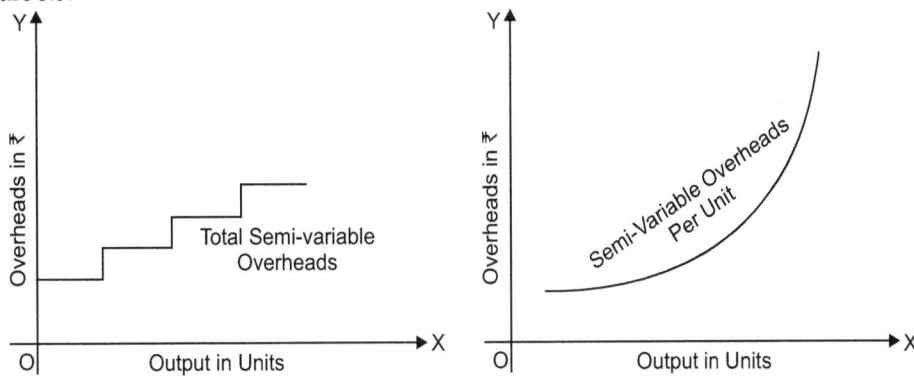

Fig. 3.5 : Features of Semi-Variable Overheads

Example :

Semi-variable Overheads of ₹ 1,50,000 are constant upto 75% capacity (7,500 units) but increases by 10% over 75% but upto 85%, and then increases by 20% over 85% but upto 100% capacity.

Capacity	Output in units (A)	Total Semi-variable Overheads in ₹ (B)	Semi-variable Overheads per unit in ₹ (C = B/A)
50%	5,000	1,50,000	30.00
60%	6,000	1,50,000	25.00
70%	7,000	1,50,000	21.43
80%	8,000	1,65,000	20.62
90%	9,000	1,98,000	22.00
100%	10,000	1,98,000	19.80

Thus, the above mentioned example clarifies that Semi-Variable Overhead costs vary in part with the volume of production and in part they are constant.

> Behavioural classification of overheads is highly helpful to the management for effective and efficient running of the business enterprise.

Importance of Overhead Classification according to Behaviour:

Behaviourwise cost classification is of maximum importance in planning, decision-making and control as explained below:

i) Decision-Making:

As most of the problems of decision-making relate to changes in volume, this classification acquires a special importance in managerial decision-making. This is so because fixed and variable costs behave in different ways when volume of output changes.

ii) Control of Costs:

From control point of view, cost may be controllable or uncontrollable. The fixed costs are mostly uncontrollable and if, at all, any control can be exercised, it can be done by the top management. Variable costs, on the other hand, are mostly controllable. e.g., rent of building (fixed) is not easily controllable but cost of materials (variable) may be controlled by purchasing in economic lots, seasonal purchasing etc. classifying costs into fixed and variable, therefore, helps in the effective control of costs by pointing out where management should concentrate to control.

iii) Preparation of Budget:

This classification helps in the preparation of budget. For instance, when flexible budgets are prepared for different levels of activity, the fixed cost remains constant at all levels of activity, whereas variable cost varies according to the actual level of output. This has been taken up in detail in the chapter on Budget.

iv) Absorption of Overhead:

By classifying cost into fixed and variable, separate rates of absorption of overhead may be used for fixed and variable overheads. The under / over absorption arising out of two types of overheads are different in nature and need different managerial action. For example, under absorption of fixed overhead means the existence of surplus or idle capacity so that suitable steps may be taken to effectively utilise idle capacity.

v) Marginal Costing and Break Even Analysis:

This technique is totally dependent on segregation of cost into fixed and variable.

vi) Other uses:

In addition to points stated above, fixed-variable cost classification is useful in many other areas. e.g., while planning capital expenditure, effect of the project on total fixed and variable costs should be studied. Moreover, differential and comparative cost analysis are based on this classification.

(d) Controlwise Classification

There are two aspects in control of overheads, one is accounting aspect of control which consists of classification, collection, apportionment and absorption of overheads and also analysis according to function and variability. This is helpful for ascertainment of overheads with accuracy and control thereof. According to controlwise classification, overheads are classified as follows:

i) Controllable Overheads:

These are the indirect costs which may be directly controlled at a given level of management authority. Variable overheads are generally controllable by the departmental heads e.g. indirect material cost may be controlled by purchasing these materials in larger quantities.

ii) Un-controllable Overheads :

These are the indirect costs which cannot be influenced by the action of a specific member of an organisation e.g. rent and taxes, office salaries, etc.

The distinction between **Controllable Overheads and Uncontrollable Overheads** can be shown as follows.

Controllable Overheads	Uncontrollable Overheads
i) These overheads are the costs which can be verified or regulate by conducting a parallel experiment or by comparing with another standard.	i) These overheads are the costs which are not able to be controlled or governed.
ii) These overheads are those which can be controlled by management with proper care and efficient planning. e.g. costs incurred due to strikes can be avoided by giving proper working facilities, due share of bonus to the workers and negotiation with the union.	ii) These overheads are those which cannot be controlled by the management and are not predictable in nature. e.g. loss of production due to earthquakes, floods, heavy rain, etc.
iii) These overheads are influenced by managerial action and are within their control.	iii) These overheads are not influenced by managerial action and are not within their control.
iv) Controllability depends upon the level of management, the time period (short-term or long-term), location of the units, etc.	iv) In case of these controllability cannot be predicted.
v) Controllable overheads incurred in a particular responsibility centre can be influenced by the action of the executive heading that responsibility centre.	v) Uncontrollable overheads not incurred in a particular responsibility centre.

While Variable Costs are controllable, Fixed Costs are not.

(e) Normality Classification

According to normality classification overheads are classified as follows :

i) Normal Overheads :

These are the expenses which are expected to be incurred in producing a given output. They cannot be avoided. They are included in production cost. e.g. indirect material cost.

ii) Abnormal Overheads :

These are the expenses which are not expected to occur in producing a given output. e.g. abnormal idle time, abnormal wastage etc. These expenses are transferred to costing profit and loss account.

The classified cost data as collected from the methods discussed above, is further analysed and interpreted by the cost accounting department on scientific basis and finally submitted to the management. The cost accountant does not make any pricing decisions of the products. Actually, pricing is the domain of top management, as it is based on demand and supply forces available in the market. The cost accountant only helps the management in providing significant cost data and determines the financial effects of price fixation or change in prices on the overall profitability of the manufacturing unit.

Therefore, classification of overhead cost is of utmost importance, as it helps the management to perform their peculiar functions of planning, controlling and decision-making more effectively and efficiently.

3.3 ACCOUNTING OF OVERHEADS

In order to ascertain the manufacturing cost of goods produced which is a pre-requisite to determine the cost of sales, fixation or revision of selling price etc. it is necessary to add production overheads to the prime cost. That means,

Prime Cost + Production Overheads = Manufacturing Cost (of goods produced)

Therefore,

Production Overheads = Manufacturing Cost (−) Prime Cost

Actually, Production Overheads = (Factory Indirect Material Cost + Factory Indirect Labour Cost + Other Factory Indirect Expenses).

From the above, it is observed that the production overheads represent all indirect costs incurred in the production of goods and services. This is in addition to the direct cost or prime cost. These production overheads cannot be allocated directly to the cost units like the direct material cost and direct wages. Therefore, a systematic procedure is to be followed to account for production overheads. Accounting treatment required following important steps for the same.

- Classification and **collection of overheads.**
- **Allocation and apportionment of overheads** to production and service departments.
- **Re-apportionment** of service department costs to production departments and
- Absorption of overheads.

Overheads Accounting :

Direct costs are charged directly to the cost centre or cost units without any difficulty. But this is not possible in overhead costs. Distribution of overhead costs to cost units is one of the most complicated problems of cost accounting. This is because overhead costs cannot be identified with individual cost units and there are no accounting means of exact distribution. Therefore, such costs are analysed and distributed to various cost centres and cost units on an arbitrary basis. For e.g., it is not possible to exactly calculate the amount of rent that should be charged to a particular cost unit and thus it has to be distributed on the same arbitrary basis. The cost accountant is constantly searching for equitable basis to distribute overheads costs to units and divisions of business enterprises and quite often he needed to exercise his own judgement in this regard. e.g., he may apportion rent to various departments of the factory on the basis of area occupied by each and such department, similarly, labour welfare expenses may be apportioned on the basis of number of workers in each department. The procedure of distribution of overheads costs in overhead accounting is as follows :

Steps in Overhead Accounting :

Unlike direct materials and direct wages, overheads cannot be allocated to cost units directly. The various steps involved in the distribution of overhead costs are as follows :

1) Collection and Classification of Overheads.
2) Allocation of Overheads.
3) Apportion of Overheads.
4) Re-apportionment of Overheads and
5) Absorption of Overheads.

Figure 3.6 shown below indicates the steps involved in Overheads Accounting i.e. Panchsutri of Overheads Accounting.

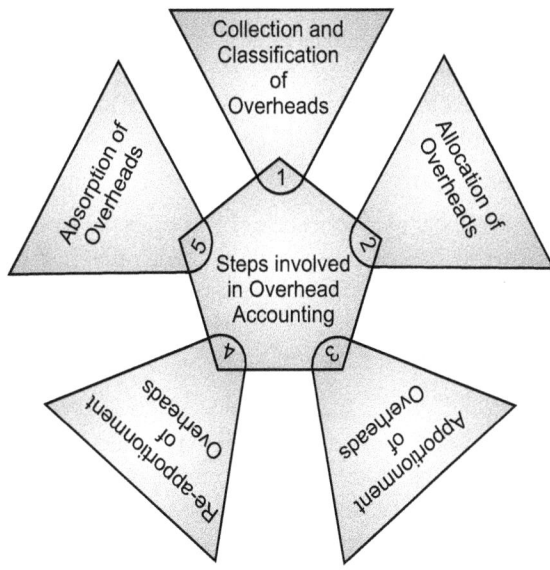

Fig. 3.6 : Steps involved in Overheads Accounting i.e. Panchasutri of Overheads Accounting

1) Collection and Classification of Overheads :

a) Collection of Overheads :

It is a routine procedural work concerned with the collection of overhead expenses under correct accounting heads already provided for. Usually, the overhead expenses are collected through a system of 'standing orders', under which a standing order denotes sanction for overhead expenses under various heads of expenses. The important sources from which overhead expenses are collected regularly are: i) Purchase Day Book; ii) Invoice; and iii) Stores Requisitions.

These three are meant for collection of indirect material costs;

iv) Wages Analysis book for indirect wages; v) Cash book and Petty Cash Book. vi) Nominal Ledgers and vii) Other Registers like Plant and Machinery Registers and Reports. These four are meant for collection of indirect expenses including depreciation of plant and machinery.

b) Classification of Overheads :

Overheads classification is the systematic process of grouping of overheads on the basis of common characteristics and specific objectives.

There may be three broad categories of factory overheads viz. : i) Plant overheads; ii) Overheads relating to production cost centres and; iii) Overheads relating to service cost centres.

All the factory overheads are to be classified to suit the basic purpose of cost accounting. Standing order numbers are used for covering the factory overheads. Cost account numbers are used for covering the administration, selling and distribution overheads.

2) Allocation of Overheads :

Allocation is the allotment of whole items of cost to cost units or cost centres, whether they may be production cost centres or service cost centres, e.g., indirect wages of production department 'A' is to be allocated to Department 'A' only. Similarly, wages of services department 'S' is to be allocated to Department 'S' only.

3) Apportionment of Overheads :

Apportionment is the allotment of proportion of items of cost to cost centres or cost units on a suitable basis after they are collected under separate standing order numbers. It may be the basis of services rendered by a particular item of expense to different departments or by survey method. Sometimes, the basis will be the 'Ability to pay method' i.e. ability of the department to bear such share of items of overheads.

4) Re-apportionment of Overheads :

The service departments do not engage directly in the production of goods and services. But they render valuable services to the production departments which produce goods and services. Hence, it is necessary to distribute the costs of service departments to the production departments on some suitable bases so that the product, output, job etc. bear ultimately, an equitable share of costs of service departments. This is called secondary distribution or secondary overhead distribution summary.

5) Absorption of Overheads :

Charging overheads to individual product or job is known as absorption. Thus, purpose behind absorption is that, expenses allocated and apportioned to departments or cost centres should be absorbed in the cost of output of the given period.

3.3.1 COLLECTION OF OVERHEADS

The first step involved in the accounting of overheads is **collection and classification of overheads**. Systematic classification and codification are a pre-requisite to the collection of overheads.

Production overheads should be collected through standing order numbers. The main sources from which overhead costs are collected are as follows :

i) **Invoice :**

For collection of indirect expenses like rent, insurance etc.

ii) **Stores Requisitions :**

For collection of indirect materials.

iii) **Wages Analysis Sheet :**

For collection of indirect wages.

iv) **Journal Entries :**

For collection of those overheads items which do not result in current cash outlay and need some adjustment, for e.g., depreciation, charge in lieu of rent, outstanding rent etc.

To understand the systematic procedure of assigning standing orders numbers, there is a need to know about **'Standing Order System'**.

Standing Order System :

The production overheads are usually collected through a system of standing order numbers. **Standing Order System** is a system under which a distinct number is allocated to each item of cost for the purpose of identification.

Standing Order Numbers :

After overheads are classified, it is found useful to allot each group of expenses a number of symbols so that each such group is easily distinguished from others. Such number of symbols are codes for overheads and are sometimes called 'standing order numbers'. Each standing order number denotes a particular type of expenditure so that items of expenses of similar nature, as and when they are incurred are appropriately classified into one of these. A schedule or manual is maintained enlisting all standing order numbers. There cannot be a standard list of standing order number as the number and type under which overheads may be sub-grouped vary with the size of the factory, type of expenses, and the extent of control necessary.

An essential requisite for an effective system of standing order number is that such numbers should be clearly defined so that individuals responsible for booking expenditure may easily understand the classification. Secondly, the classification into standing order numbers should have the quality of flexibility, so that as and when the need arises, suitable changes can be incorporated without seriously dislocating the existing system.

Methods of Allotting Standing Order Numbers :

Each standing order number is identified by a code number or symbol. The allocation of code numbers or symbols can be done by any of the following methods :

Methods of Coding :

The important methods of coding are as follows :

a) Serial number system, b) Decimal system, c) Alphabetical system, d) Combination of Alphabetical and Numerical system, and e) Field method or Numerical code.

a) Serial Number System:

In this method, each type of expenditure is allotted a number in serial order as shown below:

Standing Order Number	Expenditure
01	Furnace Oil
07	Works Manager Salary
23	Power
34	Factory Lighting
52	Factory Rent

A group of numbers is set apart to classify the items under a broad head. e.g., 1 to 20 for indirect materials, 21 to 40 for indirect labour, and so on.

b) Decimal System:

This is also a numerical system with the difference that instead of full numbers, decimals are used. The whole numbers are used to indicate the main group and the decimal represents the sub-groups. For example,

Sr. No.	Item	Standing Order Number	Item
1.	Factory Overheads		
1.1	Indirect material	1.2	Indirect Labour
1.1.1	Furnace Oil	1.2.1	Inspectors
1.1.2	Lubricating Oil	1.2.2	Foremen
1.1.3	Cotton Waste, etc.	1.2.3	Sweepers
1.1.4	Repairs and Maintenance, Stores	1.2.4	Repair Wages
1.1.5	Tools For General Use	1.2.5	Idle Time Wages
Similarly,			
2.	Administration Overheads	2.2.	Accounting Services
2.1.1	Travelling expenses	2.2.1	Salaries
2.1.2	Salaries / Honorarium	2.2.2	Depreciation of accounting Machine
2.1.3	Maintenance of cars		
2.1.4	Telephone expenses	2.2.3	Stationery, Xerox
		2.2.4	Postage / Courier

c) Alphabetical System:

This system has the advantage that it may be formed into a mnemonic code. e.g.,

P = Purchases
PD = Purchase Discount
PM = Purchase Manager
PO = Purchase Outdoor
PR = Purchase of Raw Material
PI = Purchase Indoor
PC = Purchase Components

On account of limited number of alphabets, this method has a limited coverage and lacks of flexibility.

d) Combination of Alphabets and Numbers System :

The alphabet denotes the main group and the sub-group or type of expenditure is indicated by the numerical 1. The following codes illustrate this method :

R1 –	Repairs to Plant and Machinery		D1 –	Depreciation to Plants and Machinery
R2 –	Repairs to Buildings		D2 –	Depreciation of Buildings
R3 –	Repairs to Delivery vans		D3 –	Depreciation of Delivery Vans
R4 –	Repairs to Office cars		D4 –	Depreciation of Office Cars

e) Field Method or Numerical Code :

Under this method, codes used are numeric in nature and each code number usually consists of nine digits. The first two digits indicate the nature of expenses viz. variable or fixed, the next three digits indicate head of expenses, the next two digits stand for the analysis of expenses, and last two digits indicate the cost centre, where expenses have been incurred. e.g., in code 223035985, 22 stands for variable costs, 303 for idle time, 59 for waiting for materials and 85 for lathe shop.

Code	Particulars
22/303/59/85	Variable Cost/Idle Time/Waiting for Material/Lathe Shop.

3.3.2 ALLOCATION OF OVERHEADS

Certain items of overhead costs can be directly identified with a particular department or cost centre as having been incurred for that cost centre. Allotment of such costs to departments or cost centres is known as **allocation**. Thus, **allocation** may be defined as *"the allotment of whole items of cost to cost centres or cost units"*. In other words, allocation is charging to a cost centre those overheads that result solely from the existence of that cost centre. A point to be clearly understood is that allocation can be made only when the exact amount of overhead incurred in a cost centre is definitely known. For example, rent cannot normally be allocated since rent is payable for the factory as a whole and exact amount for each department cannot be known. Indirect materials, on the other hand, can be easily allocated to various departments in which they are incurred. Other items which are allocated include indirect wages, overtime and idle time cost, power (when sub-metres are installed in departments), depreciation of machinery, supervision etc. In brief, in order that an overhead can be allocated, it should meet both of the following conditions :

   i) the cost centre must have caused the overhead to be incurred; and
   ii) the exact amount incurred in a cost centre must be known.

   Allocation of Overheads is always direct

In short, **Allocation of Overheads** is the process of charging the full amount of an individual item of cost directly to a cost centre for which this item of cost was incurred. The usual format of statement showing allocation of overheads is as follows :

In the books of a Co. ......
Statement showing Allocations of Overheads

Particulars	Production Departments		Service Departments	
	P_1 ₹	P_2 ₹	S_1 ₹	S_2 ₹
Direct Material			–	–
Direct Wages			–	–
Direct Expenses			–	–
Indirect Material	–	–	–	–
Indirect Wages	–	–	–	–
Indirect Expenses	–	–	–	–
∴ Total	–	–	–	–

It should be noted that, all costs of service departments only are considered as overheads.

Example

Atlas Ltd., Anand has two production departments and two service departments, they provide you the following data for the period ended 31st March, 2015.

Particulars	Production Departments		Service Departments	
	P_1 ₹	P_2 ₹	S_1 ₹	S_2 ₹
Direct Material	30,000	20,000	20,000	10,000
Direct Wages	20,000	15,000	10,000	5,000
Direct Expenses	10,000	10,000	5,000	2,500
Indirect Material	8,000	8,000	8,000	8,000
Indirect Wages	2,500	2,500	5,000	2,500
Total	10,500	10,500	48,000	28,000

Common Indirect Expenses during period were ₹ 20,000. You are required to prepare the Statement showing Allocation of Overheads for the period ended 31st March, 2015.

Answer

In the books of Atlas Ltd., Anand
Statement showing Allocation of Overheads for the period ended 31st March, 2015

Particulars	Production Departments		Service Departments	
	P_1 ₹	P_2 ₹	S_1 ₹	S_2 ₹
Direct Materials	–	–	20,000	10,000
Direct Wages	–	–	10,000	5,000
Direct Expenses	–	–	5,000	2,500
Indirect Materials	8,000	8,000	8,000	8,000
Indirect Wages (+)	2,500	2,500	5,000	2,500
Total	10,500	10,500	48,000	28,000

3.3.3 APPORTIONMENT OF OVERHEADS

Certain overhead costs cannot be directly charged to a department or cost centre. Such costs are common to a number of cost centres or departments and do not originate from any specific department. Distribution of such overhead costs to various departments is known as 'apportionment'. Thus, **apportionment** may be defined as *"the allotment of proportions of items of* *cost to cost centres or cost units*". In other words, it is charging to a cost centre as fair share of an overhead. Where an item of overhead is common to various cost centres, it is allotted to different cost centres, proportionately on some equitable basis. Again taking the case of rent, as it cannot be allocated, it is apportioned to various departments on some equitable basis e.g. in the ratio of area occupied. Similarly, salary of a general manager cannot be allocated wholly to anyone department as he attends in general to all the departments. It should, therefore, be apportioned on some equitable basis. Other items which generally cannot be allocated but are apportioned include fire insurance, lighting and heating, time keeping expenses, canteen expenses, medical and other welfare expenses etc.

In short, apportionment of overheads is the process of charging the proportion of common items of cost to two or more cost centres on some equitable basis i.e. actual benefit/or potential benefit/or ability to pay/or service or use etc. e.g.
  i) Where only one electric meter is installed in a factory, the common electricity charges should be apportioned to all the departments on the basis of number of light points or floor area occupied.
  ii) Factory Rent is incurred for the factory as a whole and benefits all the departments in the factory. Hence, it should be apportioned to all the departments on the basis of floor area occupied.

Distinction between 'Allocation of Overheads' and 'Apportionment of Overheads':

The distinction between Allocation of Overheads and Apportionment of Overheads can be shown as follows:

Allocation of Overheads	Apportionment of Overheads
i) It deals with the whole items of costs.	i) It deals with proportions of items of cost.
ii) Here, the cost is allotted directly.	ii) Here, the costs are distributed on a proportionate basis.
iii) It is a direct process.	iii) It is an indirect process according to suitable basis.
iv) Overheads cannot be allocated directly to the products.	iv) It is possible to charge the expenses indirectly through apportionment and absorb the cost in the final products.
v) Overheads should always be allocated, if possible.	v) If overhead cannot be allocated, it is apportioned.
vi) This is known as 'Departmentalisation of Overheads' or 'Primary Distribution of Overheads'.	vi) This is also a part of primary distribution of overhead costs.
vii) It is the process of alloting or charging the whole amount of an item of overhead to a department or cost centre.	vii) It is the 'allotment of proportions or items of cost to cost centres or cost units'. It is the distribution of common costs to different department on some suitable basis.
Allocation and Apportionment of Overheads aims at ascertaining the exact cost of cost units	

Types of Department:

The organisation of business enterprise is administratively classified into different sub-divisions, termed as 'departments'. These departments are classified as either production or service department. A **production department** is one that engages in the actual manufacture of the product by changing the shape, form or nature of material worked upon or by assembling the parts into finished product. A **service department**, on the other hand, is one rendering a service that contributes in an indirect manner to the manufacture of the product but which does not itself change the shape, form or nature of material that is converted into the finished product. Examples of production departments and service departments are as follows :

Production Departments	Service Departments
• Weaving Department	• Purchasing Department
• Spinning Department	• Stores Department
• Crushing Department	• Time-Keeping Department
• Mixing Department	• Personnel Department
• Grinding Department	• Inspection Department
• Annealing Shop	• Canteen
• Picking Shop	• Labour Welfare Department
• Polishing Department	• Production Control Department
• Finishing Department	• Internal Transport Department
• Kiln Burning Shop	• Tool Room
• Melting Shop	• Accounting Department

The distinction between **Production Department** and **Service Department** can be shown as follows :

	Production Department		Service Department
i)	It is one that is engaged in the actual manufacturing of the product by changing the shape, form or nature of material worked upon or by assembling the parts into finished product.	i)	It is one rendering a service that contributes in an indirect manner to the manufacture of product but which does not, itself change the shape by form or nature of material, that is converted into finished product.
ii)	Weaving department, spinning department, mixing department, grinding department, etc. are some of the examples of production department.	ii)	Time-keeping department, canteen, stores department, labour welfare department, etc. are some of the examples of service department.
iii)	It works on things.	iii)	It works on people.
iv)	It produces goods, goods can be stored in inventory until sold at a later date.	iv)	It produces on output that is by nature, intangible. Its services are perishable, and cannot be stored.

Partly Producing Department :

There may be certain departments which are normally treated as service departments, but sometimes they are also required to undertake direct production work. These may be known as **partly producing or partly service departments**. For example, **a carpentry shop** which is mainly engaged in the work of repairs and maintenance of fittings and fixtures, is a service department but may be occasionally required to manufacture wooden boxes for packing of goods which may be charged direct to output. Similarly tool room, though a service department, may manufacture special tools against job orders. As these departments are sometimes engaged in direct manufacturing activities, they are called **partly producing departments**.

Principles of Apportionment :

Apportionment of overheads to various production and service departments is based on the following principles :

a) Service or Use :

This is the most common basis of apportionment of overhead costs. It is based on the theory that greater the amount of service or benefit received by a department, the larger should be the share of the cost to be borne by that department. e.g. rent is apportioned to various departments according to the floor space occupied, telephone charges according to the number of extension telephones in each department and so on. The guiding principles of apportionment of common overheads on the basis of service or use are as follows :

i) Actual Benefit :

According to this principle, common overheads are apportioned on the basis of actual benefit received. This method is adopted where measurement of actual benefit is possible. e.g. rent can be apportioned on the basis of area occupied by each department.

ii) Potential Benefit :

According to this principle, common overheads are apportioned on the basis of potential benefit i.e. benefit likely to be received. This method is adopted where measurement of actual benefit is not possible at all or if possible, is uneconomical. e.g. cost of transport for workers, can be apportioned on the basis of the number of employees in each department.

b) Survey Method :

This method is used for those overhead costs that are not closely related to departments and whose remoteness necessitates an arbitrary distribution. For e.g., salary of a General Manager of a company may be apportioned on the basis of the results of a survey which may reveal that 30% of his salary should be apportioned to sales, 10% to administration and 60% to various producing departments. Similarly, lighting expenses may be apportioned on the basis of a survey of the number of lights, size, estimated hours of use etc.

c) Ability to Pay Method :

This is based on the theory of taxation which holds that those who have the largest income should bear the highest proportion of the tax burden. In overhead distribution, those departments which have the largest income may be charged the largest amount of overhead. This method is generally considered inequitable because it penalises the efficient and the profitable units of the business to the advantages of inefficient ones.

> If allocation of overheads is not possible, they should be apportioned to different cost centres on the most equitable basis.

Common Bases of Apportionment of Overheads :

The following table indicates the various basis of apportionment for the usual items of factory overheads.

Common Items of Factory Overheads	Basis of Apportionment
1) a) Factory Rent, Rates and Taxes	• Floor area occupied
b) Repairs and Maintenance of Factory Buildings, Air conditioning	• Floor area occupied
c) Insurance of Factory Buildings	• Floor area occupied
d) Depreciation of Factory Buildings, if owned	• Floor area occupied
2) a) Repairs and maintenance of plant and machinery	• Capital cost of Plant and Machinery or Machine hours
b) Insurance of Plant and Machinery	• Capital cost of Plant and Machinery
c) Depreciation of Plant and Machinery	• Capital cost of Plant and Machinery
3) Insurance of Stock	• Insured value of stock
4) a) Supervision	• Number of workers/Direct labour hours
b) Canteen, Staff welfare expenses	• Number of workers
c) Time-keeping and Personnel Office Expenses	• Number of workers
d) Medical Expenses	• Number of workers
5) a) Compensation to workers	• Wages
b) Employees' State Insurance Contribution	• Wages
c) Provident Fund Contribution	• Wages
6) Stores Overhead or Store keeping Expenses	• Value of direct materials
7) Material Handling Charges	• Weight of direct materials
8) Lighting and Heating	• Number of light points or floor area occupied or kilowatt hours.
9) Power or Steam consumption	• Horse power of machines or machine hours.
10) Technical Estimates	• For apportioning the expenses for which it is not possible to use any conventional basis. The apportionment is made on the basis of the assessment made by the technical experts.
11) Fire Insurance	• Value of Asset
12) Machine Shop Expenses	• Machine hours or Labour hours
13) General Expenses	• Direct wages or number of employees
14) Audit Fees	• Sales or Total cost.

The basis of apportionment can be arrived at on a trial basis and reviewed annually. It should be noted that some overheads in the above list can be apportioned on more than one basis. The choice of an appropriate basis is really a matter of judgement. e.g., welfare expenses may be apportioned on the basis of employees or total wages. Similarly, lighting expenses may be apportioned on the basis of number of light points in each department or on the basis of technical estimates or on the basis of floor area. General format of statement showing the apportionment of overheads is as follows :

Statement showing Apportionment of Overheads

Particulars	Basis of Apportionment	Production Departments			Service Departments	
		P_1 ₹	P_2 ₹	P_3 ₹	S_1 ₹	S_2 ₹
Fixed Power Generation Cost	Normal Capacity	...	...	...	...	...
Variable Power Generation Cost	Actual Power Consumption (kwh)	...	...	...	...	...
Lighting	Number of Light Points	...	...	...	...	...
Depreciation	Asset Value	...	...	...	...	...
Insurance	Asset Value	...	...	...	...	...
Rent, Rates and Taxes	Floor Area	...	...	...	...	...
Repairs	Floor Area	...	...	...	...	...
Stores Overheads	Direct Material	...	...	...	...	...
Employee's Insurance Charges	Direct Wages	...	...	...	...	...
Staff Welfare Expenses	Number of Workers	...	...	...	...	...
Supervision Expenses	Number of Workers (+)	...	...	...	...	...
∴ Total		...	...	...	...	...

Departmentalisation of Overheads :

After overhead costs have been collected under various standing order numbers, the second step is to allocate and apportion the overheads to production and service departments. This is also known as **Departmentalisation or Primary Distribution of Overhead**.

Departmentalisation of Overheads is the process of allocation and apportionment of overheads to different departments or cost centres. For smooth and efficient working, a factory is sub-divided into a number of departments each of which denotes a particular activity of the factory. For e.g., Purchase Departments, Stores Department, Time-Keeping Department, Personnel Department, Crushing Department, Melting Shop etc. These departments are mainly of various types viz. Production Departments, and Service Departments and Production cum Service Department.

The following factors are taken into account while organising a concern into a number of departments.

i) Similarity of operations, processes, machines and equipment in a department,

ii) Location of operations and processes and the sequence of operations,

iii) Division of responsibility for control of production and control of cost, and

iv) Optimum number of centres. Too many cost centres make the system of cost accounting detailed and quite expensive, whereas too few cost centres will not be able to provide requisite cost information and thus will fail to serve the main objectives of cost accounting.

Need for Departmentalisation of Overheads :

Departmentalisation of Overheads is necessary for the following reasons :

i) Control of Overhead Costs :

Effective control of overhead costs is possible because departmentalisation makes the incurrence of costs in a department or cost centre the responsibility of someone who heads the department or the cost centre. Thus, with the help of departmentalisation, responsibility accounting can be effectively introduced for control purposes.

ii) Forecasting and Estimating :

Because of greater accuracy in cost ascertainment and cost control, departmentalisation ensures more accurate forecasting and estimating and decision-making.

iii) Ensures Greater Accuracy in Cost Ascertainment :

By proper allocation and apportionment of overheads for accurate costing of each function or operation, overhead absorption rates should be determined separately for each cost centres. This is possible only with the help of departmentalisation.

iv) Use of different Methods of Absorption :

Basis of absorption of overhead may be different for different cost centres. For e.g., machine hour rate may be suitable for one cost centre whereas direct labour hour rate may be more appropriate for another cost centres. Different basis may be used for different cost centres only when overheads are departmentalised.

v) Valuation of Work-in-Progress :

Correct cost of work-in-progress cannot be ascertained unless overheads are departmentalised.

vi) Cost of Service Departments :

Departmentalisation helps in ascertaining the cost of various service departments which is useful for making estimates and submitting quotations for those items which make use of the services of various cost centres.

EXAMPLE

Britania Ltd., Baroda has three production departments 'X', 'Y' and 'Z' and two service departments, 'A' and 'B'. The following figures are extracted from the records of the company for the period ended 31st March, 2015.

Basics of Cost Accounting — Overheads

	₹		₹
Rent and Rates	5,000	General Lighting	600
Indirect Wages	1,500	Power	1,500
Depreciation of Machinery	10,000	Sundries	10,000

The following further details are available.

Particulars		Total	'X'	'Y'	'Z'	'A'	'B'
Floor Space	(Sq. ft)	10,000	2,000	2,500	3,000	2,000	500
Light Points	(Numbers)	60	10	15	20	10	5
Direct Wages	₹	10,000	3,000	2,000	3,000	1,500	500
H.P. of Machines	(H.P.)	150	60	30	50	10	–
Value of Machinery	₹	2,50,000	60,000	80,000	1,00,000	5,000	5,000

Apportion the costs to various departments on the most equitable basis.

ANSWER

In the books of Britania Ltd., Baroda
Primary Departmental Distribution Summary for the period ended 31st March, 2015

Particulars	Basis of Apportionment	Total ₹	X ₹	Y ₹	Z ₹	A ₹	B ₹
Direct Wages	Actual	2,000	–	–	–	1,500	500
Rent and Rates	Floor Space	5,000	1,000	1,250	1,500	1,000	250
General Lighting	Light Points	600	100	150	200	100	50
Indirect Wages	Direct Wages	1,500	450	300	450	225	75
Power	H.P. of Machines	1,500	600	300	500	100	–
Dep. of Machinery	Value of Machine	10,000	2,400	3,200	4,000	200	200
Sundries	Direct Wages (+)	10,000	3,000	2,000	3,000	1,500	500
∴ Total		30,600	7,550	7,200	9,650	4,625	1,575

EXAMPLE

Coment Ltd., Chembur, has two production departments and two service departments and provides you the following data for the period ended 31st March, 2015.

Particulars		Production Departments		Service Departments	
		P_1 ₹	P_2 ₹	S_1 ₹	S_2 ₹
Direct materials	₹	40,000	30,000	20,000	10,000
Direct Wages	₹	15,000	20,000	5,000	10,000
Floor Area	(sq. feet)	5,000	4,000	3,000	2,000
Value of Plant and Machinery	₹	1,00,000	1,20,000	40,000	20,000
Value of Stock	₹	35,000	25,000	5,000	5,000
Number of workers	No.	100	50	25	25
Number of light points	LP	200	50	25	25
Horse power of machines	HP	50	25	15	10

The indirect expenses for the period were :

	₹
Factory Rent, Rates, Taxes and Repairs	14,000
Depreciation, Insurance and Repairs of Machinery	56,000
Insurance of Stock	700
Supervision and Staff Welfare Expenses	2,000
Stores Overheads	1,000
Lighting and Heating	3,000
Power	1,000

Prepare the Statement showing the Apportionment of Overheads for the period ended 31st March, 2015.

ANSWER

In the books of Coment Ltd. Chembur
Statement showing Apportionment of Overheads for the period ended 31st March, 2015

Particulars	Basis of Apportionment	Total	Production Department		Service Departments	
			P_1 ₹	P_2 ₹	S_1 ₹	S_2 ₹
• Factory Rent, Rates, Taxes and Repairs	Floor Area	14,000	5,000	4,000	3,000	2,000
• Depreciation, Insurance and Repairs of Machinery	Value of Plant and Machinery	56,000	20,000	24,000	8,000	4,000
• Insurance of Stock	Value of Stock	700	350	250	50	50
• Supervision and Staff Welfare Expenses	Number of workers	2,000	1,000	500	250	250
• Stores Overhead	Value of Materials	1,000	400	300	200	100
• Lighting and Heating	Number of light points	3,000	2,000	500	250	250
• Power	H.P. of Machinery (+)	1,000	500	250	150	100
∴ Total		77,700	29,250	29,800	11,900	6,750

3.3.4 RE-APPORTIONMENT OF OVERHEADS

Once the overheads have been allocated and apportioned to production and service departments and totalled, the next step is to **re-apportion** the service department costs to production departments. This is necessary because our ultimate object is to charge overheads to cost units, and no cost units pass through service departments. Therefore, the costs of service departments must be charged to production departments which directly comes in contact with cost units. This is called '**Secondary Distribution of Overheads'**. The method of re-apportionment of service department costs is similar to apportionment of overheads as mentioned above. Some of the important bases of re-apportionment of service department costs are as follows.

Basis of Re-apportionment of Overheads of Service Departments :

The following is the general summary of the basis of re-apportionment of some common items of overheads of service departments.

	Service Department	Basis of Re-apportionment
i)	Purchase Dept.	• Number of purchase orders or number of purchase requisitions or value of materials purchased.
ii)	Stores Dept.	• Number of material requisitions or value of materials issued.
iii)	Time-keeping Dept., Payroll Dept.	• Number of employees or total labour hours or machine hours
iv)	Personnel Dept., Canteen, Welfare, Medical and Recreation Dept.	• Number of employees or total wages.
v)	Repairs and Maintenance	• Number of hours worked in each department.
vi)	Power House Dept.	• Meter reading or H.P. hour for powers. Meter reading or floor space for lighting, heat consumed.
vii)	Inspection Dept.	• Inspection hours or value of items inspected.
viii)	Drawing Office Dept.	• Number of drawings made or man-hours worked.
ix)	Accounts Dept.	• Number of workers in each department or time devoted.
x)	Tool Room Dept.	• Direct labour hours or Machine hours or wages.
xi)	Factory Office Dept.	• Number of employees.
xii)	Boiler House Dept.	• Percentage of steam utilised.
xiii)	Internal Transport Dept.	• Weight and distance.

Secondary Distribution of Overheads :

Secondary distribution of overheads means the re-apportionment of overheads of service departments among the production departments on some suitable basis.

The costs of service departments are re-apportioned on the basis of services rendered i.e. the benefits received by the beneficiary departments. The various methods of Re-apportionment of Service Department Costs are summarised in this chart shown in Figure 3.7.

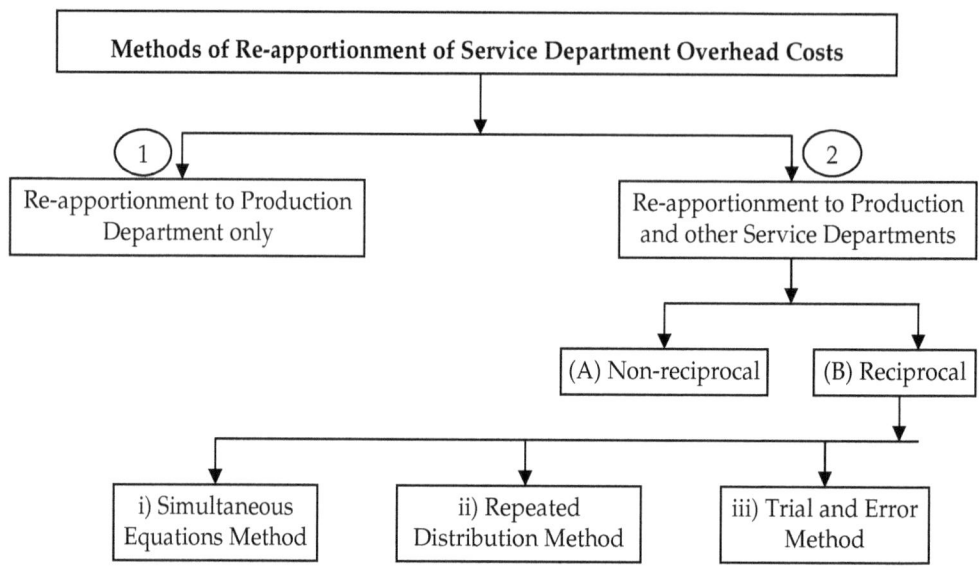

Fig. 3.7 : Methods of Re-apportionment of Service Department Overhead Costs

1) Re-apportionment to Production Departments Only :

In this case, cost of a service department is re-apportioned only to production departments without re-apportioning it to other service departments.

EXAMPLE

Continuing the example given on page number 3.25 by taking the total overhead as per departmental distribution summary and the following additional information, apportion the service department costs to production departments, only ignoring inter-service departmental transfer.

		'X'	'Y'	'Z'
Number of Employees	No.	75	30	45
Value of Materials Purchased	₹	10,000	8,000	7,000

Further assume that Service Department 'A' is Purchasing Department and 'B' is Time-keeping Department.

ANSWER

In the books of Britania Ltd., Baroda
Secondary Distribution Summary for the period ended 31st March, 2015

Particulars	Basis of Re-apportionment	Total ₹	Production Depts.			Service Depts.	
			'X' ₹	'Y' ₹	'Z' ₹	'A' ₹	'B' ₹
Total as per Primary Summary	—	30,600	7,550	7,200	9,650	4,625	1,575
Service Dept. A	Value of materials purchased	—	1,850	1,480	1,295	(–) 4,625	—
Service Dept. B	Number of employees (+)	—	788	315	472	—	(–) 1,575
∴ Total		30,600	10,188	8,995	11,417	—	—

2) Re-apportionment to Production as well as Other Service Departments :

Quite often, a service department renders service not only to production department but also to other service departments. For example, maintenance department looks after not only the plant and machinery of production department but also the equipment of other service departments like power house, materials handling, etc. Similarly, power house supplies electricity not only to production departments but also to canteen, maintenance department etc. This type of inter-service department apportionment may be either on reciprocal basis or non-reciprocal basis :

A) Re-apportionment on Non-reciprocal basis :

This is done when service departments are not interdependent. In this method, the service departments are arranged in the descending order of their serviceability. The cost of the most serviceable departments i.e. the department which serves the largest number of departments is first apportioned to other service departments. The service department whose services are the next largest is taken up next and its cost (including the prorated cost of the first service department) is apportioned to other service and production departments excepting the first service department. In the same way, while apportioning the third service department in this order, the first two service departments are ignored. This process is continued till the cost of the last service department is apportioned. It should be noted that the cost of the last service department is apportioned only to production department.

EXAMPLE

This method has been illustrated with assumed figures which are as follows :

Secondary Distribution Summary for the period ended 31st March, 2015

Total	Production Depts.			Service Depts.			
	'X'	'Y'	'Z'	'A'	'B'	'C'	'D'
₹	₹	₹	₹	₹	₹	₹	₹
25,350	8,000	7,250	5,600	1,200	1,000	800	1,500
	350	250	300	300	200	100	(–) 1,500
	300	250	200	150	–	(–) 900	–
	200	350	400	250	(–) 1,200	–	–
	600	700	600	(–) 1,900	–	–	–
25,350	9,450	8,800	7,100	–	–	–	–

It is assumed that the descending order of serviceability of service departments is 'D', 'C', 'B' and 'A'. This means service department 'D' is the most serviceable department i.e. it renders service to the largest number of production as well as other service departments. It does not receive any service from other service department. Therefore, cost of ₹ 1,500 of service department 'D' is apportioned to all other departments in the ratio it renders its services. The next most serviceable department is 'C' which renders its services to all other departments except 'D'. Therefore, its cost is apportioned to all departments except service department 'D'. Then 'B' department's cost is apportioned which is next in the order of serviceability and lastly A's cost is apportioned.

Basics of Cost Accounting   3.31   Overheads

B) Re-apportionment on Reciprocal basis :

This method is used when service departments are mutually dependent. Thus, in the above example, position will be different if in addition to serving production departments, each service department also renders services to each other service department. For example, service department 'A' renders service to 'B', 'C' and 'D', service department B renders service to 'A', 'C' and 'D' department and so on. In such a case, until B's charge to A, C and D is known A, C and D cannot allot any cost to B. Similarly, until A's charge to 'B', 'C' and 'D' is known, 'B', 'C' and 'D' cannot allot any costs to 'A'. Thus, there are many unknown variables as the number of service departments.

There are three methods for breaking this vicious circle which are, **i) Simultaneous Equations Method, ii) Repeated Distribution Method and iii) Trial and Error Method.**

i) Simultaneous Equations Method :

In this method, the following algebraic equations help in finding out the unknowns :

$$X = a + by$$
$$Y = a + bx$$

This is illustrated as follows :

EXAMPLE

The departmental distribution summary showed the following departmental totals :

Particulars	Production			Service	
Departments	'X'	'Y'	'Z'	'A'	'B'
Amount ₹	7,550	7,200	9,650	4,625	1,575

The costs of Service Depts. A and B are to be charged on the basis of the following percentage :

Departments	'X'	'Y'	'Z'	'A'	'B'
'A'	20%	30%	40%	–	10%
'B'	40%	20%	30%	10%	–

Find the total overheads of production departments as per Simultaneous Equation Method.

ANSWER

Let X denote the total overheads of Service Dept. 'A'

Y denotes total overheads of Service Dept. B

$$X = ₹4{,}625 + \frac{10}{100}Y \quad \ldots \text{(i)}$$

$$Y = ₹1{,}575 + \frac{10}{100}X \quad \ldots \text{(ii)}$$

or $X = ₹4{,}625 + 0.10\,Y \quad \ldots \text{(i)}$

$$-X + 10Y = ₹15,750 \quad \ldots \text{(ii)}$$

Again multiplying equation (ii) by 10 to eliminate X and adding :

$$10X - Y = ₹46,250 \quad \ldots \text{(i)}$$
$$\underline{-10X + 100Y = ₹1,57,500} \quad \ldots \text{(ii)}$$
$$99Y = ₹2,03,750$$
$$Y = \frac{₹2,03,750}{99}$$
$$\therefore Y = ₹2,058$$

Substituting the value of Y in equation (i)

$$10X - ₹2,058 = ₹46,250$$
$$10X = ₹46,250 + ₹2,058$$
$$10X = ₹48,308$$
$$X = ₹4,830.8 \text{ or } ₹4,831 \text{ (Approx.)}$$

Thus, X = ₹4,831 and Y = ₹2,058.

Statement showing Secondary Distribution as per Simultaneous Equation Method for the period ended …

Particulars	Total ₹	Production Depts.		
		'X' ₹	'Y' ₹	'Z' ₹
Total as per Primary Distribution Summary	24,400	7,550	7,200	9,650
Service Department 'A' (₹4,831)				
Less : 10% to Dept. 'B'	4,348	966	1,450	1,932
Service Department 'B' (₹2,058)				
Less : 10% to Dept. 'A'	1,852	823	411	618
∴ Total	30,600	9,339	9,061	12,200

This method of simultaneous equations gives scientific and more accurate results. But when the number of service departments exceeds two, calculations become cumbersome and tedious.

ii) **Repeated Distribution Method :**

In this method, the following steps are taken to apportion the service departments costs :

a) The costs of the first service department are apportioned in the normal way according to the given percentages. This will close the amount of the first service department.

b) Then apply the given percentages to the apportionment of second service department costs which includes its own total plus amount apportioned from the first service department. This closes the account of the second service department but re-opens the account of the first service department.

c) The same procedure should be followed in the case of all other service departments.

d) The procedure should be repeated again starting with the first service department whose total now consists only of amounts apportioned from other service departments. In this way, service department costs keep on reducing with each process of distribution because each time a substantial amount is charged to the production departments.

e) This process is continued until the amounts involved become insignificant.

The operation of this method is explained below continuing example given on page number 3.31.

EXAMPLE

Statement showing Secondary Distribution as per Repeated Distribution Method for the period ended ...

Particulars	Total ₹	Production Depts.			Service Depts.	
		'X' ₹	'Y' ₹	'Z' ₹	'A' ₹	'B' ₹
Total as per Primary Summary	30,600	7,550	7,200	9,650	4,625	1,575
Dept. 'A'		925	1,387	1,850	– 4,625	463
Dept. 'B'		815	408	611	204	– 2,038
Dept. 'A'		41	61	82	– 204	20
Dept. 'B'		9	4	7	–	(–) 20
∴ Total	30,600	9,340	9,060	12,200	–	–

Working Note : In the above statement, first of all the cost of service department 'A' is apportioned to 'X', 'Y', 'Z' and 'B' in the ratio given. Then the cost of service department 'B' ₹ 2,038 (i.e. 1,575 + 463) has been apportioned to departments 'X', 'Y', 'Z' and A in the given percentage. The account of department A is again open with ₹ 204, whose amount is distributed to 'X', 'Y', 'Z' and B in the given ratio. Then ₹ 20 allotted to department 'B' is distributed to departments 'X', 'Y', 'Z'. Nothing has been allotted to department 'A' as the share of department 'A' is quite negligible. In this way, the entire costs of service departments 'A' and 'B' are apportioned to production departments 'X', 'Y' and 'Z'.

It should be noted that, unlike Simultaneous Equations method, this method produces approximate results. But the advantage of this method is that it can be conveniently applied where the number of service departments is more than two.

iii) Trial and Error Method :

In this method, the cost of first service department is apportioned to other service departments in the given ratio. The cost of the next service department is apportioned to first and other service departments. In this way, when the costs of all service departments has been apportioned, the process is repeated till the service department costs are negligible.

The distinction between Apportionment of Overheads and Re-apportionment of Overheads can be shown as follows.

Apportionment of Overheads	Re-apportionment of Overheads
i) It is the process to allot costs to the cost centres or cost units for ascertaining the total costs. Apportionment does not depend upon the nature of expenses to be incurred, but depends upon the relationship with cost centre or cost unit to which it is required to be charged.	i) After 'primary distribution' the cost of service department is borne by the production departments. The process of redistribution of the service department costs to the production department is known as 'Re-apportionment' or 'secondary overhead distribution summary'.
ii) This is necessary because certain overhead costs cannot be directly charged to department or cost centre.	ii) This is necessary because the ultimate aim is to charge overheads to cost units, and no cost unit pass through service department.
iii) There is no hard and fast rule as regards the bases of apportionment of overheads. It depends on the nature of overhead incurred.	iii) It is done on the basis of the benefits received by each department.
iv) There are some common bases for apportionment of overhead costs on some equitable basis which is known as primary distribution method.	iv) For selecting a suitable base for re-apportioning the cost of service department, the same principles of apportionment may be applied here also.

3.3.5 ABSORPTION OF OVERHEADS

The process of apportioning the total overhead expenses of production department among the units produced in that department is termed as **'Overhead Absorption'**. In other words, **absorption of overhead expenses** refers to a systematic process of distributing the overheads among the units produced by production departments. **Overhead absorption** is also called as **overhead application, overhead recovery, levy of overhead, overhead costing** etc. After apportionment and re-apportionment of overheads to production departments, these overheads are to be charged to cost units. In essence, the procedure is to take each production department and distribute its overheads among all cost units passing through that particular department, this is technically known as **'Absorption'**.

After studying the methods of allocation and apportionment of overhead costs to cost centres, the next step in accounting of overheads is **absorption of overheads** in the cost of production i.e. recovery of overheads in the cost of production. All jobs, processes or services pass through one or more producing cost centre. The overhead expenses are ultimately charged to cost centre in such a manner that the cost of production of each unit includes an appropriate or equitable share of overheads of the cost centre. This method of apportionment of overhead expenses of the cost centres to cost units is called **absorption of overheads** which is also known as **application, levy or recovery of overheads**.

Following are some of the important definitions of **'Overhead Absorption'**.

i) *The Institute of Cost and Management Accountants, U.K. :*

"It is the allotment of overhead to cost units".

ii) *The Institute of Cost and Works Accountants, India :*

"It is the allotment of overheads to cost units by means of rates separately calculated for each cost centre".

The distinction between **Apportionment of Overheads** and **Absorption of Overheads** can be shown as follows :

Apportionment of Overheads	Absorption of Overheads
i) It may be defined as "allotment of proportions of items of cost to cost centre or cost units. In other words, distribution of common costs to different department on some suitable bases is called **apportionment** of overheads.	i) After apportionment and re-apportionment of overheads to production departments, these can be charged to cost units. In essence, the procedure is to take each production department and distribute its overheads among all cost units passing through that particular department. This is technically known as 'absorption' and is defined as **charging of overheads to cost units.**
ii) It is the second step in the distribution of overheads.	ii) It is the last step in the distribution process of overheads.
iii) It is the process to allot costs to the cost centre or cost units for ascertaining the total cost.	iii) It is the charging of overheads to the cost units.
iv) There are some common bases for apportionment of overheads cost on some equitable basis which is known as primary distribution method.	iv) It is known as levy, recovery or application of overheads.

3.3.5.1 UNDER AND OVER-ABSORPTION OF OVERHEADS

Meaning and Definition :

Overheads may be absorbed either on the basis of actual rates or pre-determined rates. When actual rates are used, the overheads absorbed must, if all the calculations are correctly made, exactly equal to the overheads incurred. In such a case, there is no problem of under or over-absorption of overheads. But when a predetermined rate is employed, overheads absorbed may not be equal to the amount of actual overheads incurred. Thus, whenever the overheads absorbed are not equal to the amount of actual overheads, it is a case of either **Under-absorption or Over-absorption of Overheads**. It should be noted that the overhead absorption rates are pre-determined.

$$\text{Pre-Determined Rate} = \frac{\text{Factory Overheads Estimated}}{\text{Basis i.e. units of output etc.}}$$

Where a pre-determined rate is adopted, the overhead absorption may not be the same as overhead incurred actually for e.g..

i) Actual factory overheads incurred are ₹ 5,500, whereas, factory overheads absorbed to the final output are ₹ 5,000 @ ₹ 2 per unit on the actual output of 2,500 units. Thus, there is under-absorption of factory overheads to the extent of ₹ 500, which means overhead absorbed to the final output is less than the actual overheads incurred.

ii) Actual factory overheads incurred are ₹ 4,500, whereas, factory overheads absorbed to the final output are ₹ 5,000 i.e. @ ₹ 2 per unit on the actual output of 2,500 units. Thus, there is over-absorption of factory overheads to the extent of ₹ 500, which means overhead absorbed to the final output is more than the actual overheads incurred i.e. the cost absorbed is more than the actual cost incurred.

i) **Under-absorption :**

It may be defined as "when the amount of overheads absorbed is less than the amount of overheads incurred, it is called **under-absorption or under-recovery**". This has the effect of under-stating the cost because the overheads incurred are not fully recovered in the cost of jobs, processes etc.

ii) **Over-absorption :**

It may be defined as, "when the amount of overhead absorbed is more than the amount of overhead incurred, it is known as **over-absorption or over-recovery**". This has the effect of over stating the cost of jobs processes etc.

Reasons :

Under or over-absorption of overheads may arise due to one or more of the following **reasons**.

i) Faulty estimation of overheads costs (or overhead incurred exceed the estimates) or outputs are less than anticipated).

ii) Faulty estimation of the quantity of output.

iii) Seasonal fluctuation in the amount of overhead in certain industries.

iv) Unforeseen changes in the production capacity.

v) Unexpected changes in the method of production affecting changes in the amount of overhead.

vi) Non-utilisation of normal capacity.

Whatever may be the reason, under or over-absorption is caused mainly due to the wrong estimation either of the costs incurred or of the production over which they are to be absorbed.

The **distinction between under-absorption of Overheads and Over-absorption of Overheads** can be shown as follows :

Under-absorption of Overheads	Over-absorption of Overheads
i) When the amount of overheads absorbed is less than the amount of overhead incurred it is called "under-absorption or under-recovery".	i) When the amount of overhead absorbed is more than the amount of overhead incurred it is known as "over-absorption or over-recovery".
ii) This has the affect of understating the cost because the overhead incurred are not fully recovered in the cost of jobs, processes, etc.	ii) This has the overstating cost of jobs, processes, etc.
iii) In case of under-absorption, supplementary rate is computed by dividing the under-absorbed production overheads by the actual value of the base. This is supplementary rate may be formed positive, supplementary rate as the under-absorbed overheads is to be added.	iii) In case of over-absorption, supplementary rate is computed by dividing the over-absorbed production overheads by the actual value of the base. This supplementary rate may be called negative supplementary rate as over-absorbed amount is to be subtracted.
iv) In case of under-absorption, under absorbed production overheads are to be added, applying positive supplementary rate, to the cost of various categories.	iv) In case of over-absorption, over-absorbed production overheads are to be deducted from the cost of work in progress, unsold stock and units sold.

Accounting Treatment :

The methods of Accounting Treatment for disposal of Under or Over-absorbed Overheads are shown below in Figure 3.8.

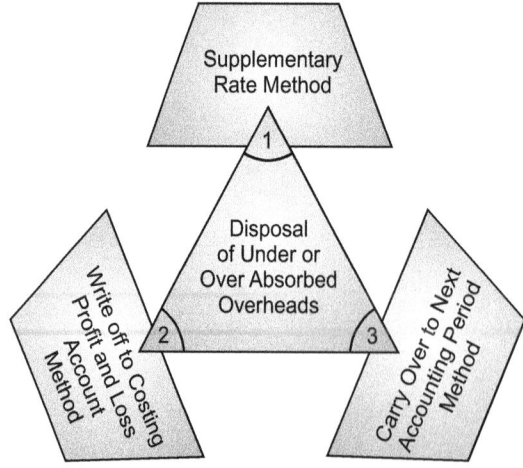

Fig. 3.8 : Accounting Treatment for Disposal of Under or Over-absorbed Overheads

1) **Supplementary Rate Method :**

   a) **When to use :**

   This method is usually used when,

   i) the amount of under/over-absorption of overheads is quite large and

   ii) the under or over-absorption of overheads is **due to normal reasons** like increase in material prices or labour rates. Supplementary rate may be calculated as follows :

   $$\text{Supplementary Rate} = \frac{\text{Amount of under/over-absorbed overheads}}{\text{Actual Base}}$$

   b) **How to use :**

   i) In case of under-absorption

   - The cost of sales, stocks of finished goods and work-in-progress are increased by applying positive supplementary rate.

   ii) In case of over-absorption

   - The cost of sales, stocks of finished goods and works-in-progress are reduced by applying negative supplementary rate.

2) **Write off to Costing Profit and Loss Account Method :**

   a) **When to use :**

   This method is usually used when,

   i) the amount of under/over-absorbed overheads is not very large, or

   ii) the under or over absorption of overheads is **due to abnormal reasons** like defective planning, idle capacity etc. In this case, even large amounts are written off to Costing Profit and Loss Account.

   b) **How to use :**

   The amount of under-absorbed overheads is transferred to the debit of costing profit and loss account and amount of over-absorbed overheads is transferred to the credit of costing profit and loss account.

3) **Carry Over to Next Accounting Period Method :**

   a) **When to use :**

   This method is usually used when,

   i) the period of normal business cycle is more than 1 year and overhead rates are determined on a long-term basis.

   ii) in case of new projects, more output in the next period(s) than that in initial stages is expected.

   b) **How to use :**

   The amount of under-absorbed overheads is transferred to the debit of overhead reserve or suspense account and the amount of over-absorbed overheads is transferred to the credit of overhead reserve or suspense account.

The under or over-recovered amounts are disposed off in accordance with any of the following methods depending upon the circumstances.

1) Use of Supplementary Rates :

Where the amount of under or over-absorbed overhead is not negligible, a supplementary overhead absorption rate is calculated to adjust this amount in the cost. However, adjustment is made in the cost of i) work-in-progress, ii) finished stock, and iii) cost of sales.

In the case of under-absorption, the overhead is adjusted by a plus rate since the amount is to be added, whereas, over-absorption is adjusted by a minus rate since the amount is to be deducted.

EXAMPLE

Pre-determined overhead rate	:	₹ 10 per machine hour
Actual machine hours	:	Hrs. 1,500
Actual overheads	:	₹ 18,000

ANSWER

Overhead absorbed	=	Hrs. 1,500 × ₹ 10 = ₹ 15,000
Under-absorption	=	₹ 18,000 – ₹ 15,000 = ₹ 3,000
Under Supplementary Rate	=	$\frac{₹ 3,000}{1,500 \text{ units}}$ = ₹ 2 per unit

This is a plus rate because it is for under-absorbed overheads and will be used to add to the overhead already recovered.

$$\text{Supplementary Overhead Rate} = \frac{\text{Under-absorption of Factory Overhead}}{\text{Units of Output}}$$

$$= \frac{₹ 3,000}{1,500 \text{ Units}}$$

$$= ₹ 2.00 \text{ per unit.}$$

Accounting Entry :

Work-in-Progress A/c Dr.	3,000	
To Factory Overhead Control A/c		3,000

2) Writing-off to Costing Profit and Loss Account or Transfer to Current year's Costing Profit and Loss Account :

The method is used when the under or over-absorbed amount is quite negligible and it is not worthwhile to absorb it by supplementary rates. Under-absorption due to abnormal factors like idle capacity, defective planning etc. is also transferred to Costing Profit and Loss Account. This method suffers from the shortcoming that stocks of work-in-progress and finished goods remain under or over-valued and are carried over to the next accounting period at such values.

EXAMPLE

Considering the above example, pass the Accounting Entry for the same.

ANSWER

Accounting Entry :

Costing Profit and Loss A/c Dr.	3,000	
To Factory Overhead Control A/c		3,000

3) Carry over to the next year :

Under this method, the under or over-absorbed amount is transferred to Overhead Reserve Account or Suspense Account for carry over to the next accounting year. This procedure is open to criticism on the ground that it is not logical to carry over the overhead of one year to the subsequent years for absorption. But, this method can be usefully employed where normal business cycle extends over more than one year and overheads are determined on a long-term basis.

EXAMPLE

In a manufacturing unit, overhead was recovered at a pre-determined rate of ₹ 25 per man day. The total factory overhead expenses incurred and the man-days actually worked were ₹ 41,50,000 and 1,50,000 days respectively. Out of the 40,000 units produced during a period, 30,000 were sold. On analysing the reasons, it was found that 60% of the unabsorbed overheads were due to defective planning and the rest were attributable to increase in overhead costs.

How would unabsorbed overheads to be treated in cost accounts ?

ANSWER

Particulars		Amount ₹
Actual overhead expenses incurred		41,50,000
Overhead expenses absorbed (₹ 25. × 1,50,000 days)	(−)	37,50,000
Unabsorbed overheads		4,00,000

60% of this amount of unabsorbed overheads which is due to defective planning (controllable reasons) should be charged to Costing Profit and Loss Account and the remaining 40% should be adjusted to the Cost of Sales and Closing Stock in the ratio of units sold and units in stock respectively.

	Particulars		Amount ₹
	Charge to Costing Profit and Loss Account : 60% of ₹ 4,00,000		2,40,000
Add :	Adjustment to the Cost of Sales : 40% of ₹ 4,00,000 = ₹ 1,60,000 ₹ 1,60,000 × $\dfrac{30,000 \text{ units}}{40,000 \text{ units}}$ = ₹ 1,20,000		1,20,000
Add :	Adjustment to Closing Stock : ₹ 1,60,000 × $\dfrac{10,000 \text{ units}}{40,000 \text{ units}}$	(+)	40,000
∴	Unabsorbed Overhead		4,00,000

QUESTIONS FOR SELF STUDY

I. Theory Questions :

i) Define the term 'Overheads'. State the important features of Overhead Costs.

ii) What is 'Overheads' ? Explain the various methods of classification of overheads.

iii) Explain the concept 'classification of overheads'. Describe in brief the following methods of classification of overheads giving suitable examples of the same.

a) Functional classification, b) Elementwise classification and c) Behaviourwise classification.

iv) What is 'Behaviourwise classification of overheads' ? Explain the importance of overheads classification according to behaviour.

v) What is 'Overhead Accounting' ? Explain the necessary steps involved in Accounting of Overheads'.

vi) What is 'Collection of Overheads' ? Explain the important sources from which overhead costs are collected.

vii) What is 'Allocation of Overheads' ? How it is different from 'Apportionment of Overheads' ?

viii) Define the term 'Apportionment of Overheads'. State the important principles of Apportionment of Overheads.

ix) What is 'Production Department' ? How it differs from a 'Service Department' ? Give atleast five examples of each department.

x) What is meant by 'Re-apportionment of Overheads' ? Explain the methods of Secondary Distribution of overhead costs.

xi) What is 'Departmentalisation of Overheads' ? Explain the need for departmentalisation of overheads.

xii) Explain various methods of 'Reapportionment of Overheads' on non-reciprocal basis.

xiii) What is 'Overhead Absorption ? How it differs from Apportionment of Overheads ?

xiv) What is 'Under-absorption' and Over-absorption of Overheads' ? State the reasons for under and over-absorption.

xv) Define the term 'Under-absorption of Overheads'. State the methods of disposal of under absorption of overheads.

xvi) Differentiate between :

a) Fixed Overheads and Variable Overheads, b) Selling Overheads and Distribution Overheads, c) Controllable and Uncontrollable Overheads, d) Normal Overheads and

Abnormal Overheads, e) Allocation of Overheads and Apportionment of Overheads, f) Production Department and Service Department, g) Apportionment of Overheads and Reapportionment of Overheads, h) Apportionment of Overheads and Absorption of Overheads, i) Under-absorption of Overheads and Over-absorption of Overheads.

xvii) Write short notes on :

a) Overheads costs, b) Features of Overheads costs, c) Elementwise classification of overheads, d) Importance of Overhead classification according to behaviour, e) Importance of Overheads Accounting, f) Collection of Overheads, g) Allocation of Overheads, h) Apportionment of Overheads, i) Reapportionment of Overheads on Reciprocal basis, j) Overhead Absorption, k) Reasons for Under and Over absorption of Overheads.

Unit ... 4

METHODS OF COSTING

4.1 Contract Costing
    4.1.1 Meaning
    4.1.2 Features
    4.1.3 Contract Costing Concepts
        4.1.3.1 Work Certified
        4.1.3.2 Work Uncertified
        4.1.3.3 Escalation Clause
        4.1.3.4 Cost Plus Contract
        4.1.3.5 Work-in-Progress
        4.1.3.6 Profit on Incomplete Contracts
* Illustrations
* Questions for Self-Study

4.2 Process Costing
    4.2.1 Meaning
    4.2.2 Features
    4.2.3 Preparation of Process Accounts including Normal and Abnormal Loss or Gain
        4.2.3.1 Preparation of Process Accounts
        4.2.3.2 Normal and Abnormal Loss or Gains
* Illustrations
* Questions for Self-Study

4.3 Service Costing
    4.3.1 Meaning
    4.3.2 Features
    4.3.3 Application
    4.3.4 Cost Unit : Simple and Composite
    4.3.5 Preparation of Cost Sheet for Transport Service
* Illustrations
* Questions for Self-Study

Methods of Costing

Costing is simply a method of cost finding. It is the technique and process of ascertaining the costs. It is the classifying, recording and appropriate allocation of expenditure for the determination of costs of products or services and for the presentation of suitably arranged data for the purposes of control and guidance of the management. It includes ascertainment of the cost of every order, job, batch, contract, process, service or unit as may be appropriate. It deals with the cost of production, selling and distribution. Thus, costing is the proper allocation of expenditure whereby reliable cost may be ascertained appropriately and suitably presented to afford guidance to the manufacturers, traders or service-providers in control of their respective businesses.

Cost Accounting is the process of accounting for cost, from the point at which expenditure is incurred or to be incurred to the point of charging to the cost centres and cost units. It has many uses which includes the preparation of statistical data, the application of cost control methods and the ascertainment of the profitability of activities carried out or planned. It is the means which consists of concepts, methods and procedures used to measure, analyse or estimate the cost, profitability and performance of individual products, departments and other sectors of a company's operations. It has internal and external use or both and it answers to all the questions to the concerned parties. Thus, Cost Accounting is the process and technique of determination of a product cost. It is a system of cost accumulation, ascertainment and classification for product costing and managerial planning, control and decision-making process. In short, Cost Accounting is a dynamic and diverse field of activity.

In **modern manufacturing world** of severe competition, industries are usually classified as **mass production industries** and **jobbing industries**.

In **mass production industries**, identical units are produced on a large scale and on a continuous basis. Manufacturing of standard product is made without any customers order or specifications. Thus, mass production industry is characterised by the continuous production of uniform products as per standard specifications. Mass production includes coal mines, products, cement, steel, paper, chemicals, bricks, rubber production. Their costing is made for entire output of a uniform product produced during a specific period.

On the contrary in **jobbing industries** production is made only against special orders from customers. Production of non-standard jobs is made strictly as per the specific requirements of customers, where each job is clearly distinguished from other jobs. Thus, jobbing industry is characterised by irregular production of non-standard products as per customer's specifications. Special job order production includes printing press, construction work, heavy machinery, foundry, general engineering works, machine tools, interior decoration, repairing works, furniture makers. Their costing is made separately for each job as per customer specifications.

The **method of cost accumulation** and identifying them to products and services depends upon the nature of operations in an enterprise. Cost accounting procedure varies from one company to another company. e.g., a non-manufacturing enterprise may not follow the procedure of accumulating costs with specific customer orders. Similarly, a hospital may prefer to accumulate costs in a manner as to provide the cost of out-patient treatment or a specific medical treatment. A concern organising exhibitions and fairs may be interested in knowing the cost of an exhibition to be organised in a particular season. On the contrary, a contractor accumulates costs for each separate contract. Although the procedure of accumulating costs may differ among different types of organisations, the basic principles underlying cost accumulating procedures are applicable to all types of organisations. Each cost accounting system aims to provide information that is required by the management.

A standard method of costing cannot be used for all types of industries.

Need for Various Methods of Costing

Methods of Costing indicates a systematic procedure established for ascertaining cost of a product, job process or services by using the principles of costing. A Cost Accounting method is merely the process of 'collecting and presenting costs. The nature of industries differs. Some are very simple and produce only one product e.g. brick-making. Some industries may produce only one product but it may really be an assembly of numerous components e.g. bicycle, motor car etc. Again there may be a homogeneous product but involving many distinct stages and processes such as vegetable oil. In some case there may be important by-products or joint products e.g. petroleum products, sugar etc. It is therefore, natural that the exact method employed to ascertain cost per unit should depend on the nature of the industry. The general principle of ascertaining cost of production per unit are the same, but the methods ascertaining and presenting the costs vary with the type of production. One standard method of costing may not be applied suitably to various types of industries because they differ in type of products, methods of production, nature of industry, scale of operation, volume of output etc. Hence, there is a **need for introducing various methods of costing** which can be applied more suitably to a manufacturing business.

Various Methods of Costing

In manufacturing organisations, the principles of cost accumulation and their identification with products are more clear and visible and therefore the principles used by a manufacturing enterprise is often used by other organisations also for accumulating costs. In manufacturing concerns, costs are accumulated and assigned to products on the basis of the following cost accounting methods viz. A) Specific Order Costing and B) Operations Costing.

But according to **Mr. Batty**, "Many costing systems do not fall neatly into the category of either job or process costing. Often, systems use some features of both the main costing systems". It is, for this reason, that he uses the term "hybrid costing systems" for all those methods that combine the features of the basic costing methods. The Figure 4.1 indicated below shows **Various Methods of Costing.**

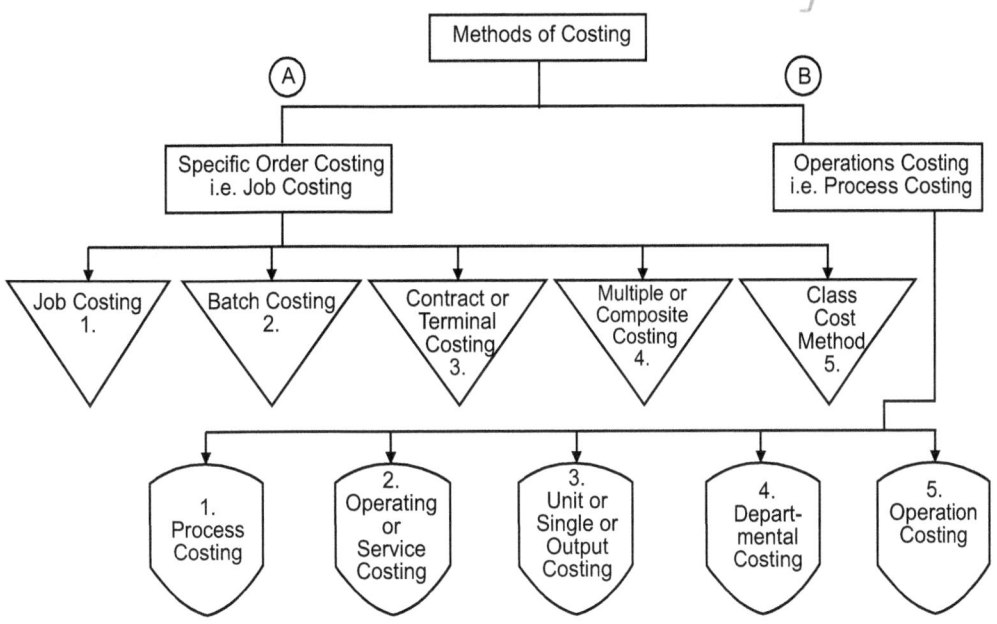

Fig. 4.1 : Various Methods of Costing

A) Specific Order Costing :

The terminology of **I.C.M.A.** defines **Specific Order Costing** as, "the category of basic costing methods applicable where the work consists of separate contracts, jobs or batches each of which is authorised by a special order or contract".

This method is adopted in made-to-order type of products which depends entirely on the specification of customers. As such there is no standardisation in the production process for want of uniformity. The following are the different methods of costing which fall under the category of specific order costing.

1) Job Costing :

The terminology of **I.C.M.A.** defines **Job Costing** as, "that form of specific order costing which applies where work is undertaken to customers' "special requirements".

Under this method, costs are collected and accumulated for each job, work order or project separately. Each job can be separately identified, so it becomes essential to analyse the cost according to each job. A Job Card is prepared for each job for cost accumulation. This method is applicable to printers, machine tool manufacturers, foundaries and general engineering workshops, interior decorator, painters, repair shops etc.

2) Batch Costing :

The terminology of **I.C.M.A.** defines **Batch Costing** as, "that form of specific order costing which applies where similar articles are manufactured in batches either for sale or use within the undertaking".

This method is a variation of Job Costing. In this method, the cost of a batch or group of identical products is ascertained and, therefore, each batch of products is a unit of cost for which costs are accumulated. This method is used in biscuit factories, bakeries, ready-made garments, hardwares like nuts, bolts, screws, shoes, toys, drugs and pharmaceuticals etc.

3) Contract or Terminal Costing :

The terminology of **I.C.M.A.** defines **Contract Costing** as, "that form of specific order costing which applies where work is undertaken to customers' special requirements and each order is of long duration".

The cost unit here is a contract which is of a long duration and may continue over more than one financial year. A separate account is kept for each contract. This method is used by builders, civil engineering contractors, constructional and mechanical engineering firms etc.

4) Multiple or Composite Costing :

It is an application of more than one method of cost ascertainment in respect of the same product. This method is used in industries where a number of components are separately manufactured and then assembled into a final product. In such industries each component differs from the others as to price, material used and process of manufacture undergone. So it will be necessary to ascertain the cost of each component for this purpose, process costing may be applied. To ascertain the cost of the final product, batch costing may be applied. This method is used in factories manufacturing cycles, automobiles, engines, radios, TVs, typewriters, aeroplanes etc. This method has been completely dropped out from the latest I.C.M.A. Terminology.

5) Class Cost Method :

It is the method of Job Costing where the costing of goods is done by classes instead of the unit or a piece. Instead of the cost being separately accumulated for each article or piece, the cost will cover a group of orders of the same class of product.

B) Operations Costing :

The terminology of **I.C.M.A.** defines **Operations Costing** as, "the category of basic costing methods applicable where standardised goods or services result from a sequence of repetitive and more or less continuous operations or process to which costs are charged before being averaged over the units produced during the period".

The following are the different methods of costing which fall under the category of Operations Costing.

1) Process Costing :

The terminology of **I.C.M.A.** defines **Process Costing** as, "that form of operation costing which applies where the standardised goods are produced".

It is a method of costing where cost is ascertained at the stage of every process and also after completing the finished production. It is used in concerns where production follows a series or sequential process. Process type of industries do not manufacture individual items to the specific requirements of customers. As such, production is not intermittent but continuous. Each process represents a distinct stage of manufacture and the output of one process becomes the input of the following process. The unit cost is arrived at by averaging the cost over the units produced, and cost per unit of each process is ascertained. This method is used in a variety of industries such as chemicals, oil refining, paper making, flour milling, cement manufacturing, sugar, rubber, textiles, soap, glass, food processing etc.

2) Operating or Service Costing :

The terminology of **I.C.M.A.** defines Service Costing as, "that form of Operation Costing which applies where – standardised services are provided either by an undertaking or by a service cost centre within an undertaking".

This method of costing is used by those undertakings which render service as against manufacturing and supply of tangible products. It is an essential method of costing where only the services are rendered. It ascertains the cost of one unit of service rendered. This method is applicable to transport undertakings, electricity supply undertakings, hospitals, hotels, canteen, water works, gas companies, educational institutions etc. The cost unit depends upon the service provided. Usually, in service undertakings a composite cost unit is used. e.g. tonne kilo-metre passenger kilo-metre, patient per day or bed per day, KWH (kilo-watt-hours), meal served, student hours etc.

3) Unit or Single or Output Costing :

It is a method of costing by the unit of production, where manufacturing is continuous and the units are identical. In some cases the units may be differ in terms of size, shape, quality etc. This method is also called as **Single Costing** because only one type of product alone is manufactured. Examples of industries where this method is applicable are collieries, quarries, flour-mills, paper mills, textile mills, brick-making, radio, cameras, pencils, slates, diary products etc. No separate set of books is generally required and costing information is presented in the form of a statement known as Cost Sheet.

4) Departmental Costing :

A factory may be divided into a number of departments and sometimes good results are obtained by allocating expenditure first to different departments and then to different products manufactured in that department. Under this method, the cost incurred in maintaining a particular department is ascertained. There are two objectives for using this method viz. to control the cost of department and to charge the cost of a department or to the finished product.

5) Operation Costing :

It is a special type of Process Costing. It refers to the determination of cost of operations, the cost unit is the 'operation' instead of the process. The per unit cost is arrived at by dividing the cost of an operation by the number of units completed in the operation centre. For large undertakings it is frequently necessary to ascertain the cost of various operations. Cost control can be exercised more effectively with operation costing.

4.1 CONTRACT COSTING

It is that form of specific order costing which is applied where the work is undertaken according to special requirement of customers, each order is of long duration and the completion of the same takes usually more than one accounting period. It is a special type of job costing. In contract costing, similar accounting principles of job costing are followed. Here 'contract' means long-term contracts relating to engineering projects and construction activity. Each contract becomes basically a separate cost unit and for the purpose of exercising strict control, it is regarded as a cost centre.

4.1.1 Meaning

Contract is a special type of Job Costing where the unit of cost is a single contract. This method is also termed as 'Terminal Costing' as when the work is terminated the cost-sheet has to be completed. It is a variant of Job Costing. In this method it is desired to find out the cost of carrying out a complete contract for a customer involving numerous jobs and batches of jobs. The costs are ascertained and analysed with respect to the contract accepted for execution. This method of costing is adopted by those concerns undertaking definite contracts e.g. builders, contractors and civil engineers who undertake long-term projects like construction of roads, bridges, houses, large estates, irrigation schemes etc. It is also adopted by the concerns where the unit of output is heterogeneous e.g. ship building companies, turbines and boilers manufacturing company, motion pictures etc. Contract Costing is that form of specific order costing under which each contract is treated as a separate cost unit and costs are accumulated and ascertained separately for that contract.

Definitions

The term 'Contract Costing' and 'Contract Cost' has been defined by different experts and professional institutions in the manner stated below.

- **The Terminology of I.C.M.A. defines Contract Costing as**, "that form of specific order costing which applies where work is undertaken to customers special requirements and each order is of long duration".

- **The Terminology of C.I.M.A. defines Contract Cost as,** "the aggregated costs relative to a single contract designated a cost unit".

Applicability

Contract Costing can **suitably be applied in**,

i) industries engaged in the construction of building, roads, ships, dams, boiler house, bridges or other construction work.

ii) industries undertaking engineering projects, civil engineering works, mechanical engineering firm.

iii) public works contractors involved in railway line contracts.

Generally, two parties are involved in a contract viz. the **contractor** – the person who undertakes the contract, and the **contractee** – the person who assigns the contract.

Under Contract Costing, a separate number is allotted for each contract and all related costs are accumulated for each contract. That means, a separate set of accounts are kept and maintained for each individual contract undertaken by the company.

4.1.2 Features

Following are the important **features of Contract Costing.**

i) The work is carried out away from contractor's premises i.e. at the contractee's work site.

ii) A contract is usually a big job of long-duration and may continue over more than one accounting period.

iii) As the contracts are of large size, a contractor usually carries out a small number of contracts in the course of a year.

iv) Contract work involves too much of risk and uncertainty.

v) A contract undertaken is treated as a cost unit.

vi) A separate account is prepared for each contract to ascertain profit or loss on each contract.

vii) Apportionment of profit on contract to different accounting periods is very difficult.

viii) In case the contract is undertaken of long-duration, a percentage of notional profit depending upon the progress of physical work may be accounted for in each year.

ix) Most of the materials are specially purchased for each contract.

x) Expenses chargeable to contracts are direct in nature, e.g. electricity, telephone charges, insurance etc.

xi) Allocation and apportionment of overhead costs is a simple task.

xii) Specialists sub-contractors may be employed for say, electrical fittings, welding works, glass work, plumbing work etc.

xiii) Plant and equipment may be purchased or hired for the duration of the contract.

xiv) Nearly all labour will be direct.

xvi) The payment is received depending on the stage of completion of work.

xviii) A contract usually includes clause for 'penalty' for delayed completion.

xix) A contract usually includes 'Escalation Clause' under which the contractor is compensated for increase in costs on account of inflation.

xx) A percentage of the value of work done is deducted from the progress payment as 'Retention Money'.

A contract is a big job whereas a job is a small contract

The difference between Job Costing and Contract Costing can be summarised as follows :

Basis of Distinction	Job Costing	Contract Costing
i) Size	A job is small in size.	A contract is big in size.
ii) Execution of work	Work under this method is performed in the premises of manufacturer.	A contract is executed generally in the premises of customer i.e. (contractee).
iii) Time	A job usually takes less time to complete.	A contract takes more time to complete.
iv) Selling price	The selling price is paid after completing the job in full.	The price is paid in various instalments depending upon the progress of work.
v) Investment	It involves heavy investment on assets initially.	Investment on assets in Contract costing is less than comparing for Job costing.

Basis of Distinction	Job Costing	Contract Costing
vi) Expenses	Expenses under job costing takes the form of both direct and indirect.	Under this method most of expenses are direct in nature.
vii) Treatment to Profit	Profit carried on Job is entirely taken to Profit and Loss Account.	In case of incomplete contract, only proportionate profit is taken to Profit and Loss Account.
viii) Number	A number of Jobs in hand may be large.	Number of contract that may be undertaken at a time may be few.
ix) Pricing	Pricing is influenced by individual condition and general policy of the organisation.	Pricing is influenced by the specific clauses of the contract.
x) Indirect Cost	Indirect costs are **higher** than those under Contract Costing.	Indirect costs are **lower** than those under Job Costing.

Basic Terms

Following are some of the important basic terms generally used in Contract Costing.

1) **Material Costs :**

   The material required for the contract are **debited** to Contract Account which includes :

   a) Materials specifically purchased for the contract.

   b) Materials issued from stores against requisition.

   c) Materials urgently required transferred from another contract.

   On completion of the contract the following types of materials should be **credited** to Contract Account.

   a) Materials returned to store.

   b) Materials in hand on site at the end of the accounting period.

   c) Materials transferred to another contract.

   d) Sale of materials.

   Any profit or loss arising out of such materials transactions must be recorded from Profit and Loss Account. Following are certain items of losses which should be **debited** to Profit and Loss Account and should be **credited** to Contract Account.

   a) Loss on sale of materials.

   b) Materials which are stolen away or destroyed by fire.

   c) Materials lost in accidents.

   d) Cost of defective materials.

2) **Labour Cost :**

   All labour actually engaged at contract site is regarded as direct labour, irrespective of the nature of the tasks performed by the workers concerned and charged to the contract. The exact labour cost that should be **debited** to a Contract Account thus includes the total remuneration paid and payable to all workers engaged on contract at the end of the accounting period.

3) **Other Direct Expenses:**

All other expenses incurred directly for the contract should be **debited** to Contract Account. e.g. Architect's or Surveyors fee, Sub-contract costs, hire charges of Plant and Machinery etc.

4) **Overhead Costs:**

There are some common indirect expenses incurred for various contracts, which cannot be charged directly to the individual contract. These expenses are divided into works expenses, office expenses and are distributed on various contracts on some appropriate basis. The ultimate proportionate industry expenses paid or payable should be **debited** to Contract Account i.e. head office expenses, expenses of central stores, establishment charges etc.

5) **Plant and Machinery Costs:**

In every Contract work some special plant, heavy machines and special tools are usually employed. The Plant and Machinery cost represents the cost for the use of Plant and Machinery and tools for the contract. These costs are treated in Contract Account with the following alternative methods.

   a) If Plant and Machinery and tools are used for the contract only for a short period, Contract Account may be **debited** with the amount of depreciation on it.

   b) If Plant and Machinery and tools are used for the contract for a long period, the full amount of it may be **debited** to Contract Account and at the end of the accounting period or completion of the contract, the residual or written down value of it may be **credited** to the Contract Account.

6) **Sub-Contract Cost:**

If the contractor has entrusted some special work to some expertise sub-contractor, the costs incurred for such sub-contract is treated as a direct charge to the contract and hence should be **debited** to Contract Account e.g. a building contractor may entrust the following types of specialised jobs as a sub-contractor to the sub-contractors e.g. task of digging foundations, electrical installation, specialised flooring, installation of lifts, painting work, plumbing work etc.

7) **Cost of Additional Work:**

If a contractor is asked to do some extra work or alteration in the work which is not included in the original contract, the cost of such additional work may be charged separately to the contract as follows:

   a) If the additional work is substantial and the amount involved is large, it is better to treat the same as a subsidiary contract and a separate contract account should be operated for the same.

   b) If the additional work is not substantial, its cost should be **debited** to Contract Account and should be added to the contract price.

8) Architect's Certificate :

In case of large contract which takes a long period, it is a normal practice for the contractor to get interim advanced payments against the actual portion of contract completed by him. The contractee appoints the architect or surveyor or engineer who works as a technical assessor. Architect visits the site periodically, inspects the work done at site, makes the necessary record in the measurement register and issues a certificate showing the stage of completion of work and the value of work done completely as on the date of issue of certificate. Thus, as per the contract agreement, the periodical payment is made to the contractor on the basis of architects certificate only.

9) Retention Money :

It is a common practice to include the clause of retention money in the contract agreement. Under this clause the contractee will not make payment of the work certified by the architect, but a certain portion thereof shall be retained by him which is called 'Retention Money'. The object of this retention money is to place the contractee in a favourable position in case of faulty work or penalty payable by the contractor. This amount will be paid to the contractor after the satisfactory completion of the work depending upon the terms of contract. Retention money is paid when it is ensured that there is no fault in the work carried out by the contractor. It is calculated as follows :

Retention Money = Value of Work Certified (−) Cash Received.

10) Cash Received :

Cash received is that portion of the value of work certified which is paid by the contractee. It is usually expressed as percentage of work certified. Cash received is calculated as follows :

Cash received = Value of Work Certified (−) Retention Money

OR

= Value of Work Certified (×) Cash Received as % of Work Certified.

OR

= Contract Price (×) % of Work Certified (×) % of Cash Received.

11) Notional Profit :

Notional Profit is the difference between the value of work-in-progress certified and the cost of work-in-progress certified.

Computation of Notional Profit :

Notional Profit is computed as follows :

Notional Profit = Value of Work Certified (−) Cost of Work Certified

OR

= Value of Work Certified (−) (Total Cost incurred till date (−) Cost of Work Uncertified)

Contract Costing Procedure

The preparation of Contract Account is the essence of Contract Costing. The Contract Account is prepared by the contractor in his books. In addition to this account he prepares Contractee's Account also. A separate account is opened for each contract. The purpose of Contract Account is to know the profit or loss on every contract executed. The basic procedure for costing of contract is as follows :

1) Contract Account Number :

Each contract is allotted a distinct number in order to distinguish it from other contracts. A separate account is opened for each contract.

2) Direct Costs :

Most of the costs of a contract can be allocated direct to the contract. All such direct costs are **debited** to the Contract Account. Direct costs for contracts include : i) Materials, ii) Labour Cost, iii) Direct Expenses, iv) Depreciation of Plant and Machinery, v) Sub-Contract Costs

i) Accounting for Material Costs :

Material Costs are accounted in the following manner :

- **For materials purchased for a contract :** Contract Account is debited and Stores Supplier's Account/Cash/Bank Account is credited.

- **For materials issued from stores :** Contract Account is debited and Stores Control Account is credited.

- **For materials returned to stores :** Stores Control Account is debited and Contract Account is credited.

- **For materials transferred to other contracts :** Transferee Contract Account is debited and Transferor Contract Account is credited on the basis of Materials Transfer Note.

- **For sale of materials :** Cash/Bank Account is debited and Contract Account is credited.

- **For abnormal loss of materials :** Costing Profit and Loss Account is debited and Contract Account is credited.

- **For materials supplied by the contractee without affecting the contract price :** Such materials should not be charged to Contract Account.

ii) Accounting for Labour Costs :

Labour Costs are accounted for as follows :
- **Wages paid to workers engaged on a particular contract :** Such wages are charged directly to respective Contract Account.
- **Wages paid to workers who move from one contract to another :** Such wages are distributed over the contract on the basis of time spent by workers on each contract.

iii) **Accounting for Direct Expenses :**

Direct expenses (if any) incurred are directly charged to the respective contract.

iv) **Accounting for Charge for the use of Plant and Machinery :**

The Charge for the use of Plant and Machinery may be accounted for as follows :

- **Where a plant is specifically purchased for the contract :** The Contract Account is debited with the cost of the plant at the time of purchase and is credited with the depreciated value of the plant at the end of accounting period.

- **Where a plant is issued from stores for a short period :** The Contract Account is debited with the amount of depreciation for the period of use.

- **Where a plant is taken on hire :** The Contract Account is debited with the amount of hire charges.

v) **Accounting for Sub-Contract Costs :**

Sub-contract costs are also debited to respective Contract Account.

3) **Indirect Costs :**

Contract Account is also **debited** with overheads which tends to be small in relation to direct costs. Such costs are often absorbed on some arbitrary basis as a percentage of prime cost, materials, wages etc. Overheads are normally restricted to head office and storage costs.

- **Accounting for Indirect Expenses or Overheads :**

Indirect Expenses or Overheads (such as expenses of Engineers, Surveyors, Supervisors, Storekeepers, Administration) are distributed over different contracts on some suitable basis like percentage of material cost, percentage of labour cost, percentage of prime cost, per labour hour etc.

- **Accounting for Extra Work :**

The cost of extra work should be debited to Contract Account and the amount payable for the extra work by the contractee should be added to the contract price. If extra work is substantial, it is better to treat it as a separate contract.

4) **Transfer of Materials or Plant :**

When materials, plant or other items are transferred from the contract , the Contract Account is **credited** by that amount.

5) **Contract Price :**

The Contract Account is also credited with the contract price. In some incomplete contract, the Contract Account is **credited** with the value of work-in-progress as on that date.

6) **Profit or Loss on Contract :**

The balance of Contract Account represents profit or loss which is transferred to Profit and Loss Account. In case of incomplete contract, only a part of profit arrived is taken into account and remaining profit is kept as reserve to meet any contingent loss on the incomplete portion of the contract.

4.1.3 CONTRACT COSTING CONCEPTS

Following are some important concepts to be studied in accounting of a contract.

4.1.3.1 Work Certified

It is the cost of that part of the contract work which is being completed by the contractor for which a completion certificate has been issued by the contractee's architect. The amount of work certified is **debited** to Contractee's Account and **credited** to Contract Account.

Computation of Value of Work Certified :

The value of work certified is calculated as follows :

$$\text{Value of Work Certified} = \text{Contract Price} \times \text{Work Certified as \% of Contract Price}$$

OR

$$= \frac{\text{Cash Received}}{\text{Cash Received as \% of Work Certified}}$$

Example

Calculate the value of Work Certified in each of the following cases :

a) Contract Price ₹ 5,00,000, Work Certified 60%.

b) Cash Received ₹ 2,40,000 being 80% of Work Certified.

Answer

a) Value of Work Certified = Contract Price × Work Certified as % of Contract Price
   = ₹ 5,00,000 × 60%
   = ₹ 3,00,000

b) Value of Work Certified = $\frac{\text{Cash Received}}{\text{Cash as \% of Work Certified}}$
   = $\frac{\text{Rs. 2,40,000}}{80\%}$
   = ₹ 3,00,000

4.1.3.2 Work Uncertified

It is the cost of that part of the contract work which is being completed by the contractor but not certified by the architects because of the faulty work or the work not according to the specifications. In respect of such work there will be no payment from the contractee. The cost price of each work is **debited** to Work-in-Progress Account and **credited** to Contract Account.

Computation of Work Uncertified :

The cost of Work Uncertified is calculated as follows :

Cost of Work Uncertified

$$= \text{Total Cost incurred till date} - \text{Cost of Work Certified}$$

OR

$$= \text{Total Cost incurred till date} \times \frac{\text{\% of Work Uncertified}}{\text{\% of Total Work done till date}}$$

Example

Calculate the Cost of Work Uncertified in each of the following alternative cases:
a) Total Costs incurred to date ₹ 1,20,000, Cost of Work Certified ₹ 1,00,000.
b) Total Costs incurred to date ₹ 1,20,000 to complete 60% of the contract work. However, architect gave certificate only for 50% of the contract price.

Answer

a) Cost of Work Uncertified = Total costs incurred to date − Cost of Work Certified

$$= ₹ 1,20,000 - ₹ 1,00,000$$
$$= ₹ 20,000$$

b) Cost of Work Uncertified $= \dfrac{\%\ of\ Work\ Certified}{\%\ of\ Total\ Work\ done\ till\ date} \times$ Total Costs incurred till date

$$= \dfrac{60\% - 50\%}{60\%} \times ₹ 1,20,000$$
$$= ₹ 20,000$$

The distinction between Work Certified and Work Uncertified can be shown as follows:

Work Certified	Work Uncertified
i) It is the cost of that part of the contract work which is being completed by the contractor for which a completion certificate has been issued by the contractee's architect.	ii) It is the cost of that part of the contract work which is being completed by the contractor but not certified by the architects because of the faulty work or the work not according to the specifications.
ii) The amount of work certified is **debited** to Contractee's Account and credited to Contract Account	ii) The amount of work uncertified is debited to Work-in-Progress Account and credited to Contract Account.
iii) The cost of work certified represents the total expenditure incurred on the contract to date, less cost of work-uncertified, material in hand, plant at site, etc.	iii) The cost of work uncertified represents the cost of the work which has been carried out by the contractor but has not been certified by the architect. It is always shown at cost price.
iv) Cost of work certified may be ascertained as follows: Cost of Work Certified = Cost of Work to date − (Cost of Work Uncertified + Materials on Hand + Plant at Site).	iv) The cost of Work Uncertified may be ascertained as follows: Cost of Work Uncertified = Total Cost to date ... (Cost of Work Certified + ... Materials on Hand + ... Plant at Site) ... ...

Generally, contracts may be of three types viz. fixed price contracts, contracts with escalation clause and cost plus contracts.

4.1.3.3 Escalation Clause

Escalation Clause is usually provided in the contract as a safeguard against likely changes in price and utilisation of material and labour. By adding this clause, the contractor makes it clear to his customer that price quoted is dependent on prevailing market prices of cost elements. If the prices of cost elements rise beyond a certain percentage cover the price prevailing at the time of tendering, the customer has to bear the additional cost. Thus, escalation clause protects the interest of the contractor against unfavourable changes in cost of raw materials, labour and overheads e.g. it may be agreed that if the prices of raw materials go up by 20% the contract price will be increased by 2.5% by providing for upward revision of the contract price. The escalation clause may also be added to cover the risk involved due to change in utilisation of material and labour, where the quantity of material or labour time cannot be properly assessed under the work has sufficiently advanced. Thus, the term of contract specify the procedure for making the adjustment to avoid all further disputes. Properly constructed escalation clause should cover the following points :

i) Description of the elements of cost that are subject to escalation.

ii) Stipulation of the index to be applied to each cost category.

iii) Indication of the frequency with which the contract price will be adjusted.

iv) Definition of the limits to which the cost elements concerned may be increased or decreased during specific periods or over the length of the contract.

v) The contract should indicate whether changes mean only rises or also falls in prices. The benefit of lower prices should be transferred to the cosnumer.

vi) Whether only price or rate variable should affect the total payment or also quantity variance should be taken into consideration. Normally, the quantity variance is the responsibility of the contractor and cannot be transferred to the contractee.

vii) Prices or rates variances normally means the purchase price of material or wage rates incurred by the contractor from time to time. It is imperative that the contractee should have power to investigate or audit the relevant invoices or pay roll. It may also need certain provisions in the contract, whether the contractor is incurring such expenses prudently at prevailing rates in the market.

Calculation of Escalation Claim :

Escalation Clause in a contract provides that if during the period of execution of a contract, the prices of materials, rates of labour etc. rise beyond a specified limit, the contract price will be increased by specified rate or amount. Escalation claim so far as rates are concerned may be calculated as follows :

- For Material = Standard Quantity × (Actual Price – Standard Price)
- For Labour = Standard Labour × (Actual Rate – Standard Rate)

Escalation Clause does not cover that part of increase in costs which is caused due to inefficiency or wrong estimation.

Concept of De-escalation Clause :

Conversely, De-escalation Clause may also be provided for the downward adjustment of the contract price in case the prices of materials, rates of labour etc. fall beyond a specified limit. Thus, de-escalation clause safeguards the interest of the contractee by providing for downward revision of the contract price.

4.1.3.4 Cost Plus Contract

This is a modified method of Contract Costing. Under this the contractee agrees to pay to the contractors the actual cost of work done plus an agreed percentage thereof to cover overhead expenses and profits. **Cost plus contract** method is generally employed in those cases,

i) Where the estimated cost of contract cannot be ascertained accurately because of the frequent changes in the prices of materials and labour rates.
ii) Where the work to be done is not fixed at the time of placing the contract.
iii) When the contract is totally new to the contractor.
iv) Where the contract requires fairly a long period to complete the same.

This method is commonly used in the manufacturing of exceptional articles produced very rarely e.g. aircraft component, urgent repairing of power house, constructions during war time etc.

Advantages to the Contractor :

i) The Contractor will not suffer any risk of loss as he will receive the contract price as is assured by the contractee.
ii) There is bargain in the contract price in future under this type of contract.
iii) The contractor is relieved from the botheration of preparing quotation price for the sake of submitting it to the contractee.

Advantages to the Contractee :

i) Since the contract price is governed by the contract, the contractee will also not suffer from risk of loss.
ii) The contractee also stands to benefit in a period of uncertain market condition as he is expected to pay only a reasonable price after satisfying the ruling prices.

Disadvantages to the Contractor :

i) No efforts are taken by contractor for cost reduction. Hence, he becomes inefficient.
ii) The profit percentage, though fixed, will necessarily vary in amount since it depends upon the increase in cost.
iii) The percentage of profit may either be excessive or inadequate to cover the overhead expenses also.

Disadvantages to the Contractee :

i) This method is not desirable from the point of view of the contractee because the price to be paid is depended upon the cost of contract.
(ii) Till complete execution of the contract, he cannot estimate his commitment accurately.

4.1.3.5 Work-in-Progress

Contracts in progress mean contracts which have not yet been completed. Such uncompleted contracts are also referred to as Work-in-Progress. All the expenditure incurred on the uncompleted contracts should be shown on the asset side of the Balance Sheet under the heading 'Work-in-progress'. Where profit is taken in respect of incompleted contract, the work-in-progress stated in the Balance Sheet should also include the profit i.e. valuation of work-in-progress is done by addition of the profit to the cost of the contract.

It should be shown as follows.

Balance Sheet – Asset Side

Work-in-Progress :
Cost of Contract till date –
i) Cost of Work Certified
ii) Cost of Work Uncertified

Add : Profit taken to Profit and Loss Account

Less : Cash Received from the contractee

OR

Work-in-Progress :
i) Cost of Work Certified
ii) Cost of Work Uncertified
Less : Reserve for unrealised profit
Less : Cash received from contractee

Accounting Treatment :

Depending upon the treatment of work certified, there are two methods of valuation and disclosure of work-in-progress as follows :

i) When the amount of Work Certified is debited to Work-in-progress Account	Amount ₹
A) Value of Work Certified	...
B) Cost of Work Certified	...
C) Less : Credit balance on the Contractee's Account	...
D) Less : Amount transferred to Reserve	...
E) Value of Work-in-Progress (A + B – C – D)	...
	...

ii) When the amount of Work Certified is debited to Contractee's account	Amount ₹
A) Cost of Work Uncertified	...
B) Add : Debit balance on the Contractee's Account	...
C) Less : Amount transferred to Reserve	...
D) Value of Work-in-progress (A + B – C)	...
	...

4.1.3.6 Profit on Incomplete Contracts

If contracts are started and completed during the same accounting year there is no problem as regards profit computation. But in case of those contracts which take more than one accounting year, a problem arises whether profit on such contracts should be worked out only on the completion of the contract or at the end of each accounting year on the partly completed work. If profit is computed only on the completion of the contract profit will be high in the year of completion of the contract, whereas in other years of working on contract, profit will be nil. This would result not only in distorted profit patterns, but also higher tax liability because income tax at higher rates may have to be paid accordingly. Hence, when contracts extends beyond a year, it becomes necessary to take into account the profit earned (or loss incurred) on the work performed during each year. This helps in avoiding distortion of the year to year profit trend of the business. There are two aspects of profit computation viz. i) Computation of estimated or notional profit at the end of the year when contract is not complete. ii) Computation of the portion of such profit to be transferred to Profit and Loss Account.

> It is always better to anticipate the future losses and to make the necessary provision for the same, but do not recognise any profit till they are actually realised.

Principles to be followed while taking credit for profit on incomplete contract :

These principles are as follows :

i) The costs incurred upto date should be clearly identified.

ii) The stage of contract performance completed should be reasonably estimated.

iii) The costs to complete the contract should be reasonably estimated.

iv) The total contract revenues to be received should be reliably estimated.

v) The work certified should be valued in terms of contract price and its value should be treated as contract revenue for the accounting period.

vi) The uncertified work should be valued at cost and should be treated like closing inventory at the end of accounting period.

vii) The notational profit on incomplete contract should be estimated as under :

Notational Profit = Value of Work Certified + Cost of Uncertified Work Costs incurred to date

Conventional norms for determining the profit :

The amount of profit that is to be credited to Profit and Loss Account depends upon the fact that how far the contract has advanced.

There are no hard and fast rules in this regard. However, the following are the conventional norms for determining the profit to be taken to the Profit and Loss Account at different stages of completion.

i) It should be noted that the profit should be considered in respect of work certified only. Work certified should always be valued at cost.

ii) If a very small portion of the work has been done, it is neither desirable nor sound to take into account profit on the work done and the Contract Account must then be **closed by balance.** In such a case, the amount expended on account of the contract to the date of balancing will be shown as **Work-in-Progress** on the asset side of the Balance Sheet and any cash received from the contractee on account of work will be shown by way **deduction** therefrom.

No definite rule can be laid down as to what stage of the work it would be safe to take credit for the profit on incomplete contractors. But the general rule may be laid down is that **no profit should be ascertained unless at least one fourth or less of the whole work has been completed.**

iii) When the work certified is 25% or more but less than 50% of the contract price, profit to be taken to the credit of Profit and Loss Account will be computed as follows :

$$= \text{Notional Profit} \times \frac{1}{3} \times \frac{\text{Cash Received}}{\text{Work Certified}}$$

iv) When the work certified is 50% or more but less than 90% of the contract price, profit to be taken to the credit of Profit and Loss Account will be computed as follows :

$$= \text{Notional Profit} \times \frac{2}{3} \times \frac{\text{Cash Received}}{\text{Work Certified}}$$

v) When contract is **near completion**, then the estimated profit should be calculated as of the whole contract. This is computed as follows :

	₹
Contract Price	...
Less : Total Expenditure to date	
Less : Estimated Additional Expenditure	...
∴ Estimated Profit	...

The profit to be taken to the credit of Profit and Loss Account will be computed by applying any of the following formula :

- $\text{Estimated Profit} \times \frac{\text{Work Certified}}{\text{Contract Price}}$

- $\text{Estimated Profit} \times \frac{\text{Work Certified}}{\text{Contract Price}} \times \frac{\text{Cash Received}}{\text{Work Certified}}$

OR

$\text{Estimated Profit} \times \frac{\text{Cash Received}}{\text{Contract Price}}$

- $\text{Estimated Profit} \times \frac{\text{Cost of Work to date}}{\text{Estimated Total Cost}}$

- $\text{Estimated Profit} \times \frac{\text{Cost of work to date}}{\text{Estimated Total Cost}} \times \frac{\text{Cash Received}}{\text{Work Certified}}$

vi) **For Loss on incompleted contracts :**

If the cost of work certified exceeds the value of such certificate or loss is incurred. The whole amount of such loss is to be charged to Profit and Loss Account. The entry will be passed as follows :

Profit and Loss A/c   ... Dr.
  To Contract A/c

vii) **Provision for Foreseeable Losses :**

When current estimates of total contract costs and revenue indicate a loss, provision should be made for the entire loss on the contract irrespective of the amount of work done and the method of accounting followed.

Accounting Entries :

i) **For materials issued to Contract :**
   Contract A/c ... Dr.
      To Materials A/c

ii) **For surplus materials transferred to another Contract :**
   Receiving Contract A/c ... Dr.
      To Supplying Contract A/c

iii) **For expenses incurred or payable on contract :**
   Contract A/c ... Dr.
      To Expenses A/c
      To Outstanding Expenses A/c

iv) **For Plant and Machinery and Equipments (at cost) issued to contract :**
   Contract A/c ... Dr.
      To Plant and Machinery/Equipment A/c

v) **For share of apportioned Overhead Expenses :**
   Contract A/c ... Dr.
      To Overhead A/c

vi) **For sub-contract cost :**
   Contract A/c ... Dr.
      To Sub-contract A/c

vii) **For materials at site at the end or materials returned to stores or supplier :**
   Materials A/c or Material Returned A/c ... Dr.
      To Contract A/c

viii) **For Plant and Machinery and Equipment at site at the end at written down value :**
   Plant and Machinery A/c ... Dr.
   Equipment A/c ... Dr.
      To Contract A/c

ix) **For Work Certified :**
   Contractee's A/c ... Dr.
      To Contract A/c

x) **For Work Uncertified :**
   Work-in-Progress A/c ... Dr.
      To Contract A/c

xi) **For cash received against Work-Certified from Contractee :**
   Bank A/c ... Dr.
      To Contractee's A/c

xii) **For materials or plant sold at site at profit :**
   Bank A/c ... Dr.
      To Contract A/c (cost of material/plant)
      To Profit and Loss A/c (with Profit on sale)
   If there is a loss, the above entry will be reversed.

xiii) **For materials stolen or lost and Insurance Co. admitted claim for certain account :**
   Bank A/c   ... Dr.   (Recovery for Insurance Co).
   Profit and Loss A/c   ... Dr.   (Loss on material)
      To Contract A/c

xiv) **For Abnormal Loss of materials, Plant etc. on site :**
   Profit and Loss A/c   ... Dr.
      To Contract A/c

xv) **For Sale of scrap :**
   Bank A/c   ... Dr.
      To Contract A/c

xvi) **For Profit transferred to Profit and Loss Account or Profit to be reserved :**
   Contract A/c   ... Dr.
      To Profit and Loss A/c   (with profit credited)
      To Work-in-Progress/Profit Reserve A/c   (with profit kept as Reserve)

Accounting Format :

Various ledger accounts in the books of a contractor may be shown as follows :

Format of Contract Account

Contract Account No. ...... for 1st Accounting Period

Dr.				Cr.
Particulars	₹	Particulars	₹
To Materials	...	By Materials at Site	...
To Wages incurred (Paid + O/s − Prepaid)	...	By Stores Ledger	...
To Direct Expenses (Paid + O/s − Prepaid)	...	(Return to Store)	
To Depreciation on Plant & Equipments)	...	By Bank	...
To Office and Administration Expenses incurred	...	(Sale of Materials)	
(Paid + O/s − Prepaid)		By Costing Profit and Loss	...
		(Loss on Sale)	
		By Cost of Contract C/D	...
	...		...
To Cost of Contract B/D	...	By Work-in-progress:	...
To Notional Profit C/D	...	• Value of Work Certified	
		• Cost of Work Uncertified	...
	...		...
To Profit and Loss Account	...	By Notional Profit B/D	...
To Reserve Account	...		
	...		...

Contract Account No. ...... for 1st Accounting Period

Dr.			Cr.
Particulars	₹	Particulars	₹
To Work-in-progress B/D			
Value of Work Certified ...			
Add : Cost of Work Uncertified (+) ...			
...			
Less : Reserve (−) ...	...		
Remaining portion same as in previous format			

Format of Balance Sheet of a Contractor

Dr.   Balance Sheet of …… as at ……   Cr.

Liabilities	₹	Assets	₹
Capital	…	Land and Building	…
Profit and Loss Account	…	**Less** : Depreciation	
Outstanding Expenses	…	Plant and Equipments	
		Less : Depreciation	
		• At Stores …	
		• At Site …	…
		Materials :	
		• At Stores …	
		• At Site …	…
		Work-in-Progress :	
		• Value of Work Certified …	
		• Cost of Work Certified …	
		Less : Contractee's Credit Balance …	
		Less : Transfer to Reserve …	…
		Cash and Bank Balance	…
		Prepaid Expenses	…
	…		…

Format of Contractee Account

Dr.   Contractee's Account   Cr.

Particulars	₹	Particulars	₹
To Balance B/D	…	By Bank (Part Payment)	…
	…		…
To Contract	…	By Balance C/D	…
(Contract Price)		By Bank (Final Payment)	…
	…		…

Alternative Format of Contract Account

Dr.   Contract Account   Cr.

Particulars	₹	Particulars	₹
To Work-in-Progress (Opening) :		**By Materials :**	
• Work-certified ………		• Returned to Store ………	
• Work Uncertified ………		• Transferred to other contracts ………	………
• Plant at Site ………			
• Materials at Site ………	………	By Costing Profit and Loss	………
Less : Reserve ………	………	(Loss on Sale if any)	
		By Plant returned to stores	………
		Less Depreciation	
To Materials :		By Costing Profit and Loss Account	………
		(For items stolen/lost)	
• From Stores ………		**By Work-in-Progress (Closing) :**	
• From outside (purchases) ………		• Work Certified ………	
• From Other Contracts ………	………	• Work Uncertified ………	
To Wages (including Outstanding)	………	• Plant at site ………	
To Direct Expenses (including Outstanding)	………	• Materials at site ………	………

Particulars	₹	Particulars	₹
To Plant at Cost/Tools at Cost	....	**OR**	
To Overheads (including outstanding)	....	Contractee's Account (with total contract price) (in case of contracts completed)	....
To Sub-contract costs	....		
To Cost of extra-work done	....		
To Profit and Loss A/c	....		
(Profit on sale, if any)			
To Notional Profit C/D *	....		
	....		....
To Profit and Loss A/c		By Notional Profit B/D	....
$\left(\frac{1}{3} \text{ or } \frac{2}{3} \times \text{Notional Profit} \times \frac{\text{Cash Received}}{\text{Work Certified}}\right)$	....		
To Work-in-Progress A/c (Reserve)	....		
	....		....

ILLUSTRATIONS

ILLUSTRATION 1

Amar Builders, Aurangabad is engaged on two contracts viz. A and B during the year 2014-2015. The following particulars are available on 31st March, 2015 in respect of 'Contract-A'.

	₹
Contract Price	6,00,000
Materials issued to contract	1,60,000
Materials returned to stores	4,000
Materials on site on 31-3-2015	22,000
Materials transferred to Contract B'	9,000
Direct Labour	1,40,000
Chargeable Expenses Outstanding	6,000
Wages Payable	2,000
Direct Expenses	60,000
Hire of Special Machinery	10,000
Administration Overheads	25,000
Plant installed at site at cost	75,000
Cost of contract not yet certified	23,000
Plant Installation Charges	5,000
Value of Work Certified	4,20,000
Value of plant on 31-3-2015	65,000
Cash received from Contractee	3,78,000

You are required to prepare Contract A' Account for the year ended 31st March, 2015.

SOLUTION

Working Notes:

i) **Calculation of Depreciation on Plant:**

= Plant cost + Installation charges – Value of Plant on 31-03-2015
= ₹ 75,000 + ₹ 5,000 – ₹ 65,000
= ₹ 15,000

ii) **Calculation of amount of notional profits to be credited to Profit and Loss Account:**

As the value of Work Certified (₹ 4,20,000) is more than $1/2$ of the Contract Price (₹ 6,00,000), the following formula is to be applied to find out the amount of notional profits to be credited to Profit and Loss Account.

$$= 2/3 \times \text{Notional Profits} \times \frac{\text{Cash Received}}{\text{Work Certified}}$$

$$= 2/3 \times ₹ 60,000 \times \frac{₹ 3,78,000}{₹ 4,20,000}$$

= ₹ 36,000

In the books of Amar Builders, Aurangabad,

Dr.   Contract Account for Contract A' for the year ended 31st March, 2015   Cr.

Particulars	₹	Particulars	₹
To Materials issued to Contract	1,60,000	By Materials returned to stores	4,000
To Direct Labour	1,40,000	By Materials at site on 31-3-2015	22,000
To Chargeable Expenses outstanding	6,000	By Materials transferred to Contract B'	9,000
To Wages Payable	2,000	By Cost of contract not yet certified	23,000
To Direct Expenses	60,000	By Value of Work Certified	4,20,000
To Hire of Special Machinery	10,000		
To Administration Overheads	25,000		
To Depreciation on Plant	15,000		
To Notional Profits C/D *	60,000		
	4,78,000		4,78,000
To Profit and Loss	36,000	By Notional Profits B/D	60,000
To Reserve*	24,000		
	60,000		60,000

ILLUSTRATION 2

The following balances have been extracted from the books of Shanti Constructions, Surat on 31st March, 2015.

	₹
Contract Price	6,00,000
Plant and Machinery as on 1st April, 2014	30,000
Materials	1,70,600
Labour Charges	1,48,750
Engineer's Fees	6,330
Outstanding Wages	5,380

	₹
Uncertified Work	12,000
Overhead Expenses	8,240
Materials Returned to Stores	1,600
Materials on hand at site	3,700
Plant and Machinery on hand at site on 31st March, 2015	22,000
Value of Work Certified	3,90,000
Cash Received	3,51,000

Prepare Contract Account for the year ended 31st March, 2015 showing separately the amount of profit that may be taken to the credit of Profit and Loss Account. Also calculate the amount of work-in-progress as it would appear in the Balance Sheet as on 31st March, 2015.

SOLUTION

Working Notes:

i) **Calculation of amount of notional profits to be credited to Profit and Loss Account:**

As the value of Work Certified (₹ 3,90,000) is more than $1/2$ of the Contract Price (₹ 6,00,000), the following formula is to be applied to find out the amount of notional profit to be credited to Profit and Loss Account.

$$= \frac{2}{3} \times \text{Notional Profits} \times \frac{\text{Cash Received}}{\text{Work Certified}}$$

$$= \frac{2}{3} \times ₹\,60,000 \times \frac{₹\,3,51,000}{₹\,3,90,000}$$

$$= ₹\,36,000$$

ii) **Calculation of amount of Work-In-Progress:**

		₹
	Value of Work Certified	3,90,000
Add:	Uncertified Work	(+) 12,000
		4,02,000
Less:	Cash received	(−) 3,51,000
		51,000
Less:	Reserve	(−) 24,000
∴	**Work-in-progress**	27,000

iii) **Calculation of depreciation on Plant and Machinery:**

	₹
Plant and Machinery as on 1st April, 2014	30,000
Less: Plant and Machinery on hand at site on 31st March, 2015	(−) 22,000
∴ Depreciation on Plant and Machinery	8,000

Basics of Cost Accounting 4.27 Methods of Costing

In the books of Shanti Constructions, Surat

Dr. Contract Account for the year ended 31st March, 2015 Cr.

Particulars	₹	Particulars	₹
To Depreciation on Plant and Machinery	8,000	By Uncertified Work	12,000
To Materials	1,70,600	By Materials returned to stores	1,600
To Labour Charges	1,48,750	By Materials on hand at site	3,700
To Engineer's Fees	6,330	By Value of Work Certified	3,90,000
To Outstanding Wages	5,380		
To Overhead Expenses	8,240		
To Notional Profits C/D *	60,000		
	4,07,300		4,07,300
To Profit and Loss	36,000	By Notional Profits B/D	60,000
To Reserve *	24,000		
	60,000		60,000

ILLUSTRATION 3

Ramesh Builders, Raipur took a contract to build a society hall on 1st April, 2014. The contract price was agreed at ₹ 8,00,000. They have incurred following expenditure during the year 2014-2015.

	₹
Direct Materials	50,000
Direct Labour	30,000
Direct Expenses	20,000
Plant	80,000

From the following additional information prepare a Contract Account for the year ended 31st March, 2015. Also show the amount in Work-in-Progress which will be shown in the Balance Sheet of the Contractor as on that date.

	₹
Value of Plant as on 31st March, 2015	60,000
Stock of material on hand at site	10,000
Materials returned to storehouse	2,000
Value of Work Certified	1,50,000
Cost of Work Uncertified	8,000
Cash Received	1,40,000

SOLUTION

Working Notes :

i) **Calculation of amount of notional profits to be credited to Profit and Loss Account :**

As the value of Work Certified (₹ 1,50,000) is less than $1/4$ of the Contract Price (₹ 8,00,000), nothing out of notional profits will be transferred to Profit and Loss Account, but everything will be transferred to Reserve Account.

ii) **Calculation of amount of Work-in-Progress :**
= Total Expenses – Asset in hand + Profits transferred to Profit and Loss Account.

	₹
Total Expenses	1,80,000
(Direct Materials + Direct Labour + Direct Expenses + Plant)	
(₹ 50,000 + ₹ 30,000 + ₹ 20,000 + ₹ 80,000)	
Less : Assets in hand	– 72,000
	1,08,000
Add : Profits transferred to Profit and Loss A/c	NIL
∴ Work-in-Progress	1,08,000

In the books of Ramesh Builders, Raipur

Dr.   Contract Account for the year ended 31st March, 2015   Cr.

Particulars	₹	Particulars	₹
To Direct Materials	50,000	By Stock of Materials on hand at site	10,000
To Direct Labour	30,000	By Materials returned to storehouse	2,000
To Direct Expenses	20,000	By Value of Work Certified	1,50,000
To Depreciation on Plant	20,000	By Value of Work Uncertified	8,000
(Opening – Closing)			
(₹ 80,000 – ₹ 60,000)			
To Notional Profits C/D *	50,000		
	1,70,000		1,70,000
To Profit and Loss	–	By Notional Profits B/D	50,000
To Reserve	50,000		
	50,000		50,000

ILLUSTRATION 4

Bharat Constructions, Baroda undertook a Contract No. 54 for ₹ 4,00,000 on 1st April, 2014. They incurred the following expenses during the year 2014-2015.

	₹
Materials issued from stores	36,600
Materials transferred from Contract No. 45	3,400
Materials directly purchased for the Contract	10,000
Materials in hand on site	2,500
Plant issued for contract	20,000
Wages paid directly	70,000
Architect's Fees	3,000
Wages due but not paid	1,000
Direct expenses outstandings	600
Cash received from contractee	1,44,000
Work Certified	1,80,000
Cost of Work uncertified	1,500

Of the Plant and Materials charged to contract, Plant costing ₹ 4,000 and Materials costing ₹ 3,000 were lost. On 31-3-2015 Plant costing ₹ 3,000 was returned to stores. Charge depreciation on Plant @ 15% p.a. as per written down value method.

Prepare Contract Account for the year ended 31-3-2015.

SOLUTION

Working Notes:

i) Calculation of amount of Notional profits to be credited to Profit and Loss Account:

As the value of Work Certified (₹ 1,80,000) is more than $1/4$ but less than $1/2$ of the contract price (₹ 4,00,000), the following formula is to be applied to find out the amount of notional profits to be credited to Profit and Loss Account.

$$= \frac{1}{3} \times \text{Notional Profits} \times \frac{\text{Cash Received}}{\text{Work Certified}}$$

$$= \frac{1}{3} \times ₹\,60{,}000 \times \frac{₹\,1{,}44{,}000}{₹\,1{,}80{,}000}$$

$$= ₹\,16{,}000$$

In the books of Bharat Constructions, Baroda
Contract Account for Contract No. 54 for the year ended 31st March, 2015

Dr. Particulars	₹	Particulars	Cr. ₹
To Materials issued from stores	36,600	By Materials in hand on site	2,500
To Materials transferred to Contract No. 45	3,400	By Work Certified	1,80,000
To Materials directly purchased for the Contract	10,000	By Cost of Work Uncertified	1,500
To Plant issued for contract	20,000	By Costing Profit and Loss Account	
To Wages paid directly	70,000	(i) Plant lost	4,000
To Architect's Fees	3,000	(ii) Materials lost	3,000
To Wages due but not paid	1,000	By Plant returned to stores :	
To Direct Expenses Outstandings	600	Original Cost 3,000	
		Less : Dep. @ 15% p.a. (–) 450	2,550
		By Plant in Hand :	
		Original Cost 13,000	
		Less : Dep. @ 15% p.a. (–) 1,950	11,050
To Notional Profits C/D *	60,000		
	2,04,600		2,04,600
To Profit and Loss	16,000	By Notional Profits B/D	60,000
To Reserve *	44,000		
	60,000		60,000

ILLUSTRATION 5

Cooper Constructions Pvt. Ltd., Chennai undertook a contract for construction of a library buildings. The following is the information relating to the contract during the year 2014-2015.

	₹
Materials sent to site	1,00,000
Materials purchased and issued	70,698
Materials returned to stores	1,098
Materials at site on 31-3-2015	3,766
Labour engaged on site	1,40,000
Wages accrued and due but not paid	8,750
Engineer's Fees	6,334
Direct Expenses Payable	580
General Overheads	8,252

Basics of Cost Accounting 4.30 Methods of Costing

Overheads Outstanding	9,250
Plant installed at site at cost	41,500
Erection charges on site for Plant	1,250
Scrap value of plant after its life of five years	2,750
Work Certified	3,90,000
Cost of Work not Certified	9,000
Cash received from Contractee	3,60,000

Prepare Contract Account and Contractee's Account. Also show the amount of profit which you consider might be fairly taken on the Contract and how you have calculated the same.

SOLUTION

Working Notes:

i) **Calculation of depreciation on Plant:**

$$= \frac{\text{Purchase Price} + \text{Erection charges} - \text{Scrap Value}}{\text{Estimated Life of Plant}}$$

$$= \frac{₹41,500 + ₹1,250 - ₹2,750}{5 \text{ years}}$$

$$= \frac{₹40,000}{5 \text{ years}}$$

$$= ₹8,000$$

ii) **Calculation of amount of notional profits to be credited to Profit and Loss Account:**

In the absence of Contract Price, it is assumed that the value of Work certified (₹ 3,90,000) must be more than $1/2$ of the Contract Price, the following formula is to be applied to find out the amount of notional profits to be credited to Profit and Loss Account.

$$= \frac{2}{3} \times \text{Notional Profits} \times \frac{\text{Cash Received}}{\text{Work Certified}}$$

$$= \frac{2}{3} \times ₹52,000 \times \frac{₹3,60,000}{₹3,90,000}$$

$$= ₹32,000$$

In the books of Cooper Construction Pvt. Ltd. Chennai,

Dr. Contract Account for the year ended 31st March, 2015 Cr.

Particulars	₹	Particulars	₹
To Materials sent to site	1,00,000	By Materials returned to stores	1,098
To Materials purchased and issued	70,698	By Materials at site on 31-3-2015	3,766
To Labour engaged on site	1,40,000	By Work Certified	3,90,000
To Wages accrued and due but not paid	8,750		
To Engineers Fees	6,334	By Cost of Work not Certified	9,000
To Direct Expenses payable	580		
To General Overheads	8,252		
To Overheads Outstandings	9,250		
To Depreciation on Plant	8,000		
To Notional Profits C/D *	52,000		
	4,03,864		4,03,864
To Profit and Loss	32,000	By Notional Profits B/D	52,000
To Reserve *	20,000		
	52,000		52,000

Dr.		Contractee Account		Cr.
Particulars	₹	Particulars		₹
To Work Certified	3,90,000	By Cash received		3,60,000
		By Balance C/D *		30,000
		(Balancing figure i.e. Rentention money)		
	3,90,000			3,90,000

ILLUSTRATION 6

Reliable Constructions Ltd., Raipur undertook a contract of ₹ 8,00,000 for the construction of a sports Gymkhana on 1st April, 2014. The following information is taken up from the contract ledger as on 31-3-2015 in respect of the above.

	₹
Materials directly issued from stores	1,30,000
Materials purchased	70,000
Scrap materials sold	8,000
Materials transferred to other contract	10,000
Materials in hand on site	11,000
Materials returned to stores	6,000
Direct wages paid and payable	85,000
Direct charges	45,000
Overheads charged to contract	40,000
Sub-contract cost	9,000
Cost of additional work	3,400
Outstanding direct expenses	1,600
Plant purchased on 1-4-2014 and issued directly	80,000
Annual depreciation on Plant	8,000
Plant transferred on 1-4-2014 to other contract	40,000
Cash received being 90% of Work Certified	3,60,000
Uncertified Work being 8% of certified work	

You are required to prepare : i) Contract Account and ii) Contractee's Account

SOLUTION

Working Notes :

i) Calculation of value of Work Certified :

$$\text{Work Certified} = \text{Cash Received} + \text{Retention Money}$$
$$100 = 90 + 10$$
$$? = ₹ 3,60,000$$

If 90 CR = 100 WC

∴ ₹ 3,60,000 CR = ?

$$= \frac{₹ 3,60,000 \times 100}{90}$$

$$= ₹ 4,00,000$$

ii) Calculation of cost of Work uncertified

= 8% of Work Certified i.e. ₹ 4,00,000
= ₹ 32,000

iii) Calculation of amount of notional profits to be credited to Profit and Loss Account :

As the value of Work Certified (₹ 4,00,000) is exactly half of the contract price (₹ 8,00,000) the following formula is to be applied to find out the amount of notional profits to be credited to Profit and Loss Account.

$$= \frac{2}{3} \times \text{Notional Profits} \times \frac{\text{Cash Received}}{\text{Work Certified}}$$

$$= \frac{2}{3} \times ₹ 75,000 \times \frac{₹ 3,60,000}{₹ 4,00,000}$$

$$= ₹ 45,000$$

In the books of Reliable Constructions Ltd., Raipur

Dr. Contract Account for the year ended 31st March, 2015 Cr.

Particulars	₹	Particulars	₹
To Materials directly issued from stores	1,30,000	By Scrap materials sold	8,000
To Materials purchased	70,000	By Materials transferred to other contract	10,000
To Direct wages paid and payable	85,000	By Materials in hand on site	11,000
To Direct charges	45,000	By Materials returned to stores	6,000
To Overheads charged to contract	40,000	By Plant at site on hand 40,000	
To Sub-Contract cost	9,000	Less : Depreciation (–) 8,000	32,000
To Cost of additional work	3,400	By Plant transferred to other contract on 1-4-2014	40,000
To outstanding direct expenses	1,600		
To Plant purchased and issued directly	80,000	By Value of Work certified	4,00,000
		By Cost of Work Uncertified	32,000
To Notional Profits C/D *	75,000		
	5,39,000		5,39,000
To Profit and Loss	45,000	By Notional Profits B/D	75,000
To Reserve *	30,000		
	75,000		75,000

Dr. Contractee Account Cr.

Particulars	₹	Particulars	₹
To Work Certified	4,00,000	By Cash received	3,60,000
		By Balance C/D * (Balancing figure i.e. Rentention money)	40,000
	40,000		40,000

ILLUSTRATION 7

Porwal Builders, Patna undertook several large contracts. The following are the particulars relating to Contract No. 22 for the year ended 31st March, 2015.

	₹
Materials issued from storehouse	90,000
Materials purchased	40,000
Materials transferred from Contract No. 27	25,000
Materials returned to storehouse	500
Materials at site on 31-3-2015	1,000

	₹
Plant purchased and installed at site	72,000
Freight and installation charges of plant	8,000
Operating Wages	1,22,000
Process labour outstandings	5,000
Other direct expenses	12,000
Operating expenses payable	2,000
Establishment on cost	27,000
Office expenses accrued	1,500
Work Uncertified	6,000
Contract Price	16,00,000
Cash received from Contractee	3,20,000

(represented the full amount of Work Certified less 20% as retention money).

Provide depreciation on Plant @ 10% p.a as per Reducing Balance Method.

You are required to prepare, Contract Account and Contractee's Account.

SOLUTION

Working Notes :

i) **Calculation of value of Work Certified :**

$$\text{Work Certified} = \text{Cash Received} + \text{Retention Money}$$
$$100 = 80 + 20$$
$$? = ₹ 3,20,000$$

If 80 CR = 100 WC

∴ ₹ 3,20,000 CR = ?

$$= \frac{₹ 3,20,000 \times 100}{80}$$

$$= ₹ 4,00,000.$$

ii) **Calculation of amount of notional profits to be credited to Profit and Loss Account.**

As the value of Work Certified (₹ 4,00,000) is exactly $1/4$ of the Contract Price (₹ 16,00,000) the following formula is to be applied to find out the amount of notional profits to be credited to Profit and Loss Account.

$$= \frac{1}{3} \times \text{Notional Profits} \times \frac{\text{Cash Received}}{\text{Work Certified}}$$

$$= \frac{1}{3} \times ₹ 75,000 \times \frac{₹ 3,20,000}{₹ 4,00,000}$$

$$= ₹ 20,000$$

iii) **Calculation of depreciation on Plant @ 10% p.a. as per Reducing Balance Method :**

		₹
	Plant purchased and installed	72,000
Add :	Freight and installation charges	(+) 8,000
		80,000
Less :	Depreciation @ 10% p.a.	(−) 8,000
		72,000

Dr.	Contract Account for Contract No. 22 for the year ended 31st March, 2015			Cr.
Particulars	₹	Particulars		₹
To Materials issued from storehouse	90,000	By Materials returned to storehouse		500
To Materials purchased	40,000	By Materials at site on 31-3-2015		1,000
To Materials transferred from Contract No. 27	25,000	By Work Certified		4,00,000
To Depreciation on Plant	8,000	By Work Uncertified		6,000
To Operating Wages	1,22,000			
To Process Labour Outstandings	5,000			
To Other Direct Expenses	12,000			
To Operating Expenses Payable	2,000			
To Establishment on cost	27,000			
To Office Expenses Accrued	1,500			
To Notional Profits C/D	75,000			
	4,07,500			4,07,500
To Profit and Loss	20,000	By Notional Profits B/D		75,000
To Reserve *	55,000			
	75,000			75,000

Dr.		Contractee's Account		Cr.
Particulars	₹	Particulars		₹
To Work Certified	4,00,000	By Cash received		3,20,000
		By Balance C/D * (Balancing Figure i.e. Rentention money)		80,000
	4,00,000			4,00,000

ILLUSTRATION 8

Gharkul Builders, Goregaon took a Contract No. 51 for construction of a school building on 1-4-2014. The Contract price is fixed at ₹ 15,00,000 subject to a retention of 20% of work certified. The following are the details of expenses made by the contractor on this contract during the year 2014-2015.

	₹
Productive Labour Charges	4,00,000
Unproductive Labour Charges	5,000
Outstanding Wages	7,800
Materials issued form store-room	4,20,000
Materials purchased directly	81,200
Stock of materials in hand on site	300
Materials transferred to Contract No. 52	6,000
Materials transferred from Contract No. 50	1,600
Direct Expenses	23,000
(Inclusive of unpaid chargeable expenses ₹ 3,000)	
Establishment Overheads	37,200
Plant installed at site on 30-9-2014	58,000
Installation Charges for Plant	2,000
Work Certified	11,00,000
Work Uncertified	16,500
Cash received upto 31-3-2015	8,80,000

Provide depreciation on Plant @ 40% p.a. as per Straight Line Method.
Prepare, Contract Account for Contract No. 51 and Contractee's Account

SOLUTION

Working Notes :

i) Calculation of depreciation on Plant @ 40% p.a. as per Straight Line Method :

		₹
	Plant installed at site on 30-9-2014	58,000
Add :	Installation charges	(+) 2,000
	Original Cost	60,000
Less :	Dep. @ 40% of ₹ 60,000 for 6 months	(−) 12,000
	Value of Plant at site on 31-3-2015	48,000

ii) Calculation of amount of notional profits to be creidted to Profit and Loss Account.

As the value of Work Certified (₹ 11,00,000) is more than $1/2$ of the Contract Price (₹ 15,00,000), the following formula is to be applied to find out the amount of notional profits to be credited to Profit and Loss Account.

$$= \frac{2}{3} \times \text{Notional Profits} \times \frac{\text{Cash Received}}{\text{Work Certified}}$$

$$= \frac{2}{3} \times ₹\,1{,}35{,}000 \times \frac{₹\,8{,}80{,}000}{₹\,11{,}00{,}000}$$

$$= ₹\,72{,}000$$

Dr.   Contract Account for Contract No. 51 for the year ended 31st March, 2015   Cr.

Particulars	₹	Particulars	₹
To Productive Labour charges	4,00,000	By Materials transferred to Contract No. 52	6,000
To Unproductive Labour charges	5,000	By Work Certified	11,00,000
To Outstanding Wages	7,800	By Work Uncertified	16,500
To Materials issued from store-room	4,20,000	By Stock of Materials in hand on site	300
To Materials purchased directly	81,200		
To Materials transferred from Contract No. 50	1,600		
To Direct expenses (including unpaid chargeable expenses)	23,000		
To Establishment Overheads	37,200		
To Depreciation on Plant	12,000		
To Notional Profits C/D *	1,35,000		
	11,22,800		11,22,800
To Profit and Loss	72,000	By Notional Profits B/D	1,35,000
To Reserve *	63,000		
	1,35,000		1,35,000

Dr.   Contractee's Account   Cr.

Particulars	₹	Particulars	₹
To Work Certified	11,00,000	By Cash received	8,80,000
		By Balance C/D (Balancing Figure i.e. Rentention money)	2,20,000
	11,00,000		11,00,000

Basics of Cost Accounting 4.36 Methods of Costing

ILLUSTRATION 9

The following information is relating to building contract of ₹ 50,00,000 undertaken by Niwara Builders, Nanded. The contractee has agreed to pay 90% of the work certified in cash.

Particulars	2012-13 ₹	2013-14 ₹	2014-15 ₹
Materials	7,00,000	8,00,000	4,00,000
Labour	3,20,000	4,80,000	5,00,000
Expenses – Direct	20,000	30,000	10,000
Expenses – Indirect	10,000	7,000	3,000
Work Certified	10,00,000	30,00,000	50,00,000
Work Uncertified	–	40,000	–
Plant issued	2,00,000	–	–
Value of Plant on Closing Date	1,80,000	1,60,000	1,30,000

Prepare Contract Account for the year 2012-13, 2013-14 and 2014-15 separately.

SOLUTION

Working Notes :

i) 2012-13 :

The entire amount of loss suffered during the year 2010-11 is to be transferred to Profit and Loss Account

ii) 2013-14 :

As the value of Work Certified (₹ 30,00,000) is more than $1/2$ of Contract Price (₹ 50,00,000), the following formula is to be applied to find out the amount of notional profits to be credited to Profit and Loss Account.

$$= \frac{2}{3} \times \text{Notional Profits} \times \frac{\text{Cash Received}}{\text{Work Certified}}$$

$$= \frac{2}{3} \times ₹7,03,000 \times \frac{₹27,00,000}{₹30,00,000}$$

$$= ₹4,21,800$$

3. 2014-15 :

As entire contract is completed during the year 2014-15, the total amount of profit is to be transferred to Profit and Loss Account

In the books of Niwara Builders, Nanded
Contract Account for the year ended 31st March, 2013

Dr. Particulars	₹	Cr. Particulars	₹
To Materials	7,00,000	By Work-in-Progress :	
To Labour	3,20,000	i) Work Certified	10,00,000
To Expenses – Direct	20,000	ii) Work Uncertified	–
To Expenses – Indirect	10,000	iii) Plant in hand	1,80,000
To Plant issued	2,00,000	(Closing Balance C/D.)	
		By Profit and Loss *	70,000
		(Balancing figure i.e. Actual loss)	
	12,50,000		12,50,000

Contract Account for the year ended 31st March, 2014

Dr.				Cr.
Particulars	₹	Particulars		₹
To Work-in-Progress :		By Work-in-Progress :		
i) Work Certified	10,00,000	i) Work Certified		30,00,000
ii) Work Uncertified	–	ii) Work Uncertified		40,000
iii) Plant in hand	1,80,000	iii) Plant in hand		1,60,000
(Opening Balance B/D.)		(Closing Balance C/D.)		
To Materials	8,00,000			
To Labour	4,80,000			
To Expenses – Direct	30,000			
To Expenses – Indirect	7,000			
To Notional Profits C/D *	7,03,000			
(Balancing Figure i.e. Notional Profits)				
	32,00,000			**32,00,000**
To Profit and Loss	4,21,800	By Notional Profits B/D		7,03,000
To Work-in-Progress (Reserve C/D)	2,81,200			
	7,03,000			**7,03,000**

Contract Account for the year ended 31st March, 2015

Dr.			Cr.
Particulars	₹	Particulars	₹
To Work-in-Progress :		By Work-in-Progress :	
i) Work Certified	30,00,000	(Reserve B/D)	2,81,200
ii) Work Uncertified	40,000	By Contractee's A/c	50,00,000
iii) Plant in hand	1,60,000	(Work Certified)	
(Opening Balance B/D.)		By Plant in hand	1,30,000
To Materials	4,00,000	(Closing Balance C/D)	
To Labour	5,00,000		
To Expenses – Direct	10,000		
To Expenses – Indirect	3,000		
To Profit and Loss	12,98,200		
(Balancing Figure i.e. Actual Profit)			
	54,11,200		**54,11,200**

Working Notes :

Particulars		2012-13 ₹	2013-14 ₹	2014-15 ₹
Contract Price		50,00,000	50,00,000	50,00,000
Work Certified	100%	10,00,000	30,00,000	50,00,000
Work Uncertified		–	40,000	–
Cash Received	90%	9,00,000	27,00,000	–
Retention Money	10%	1,00,000	3,00,000	–
Actual Loss/Notional Profits/Actual Profit	–	70,000 (AL)	7,03,000 (NP)	12,98,200 (AP)

ILLUSTRATION 10

The following information relates to Aditya Builders, Amravati for ₹ 10,00,000.

	2014 ₹	2015 ₹
Materials issued	3,00,000	84,000
Direct Wages	2,30,000	1,05,000
Direct Expenses	22,000	10,000
Work Certified	7,50,000	10,00,000
Work Uncertified	8,000	–
Materials at site	5,000	7,000
Plant issued	14,000	2,000
Cash received from Contractee	6,00,000	10,00,000

The value of plant at the end of 2014 and 2015 was ₹ 7,000 and ₹ 5,000 respectively.

Prepare, Contract Account and Contractee's Account for two years 2014 and 2015 taking into consideration such profit for transfer to Profit and Loss Account as you think proper.

SOLUTION

In the books of Aditya Builders, Amravati

Dr.   **Contract Account for 2014**   Cr.

Particulars	₹	Particulars	₹
To Materials issued	3,00,000	By Materials at site C/D	5,000
To Direct Wages	2,30,000	By Plant at site C/D	7,000
To Direct Expenses	22,000	By Work-in-Progress C/D	
To Indirect Expenses	6,000	Work Certified 7,50,000	
To Plant Issued	14,000	Work Uncertified (+) 8,000	7,58,000
To Notional Profits C/D *	1,98,000		
	7,70,000		7,70,000
To Profit and Loss	1,05,600	By Notional Profits B/D	1,98,000
To Work-in-Progress	92,400		
	1,98,000		1,98,000

Working Note :

Profit taken to Profit and Loss Account :

$$= \text{Notional Profit} \times \frac{2}{3} \times \frac{\text{Cash Received}}{\text{Work Certified}}$$

$$= ₹1,98,000 \times \frac{2}{3} \times \frac{₹6,00,000}{₹7,50,000} = ₹1,05,600$$

Dr.   **Contract Account for 2015**   Cr.

Particulars	₹	Particulars	₹
To Materials at site B/D	5,000	By Materials at site	7,000
To Plant at site B/D	7,000	By Plant at site	5,000
To Work-in-Progress B/D	6,65,600	By Contractee's Account	10,00,000
(₹ 7,58,000 – ₹ 92,400)			
To Materials issued	84,000		
To Direct Wages	1,05,000		
To Direct Expenses	10,000		
To Indirect Expenses	1,400		
To Plant issued	2,000		
To Profit and Loss A/c	1,32,000		
	10,12,000		10,12,000

Dr.		Contractee's Account		Cr.
Particulars	₹	Particulars		₹
2014 To Bal C/D	6,00,000	2014 By Bank		6,00,000
	6,00,000			6,00,000
2015 To Contract A/c	10,00,000	2015 By Balance B/D		6,00,000
		2015 By Bank		4,00,000
	10,00,000			10,00,000

QUESTIONS FOR SELF-STUDY

I. **Theory Questions :**

i) What is 'Contract Costing' ? State the important features of Contract Costing.

ii) State the costing procedure involved in Contract Costing.

iii) Define the term 'Contract Costing'. Name the industries where contract costing is applied.

iv) What is 'Contract Costing' ? State the accounting treatment of material cost in contract costing.

v) What is 'work certified' ? How work certified differentiate from work uncertified ?

vi) Explain the term 'Contract Costing'. State the method of ascertaining cost of work certified and cost of work uncertified.

vii) "Both job costing and contract costing are the forms of specific order costing". Discuss.

viii) What is 'Escalation Clause' ? State the importance of escalation clause to the contractor.

ix) What is 'Cost Plus Contracts' ? State the clauses in which Cost Plus Contract Method is applied.

x) State the advantages and disadvantages of Cost Plus Contract Method to the contractor.

xi) What is 'work-in-progress' ? State the method of valuation of work-in-progress in ? Contract Costing.

xii) What do you understand by the term 'Cost-Plus-Contract' ? State the implications of Cost-Plus-Contract from the point of view of manufacturer and customer.

xiii) What is 'Escalation Clause' ? State the relevance of the escalation clause provided in a contract.

xiv) What is 'incomplete contract' ? State the various methods of calculating profit on incomplete contracts.

xv) State clearly the similarities and dissimilarities between the job costing and contract costing.

xvi) What is 'Profit on Incomplete Contracts ? State the need for calculating the profit on incomplete contracts.

xvii) What is Work-in-Progress' ? State the accounting treatment of work-in-progress in contract costing.

xviii) **Write short notes on :**

a) Features of Contract Costing, b) Applicability of Contract Costing, c) Sub-contract Cost, d) Architect's Certificate, e) Objectives of Retention Money, f) Notional Profit, g) Work Certified, h) Work Uncertified, i) Escalation Clause, j) Cost Plus Contract, k) Advantages of Cost Plus Contract to the Contractor and Contractee, l) Profit on Incomplete Contract.

xix) **Differentiate between :**

i) Job Costing and Contract Costing, ii) Actual Profit and Notional Profit, iii) Work Certified and Work Uncertified, iv) Escalation Clause and De-escalation Clause.

II. Practical Problems :

i) Suyash Corporation Ltd. Mumbai is engaged on two contracts A and B during the year, 2015. The following particulars are available on 31st December, 2015 in respect of Contract 'A'.

	₹
Contract price	6,00,000
Materials issued	1,60,000
Materials returned	4,000
Materials on site 31.12.2015	22,000
Direct labour	1,50,000
Direct expenses	66,000
Establishment expenses	25,000
Plant installed at site at cost	80,000
Value of plant on 31.12.2015	65,000
Cost of contract not yet certified	23,000
Value of Work Certified	4,20,000
Cash received from contractee	3,78,000
Architects fees	2,000
Material transferred to contract 'B'	9,000

You are required to prepare Contract 'A' Account for the year ended 31.12.2015.

ii) Niwara Builders, Pune undertook a contract No. 354, for ₹ 4,00,000 on 1st January, 2015. They incurred the following expenses during the year :

	₹
Materials issued from stores	40,000
Materials purchased for the contract	10,000
Plant issued for contract	20,000
Wages paid	71,000
Other expenses paid	3,000
Other expenses payable and due on 31.12.2015	600

Cash received on account at the end of the year i.e. on 31.12.2014 amounted to ₹ 1,44,000. The work certified was ₹ 1,80,000. Of the plant and materials charged to contract, Plant costing ₹ 4,000 and Materials costing ₹ 3,000 were lost. On 31.12.2015, Plant costing ₹ 3,000 was returned to stores. The cost of work uncertified was ₹ 1,500. Materials in hand on site were ₹ 2,500. Charge depreciation on plant @ 15% p.a.

Prepare Contract Account for the year ended 31.12.2015.

Basics of Cost Accounting   4.41   Methods of Costing

iii) Gharkul Builders, Nasik, undertood a contract for ₹ 5,00,000 for construction of a library building. The following is the information relating to the contract during the year 2015.

	₹
Materials sent to site	1,00,000
Materials directly purchased	70,698
Labour engaged on site	1,40,000
Wages accured	8,750
Plant installed at site	30,000
Depreciation on plant	8,000
Direct expenses	6,334
Direct expenses outstanding	580
Overhead charges	8,252
Materials returned to stores	1,098
Work Certified	3,90,000
Cost of work not certified	9,000
Materials at site on 31.12.2015	3,766
Overhead charges payable	9,250
Cash received from contractee	3,60,000

Prepare Contract Account and Contractee's Account in the books of Gharkul Builders, Nasik.

iv) The following balances have been extracted from the books of Home Constructions, Haridwar on 31st March, 2015.

	₹
Materials issued from stores	60,000
Materials purchased	3,100
Wages paid	73,000
Outstanding wages	150
Plant and machinery purchased and installed at site on 1st July, 2014	16,000
Direct expenses	2,500
Direct expenses accrued	650
Administration on cost	6,000
Value of work certified	1,60,000
Cost of work uncertified	5,600
Material returned to stores	7,200
Cash received from contractee	1,44,000

Depreciation on plant and machinery @ 20% p.a.

Prepare Contract Account and Contractee Account for the year ended 31st March, 2015 in the books of a contractor.

v) Gemini Constructions, Ghatkopar took a contract No. 49 for the construction of a college building on 1st January 2015. The contract price is fixed at ₹ 15,00,000 subject to a retention of 20% of work certified. The following are the details of expenditure made by the contractor during the year.

	₹
Direct labour charges	4,05,000
Materials issued from store house	4,20,000
Materials directly purchased	81,200
Plant installed at site on 30th June, 2015	60,000

	₹
Direct expenses	23,000
(inclusive of direct expenses due but not paid ₹ 3,000)	
Management overheads	37,200
Materials transferred to contract No. 51	6,300
Outstanding wages	7,800
Material transferred from contract No. 48	1,600
Work certified	11,00,000
Work uncertified	16,500
Cash received from contractee upto 31st December, 2015	8,80,000

Provide depreciation on plant @ 40% p.a. on the original cost.

Prepare, Contract Account and Contractee Account

vi) Shaini Construction, Bhusawal undertook several large contracts. The following are the particulars relating to contract No. 17 for the year ended 31st December, 2015.

	₹
Materials issued from stores	90,000
Materials purchased	40,000
Materials transferred to contract No. 15	25,000
Plant purchased and installed at site	
i) Plant cost	72,000
ii) Installation cost	8,000
Direct wages paid	1,22,000
Wages due but not paid as on 31.12.2015	5,000
Chargeable expenses	12,000
Direct expenses payable	2,000
Establishment on cost	27,000
Administrative expenses accrued	1,500
Contract price	5,60,000

Cash received from contractee upto 31.12.2015 was ₹ 3,20,000 which represented the full amount of work certified less 20% as retention money. The materials at site were ₹ 7,500. Depreciate plant @ 10% p.a. on the original cost.

You are required to prepare Contract Account, Contractee Account.

vii) The following balances have been extracted from the books of Shanti Construction, Sholapur as on 31st December, 2015.

	₹
Materials issued to contract	81,000
Plant issued for contract	25,000
Wages paid	1,29,600
Wages accrued on 31.12.2015	10,400
Direct charged paid	4,800
Direct charges accrued on 31.12.2015	2,200

The work was commenced on 1.1.2015. Cash received on account on 31.12.2015 amounted to ₹ 2,00,000. The cost of Work certified was ₹ 2,50,000. Of the Plant and materials charged to the contract plant costing ₹ 5,000 and materials costing ₹ 4,000 were lost in accident.

Basics of Cost Accounting 4.43 Methods of Costing

On 31.12.2015, Plant costing ₹ 5,000 was returned to stores. The cost of work certified was ₹ 2,000. Materials costing ₹ 4,000 were in hand on site. Charge depreciation @ 10% p.a. on the plant.

Prepare Contract Account for the year ended 31.12.2015.

viii) Siddhartha Construction, Surat is engaged on two contracts M and N during the year 2015. The following particulars are obtained at the end of the year on 31st December, 2015 in respect of contract 'M'.

	₹
Cash received	2,80,000
Contract price	16,00,000
Direct material purchased	40,000
Materials issued from stores	60,000
Materials transferred from contract 'N'	10,000
Direct wages	60,000
Plant installed at site	1,60,000
Direct chargeable expenses	40,000
Stock of materials in hand on site	20,000
Materials returned to stores	4,000
Work certified	3,00,000
Cost of work not certified	16,000

Depreciate plant @ 25% p.a. on the original cost.

Prepare a Contract Account for the year 2015.

ix) The following balances have been extracted from the books of Amit Construction, Ahmedabad on 31st December, 2015.

	₹
Materials issued	81,000
Wages paid	1,29,600
Direct labour charges payable	10,400
Direct expenses	4,800
Direct expenses due but not paid	2,200
Cost of work certified	2,000
Cost of work uncertified	2,50,000
Cash received on account upto 31.12.2015	2,00,000
Plant issued for contract	25,000

The work was commenced on 1.1.2015. Of the plant and materials charged to contract, plant costing ₹ 5,000 and materials costing ₹ 4,000 were lost in accident. On 31.12.2015, Plant costing ₹ 5,000 was returned to stores. Materials costing ₹ 4,000 were in hand on site. Charge depreciation @ 10% p.a. on the plant.

You are required to prepare Contract Account and Contractee Account for the year.

x) M/s Janhavi Construction, Jaipur undertood several contracts. The following are the particulars of contract for the year ended 31st March, 2015.

	₹
Materials	1,15,000
Plant issued on 30.9.2015	80,000
Wages	1,22,000
Wages payable	33,500
Direct expenses	12,000
Establishment overheads	27,000
Contract price	6,00,000
Cash received on account	3,60,000
Work certified	4,00,000
Materials at site	7,500

Depreciation on plant @ 20% p.a.

Prepare Contract Account and Contractee Account for the year ended 31.3.2015.

xi) Sunny Contractors, Shahapur commences operations on 1.1.2015 and during the year 2015 they were engaged on a contract of which contract price was fixed at ₹ 4,00,000. The following particulars relating to the contract are available on 31.12.2015.

	₹
Materials issued	75,000
Direct wages	95,700
Chargeable expenses	5,000
Cash received on account (being 80% of work certified)	1,60,000
Work uncertified	2,000

Of the plant and material charged to the contract, plant costing ₹ 3,000 and materials costing ₹ 2,400 were destroyed by fire. On 31.12.2015 plant costing ₹ 4,000 was returned to stores and materials on hand at site were ₹ 3000. Depreciate plant @ 10% p.a. on the original cost.

You are required to prepare Contract Account and Contractee Account.

4.2 PROCESS COSTING

Process Costing is probably the most widely used costing system. Process Costing is a method of costing under which all costs are accumulated for each stage of production and the cost per unit of product is ascertained at each stage of production by dividing the total cost of each process by the normal output of that process. It represents a type of costing procedure for mass production industries producing standard products. Typically, in such industries all goods produced are for stock, units produced are identical, goods move down the production line in a continuous stream, and all factory procedures are standardised, costs are compiled for each process or department by preparing a separate account for each process. Thus, it is a method of costing used to ascertain the cost of product at each stage of manufacturing.

4.2.1 Meaning

Process Costing refers to a method of accumulating cost of production by process. It represents a method of cost procedure applicable to continuous or mass production industries producing standard products. Costs are compiled for each process or department by preparing a separate account for each process.

Definitions :

Process Costing as a method of ascertaining the cost has been defined by different experts and professional institutions in the manner stated below.

i) **According to I.C.M.A., London, Process Costing is**, "that form of operating costing which applies where standardised goods are produced".

ii) **Kohler defines Process Costing as,** "a method of cost accounting whereby costs are charged to processes or operations and averaged over units produced".

iii) **The terminology of CIMA defines Process Costing as,**

"the costing method applicable where goods or services result from a sequence of continuous or repetitive operations or processes. Costs are arranged over the units produced during the period".

Like unit costing, Process Costing is also a form of operation costing as distinguished from specific order costing. In case of unit costing, production of a single product is brought about by setting up a separate plant. In the case of Process Costing, however, production follows a series of sequential processes for either a single product or a limited range of product. The aim of Process Costing is to determine the total cost of each operation and to apply this cost to the product at each state of process. It will then be possible to ascertain cost per unit for each operation or process and in total.

Applicability :

Process Costing should be used by firms which are engaged in the manufacture of standardised products on a continuous basis. It is suitable for a large number of industries like paint works, mines and standard quarries, cotton, wool and jute textile mills, chemical plants, soap-making, paper plastics, distilleries, oil refining, screws, bolts and revets, food processing, dairy, breweries, sugar works, confectionaries, cement, flour mill or gas etc.

In short, Process Costing is easily applicable in those industries using continuous sequential processes, discontinuous processes, parallel processes and selective processes.

4.2.2 Features

Following are the important **features of Process Costing.**

i) Each plant is divided into a number of process cost centres or departments and each such division is a stage of production or a process.

ii) The finished products are uniform in all respects such as shape, size, weight, quality, colour, chemical content etc. so unit cost is calculated by dividing the total cost by the number of units produced.

iii) Output of one process is the input of the next process.

iv) It is not possible to distinguish finished products while they are in the stage of processing.

v) Costs follow the flow of production i.e. costs incurred in the earlier process are transferred to the later process alongwith the output.

vi) Total cost of the finished product in the last process is cumulative i.e. it comprises of costs of all processes.

vii) The cost of any particular unit is the average cost of manufacture over a period.

viii) Production of one article may give rise to two or more by-products.

ix) Occurrence of process losses e.g. evaporation, shrinkage, chemical reaction etc.

x) The semi-finished products are expressed in terms of complete products. This is technically termed as equivalent production.

xi) Production accumulated and reported by process.

xii) Production process is predetermined and a definite sequence of production is followed.

xiii) The unit of cost is the "Process" under this method of costing.

xiv) The production is continuous and on large scale basis in anticipation of demand.

xv) The entire production is divided in clearly defined processes.

xvi) The number of units produced in a particular process are identical.

xvii) Each process is treated as a separate cost centre.

The Difference between Job Costing and Process Costing can be summarised as follows :

	Job Costing		Process Costing
i)	Production is against specific orders and instructions from the customers.	i)	Production is in continuous flow and is for stocks.
ii)	Cost are determined separately for each unit or job.	ii)	Costs are compiled for each process or department and unit cost is the average cost.
iii)	Jobs are independent of each other.	iii)	Products lose their individual identity because of continuous flow.
iv)	Unit cost of a job is calculated by dividing the total costs incurred into the units produced in the lot or batch.	iv)	The unit of cost of a process is computed by dividing the total cost for the period into the output of the process during that period.
v)	Costs are ascertained when a job is complete.	v)	Costs are calculated at the end of the cost period.
vi)	Cost of a job is not transferred to another.	vi)	The cost of process is transferred to the next process.
vii)	There may or may not be work-in-progress at the beginning or at the end of the accounting period.	vii)	Due to continuous production, work-in-progress is a regular feature.
viii)	Cost control is comparatively difficult and needs more attention.	viii)	Production is standardised making it comparatively easier to exercise cost control.
ix)	It requires more forms and documents.	ix)	It requires less paper work.
x)	Diversification is possible in Job Costing.	x)	Diversification is not possible under process costing unless altogether a new set of machineries are installed.
xi)	In Job Costing, reporting is after completion of job.	xi)	In Process Costing, reporting is progresswise and in respect of time.
xii)	Investment of capital is less.	xii)	Investment of capital is more.

> Job Costing is considered as a labour-intensive process, whereas Process Costing is considered as a capital-intensive process.

Advantages :

Following are the important **advantages of Process Costing**.

i) It helps in computation of costs of the process as well as of the end product at short intervals.

ii) Average costs of homogeneous products can easily be computed.

iii) Allocation of expenses can be easily made and this results into a more accurate costing.

iv) It involves less clerical labour because of the simplicity of cost records.

v) Quotation can be submitted more promptly with standardisation of processes.

vi) Managerial control is possible by evaluating the performance of each process and by ascertaining the abnormal losses.

vii) It is easier to establish the standards in case of continuous production, hence, Standard costing system can be followed easily in process costing.

viii) As cost of production is ascertained periodically, management is in a position to receive various reports periodically and review the progress and efficiency of the production process.

ix) The method of cost ascertainment is simple and economical than that in job costing.

Disadvantages :

Following are the **disadvantages of Process Costing**.

i) The average cost ascertained under this method is not true cost per unit, as such, it conceals weaknesses and inefficiencies in processing.

ii) Since, it is based on historical costs, it has all the weaknesses of historical costing.

iii) The valuation of work-in-progress on the basis of the degree of completion may sometimes, be a more guess work.

iv) The emergence of joint products may present the problem of apportionment of joint cost and if apportionment is not properly done cost results may not be accurate.

v) It may not always be possible to indicate the suitable units for showing quantity figures in process cost statements.

vi) It is very difficult to estimate the normal quantity loss in process.

vii) The method does not permit evaluation of efforts of individual workers or supervisors.

viii) It involves difficulty in ascertaining closing stock value when output of one process is transferred to another process at transfer price or market price.

Collection of Costs :

The whole manufacturing industry is divided into distinct processes to which all assets of direct material, direct labour, direct expenses and overheads are debited.

i) Direct Materials :

With the help of material requisition, costs of raw materials are **debited** to the process concerned.

ii) **Direct Labour:**

Wages paid to the labourers and other staff engaged in particular process are charged to the concerned process. Sometimes, many workers are engaged in more than one process, the gross wages paid concerned are to be allocated on the basis of time spent.

iii) **Direct Expenses:**

There are certain expenses chargeable to the process concerned which are treated as direct expenses e.g. electricity bill, depreciation etc.

vi) **Overheads:**

There are many expenses which are incurred for more than two processes the total of such expenses may be apportioned either on suitable basis or at predetermined rate based on direct labour charges or prime cost etc.

4.2.3 PREPARATION OF PROCESS ACCOUNTS INCLUDING NORMAL AND ABNORMAL LOSS OR GAIN

4.2.3.1 Preparation of Process Accounts

The accounting procedure of Process Costing is as follows:

a) For the purpose of cost accounting, process industries are divided into departments, each department representing a particular process. A process may consist of a separate operation or series of operations. A foreman or supervisor is appointed for each department. He is responsible for efficient functioning of his department.

b) A separate account is maintained for each process and it is **debited** with the value of raw material, labour and overheads relating to the process.

c) Output is recorded in terms of units e.g. tons, litres, kg., etc. on daily, weekly or suitable periodical basis depending upon processing time.

d) **Items of Debit Side of Process Account:**

Each Process Account is debited with:
- Cost of Materials used in that process.
- Cost of labour incurred in that process.
- Direct expenses incurred in that process.
- Overhead charged to that process on some pre-determined basis.
- Cost of Rectification of Normal Defectives.
- Cost of Abnormal Gain (if any arises in the process).

e) **Items of Credit Side of Process Account:**

Each Process Account is credited with,
- Scrap Value of Normal Loss (if any) occurs in that process.
- Cost of Abnormal Loss (if any occurs in that process).
- Sale of By-product (if any).
- Finished Stock Account (in case of last process).
- Loss in weight (if any).

f) **Equivalent Production Units:** For incomplete physical units in progress at the end of a period, equivalent production units (i.e. notional quantity of completed units substituted for an actual quantity of incomplete units) are calculated on the basis of percentage estimate of degree of completion. e.g., if 200 units are in progress and it is estimated that they are complete only to the extent of 20%, then 200 incomplete units are considered as equivalent to 40 completed units.

g) **Calculation of Average Cost Per Unit:** Average cost per unit is found out by dividing the total cost of each process by total production of that process. In arriving at average unit costs or normal loss in production and incomplete units in the beginning and at the end of the period, are taken into consideration. An average cost per unit produced in each process is ascertained as follows :

$$\text{Average cost per unit} = \frac{\text{Total Cost } (-) \text{ Scrap Value of Normal Loss (if any)}}{\text{Input } (-) \text{ Units of Normal Loss (if any)}}$$

h) **Transfer of the Cost of output :** The cost of output of each process may be transferred either directly to next Process Account or to a Process Stock Account from where it will be transferred to the next process as and when required. Products remaining unfinished in the process at the close of the period are to be assessed in terms of equivalent completed units on the basis of percentage or degree of completion.

In making process accounts, columns are generally provided on both debit side and credit side for total cost, per unit cost and for material quantities.

Notable Calculations :

Remember, the simple calculation of various items to be recorded in process account may be made as follows :

i) **Number of Units of Expected Normal Loss**

   = Input (×) Expected Percentage of Normal Loss

ii) **Realizable Value of Units of Normal Scrap**

   = Units of Normal Scrap (×) Scrap Value per unit

   (**Note :** Units of Normal Wastage have no recoverable value)

iii) **Number of Units of Abnormal Loss**

   = Expected Output (i.e. Input (−) Normal Loss (−) Actual Output

iv) **Cost of Abnormal Loss :**

   $$= \frac{\text{Total Cost incurred } (-) \text{ Scrap Value of Normal Loss}}{\text{Input } (-) \text{ Units of Normal Loss}} \times \text{Units of Abnormal Loss}$$

   (Total Cost = Basic Raw Material Cost + Direct Material Cost + Direct Wages + Direct Expenses + Production Overheads + Cost of Rectification of Normal Defectives)

v) **Cost of Output transferred to next process :**

   $$= \frac{\text{Total Cost incurred } (-) \text{ Scrap Value of Normal Loss}}{\text{Input } (-) \text{ Units of Normal Loss}} \times \begin{array}{l}\text{Units of Output transferred to}\\ \text{Next Process Account}\end{array}$$

vi) **Cost of Output transferred to Process Stock Account :**

   $$= \frac{\text{Total Cost Incurred } (-) \text{ Scrap Value of Normal Loss}}{\text{Input } (-) \text{ Units of Normal Loss}} \times \begin{array}{l}\text{Units of Output transferred}\\ \text{to Process Stock Account}\end{array}$$

vii) **Cost of Output sold :**

   $$= \frac{\text{Total Cost incurred } (-) \text{ Scrap Value of Normal Loss}}{\text{Input } (-) \text{ Units of Normal Loss}} \times \text{Units of Output Sold}$$

viii) **Number of Units of Abnormal Gain :**

   = Actual Output (−) Expected Output (i.e. Input − Normal Loss)

ix) **Cost of Abnormal Gain :**

   $$= \frac{\text{Total Cost incurred } (-) \text{ Scrap Value of Normal Loss}}{\text{Input } (-) \text{ Units of Normal Loss}} \times \text{Units of Abnormal Gain}$$

Preparation of Process Accounts (where there is no work-in-progress)

The following steps are required to be taken for accurate ascertainment of the cost per unit of output of each process and finally the finished goods.

i) For the purpose of cost accounting, process industries are divided into departments, each department representing a particular process. A process may consist of a separate operation or series of operations. A foreman or supervisor is appointed for each department. He is responsible for the efficient functioning of his department.

ii) A separate account is maintained for each process and it is **debited** with the value of raw material, labour and overheads relating to the process.

iii) Output is recorded in terms of units (e.g. tons, litres, kg., etc.) on daily, weekly or suitable periodical basis depending upon processing time.

iv) Average cost per unit is found out by dividing the total cost of each process by total production of that process. In arriving at average unit costs / costs normal loss in production and incomplete units in the beginning and at the end of the period, are taken into consideration.

v) Cost of previous process is transferred to the subsequent process so that the total cost and unit cost of products are accumulated.

vi) Products remaining unfinished in the process at the close of the period are to be assessed in terms of equivalent completed units on the basis of percentage/degree of completion.

While preparing Process Accounts, columns are generally provided on both debit side and credit side for total cost, per unit cost and for material quantities. The Figure 4.2 indicates below shows the **Process Cost Flow.**

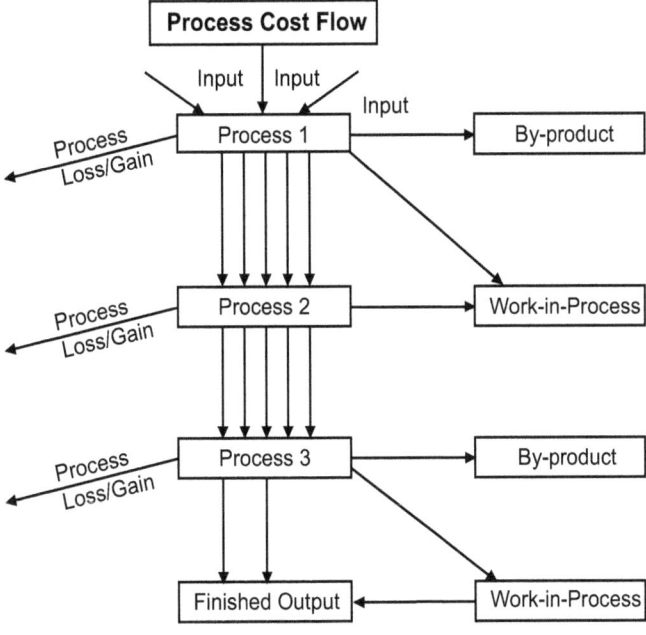

Fig. 4.2 : Process Cost Flow

Specimen of Various Accounts in Process Costing :

The following are the specimen of various accounts prepared in process costing.

In the books of a Manufacturing Company

Dr. Process Account Cr.

Particulars	Quantity Units	Cost per unit ₹	Amount ₹	Particulars	Quantity Units	Cost per unit ₹	Amount ₹
To Earlier Process (in the case of later Process Account) To Raw Materials To Direct Labour To Direct Expenses To Indirect Expenses To Abnormal Gain				By Normal Loss (% of input) By Loss in Weight By Scrap Value By Sale of By-product By Abnormal Loss By Next Process or Finished Stock (In case of last process)			

Dr. Normal Loss Account Cr.

Particulars	Quantity Units	Amount ₹	Particulars	Quantity Units	Amount ₹
To Process			By Abnormal Gain By Cash/Bank (Sale)		

Dr. Abnormal Loss Account Cr.

Particulars	Quantity Units	Amount ₹	Particulars	Quantity Units	Amount ₹
To Process			By Cash/Bank (Sale) By Costing Profit and Loss		

Dr. Abnormal Gain Account Cr.

Particulars	Quantity Units	Amount ₹	Particulars	Quantity Units	Amount ₹
To Normal Loss To Costing Profit and Loss	....	....	By Process	....	....
	....	....		....	....

4.2.3.2 Normal and Abnormal Loss or Gain

In many of the industries which employ Process Costing, a certain amount of loss or wastage occurs at various stages of production. This loss may be due to evaporation, chemical change, change in moisture content, carelessness, accident or any other reason. It is therefore, necessary to keep accurate records for both input and output of each process. Where loss occurs at a last stage of manufacture, it is apparent that financial loss is greater than the mere cost of raw materials. This is because more and more labour and overheads are expanded in process as the products move towards completion stage.

The term "**Process Loss**" may be defined *as,*

"the difference between the input quantity of raw material and the output quantity".

The I.C.M.A. defines 'waste' and 'scrap' from the recovery value point of view as follows :

- **Waste :** *"Discarded substances having no value".*
- **Scrap :** *"Discarded material having some recovery value which is usually disposed of without further treatment or re-introduced into the production process in the place of raw material".*

Process losses and wastages are usually of two types viz. Normal Process Loss and Abnormal Process Loss.

Normal Loss

Meaning :

Normal Process Loss represents the loss which is expected under normal conditions. This type of loss is unavoidable and is inherent in the process of manufacture. It is often caused by such factors as evaporation, chemical change, withdrawals for test or sampling, unavoidable spoilage quantities or other physical reasons. It often includes scrap and waste. This type of losses can be estimated from the nature of materials, nature of operation, previous experience or technical data. Normal loss is generally calculated at a certain percentage of the input of units introduced in the respective process.

Accounting Treatment :

The normal process cost is borne by the good units produced. The unit cost is calculated as under :

$$\text{Unit Cost} = \frac{\text{Total Process Cost} - \text{Value of Normal Wastage}}{\text{Good Units Produced}}$$

The units of normal wastage are recorded on the credit side of a process account in quantity column only. The value of normal wastage, if any, should be included in the amount column on the credit side as saleable value. This reduces the cost of normal output. Process loss is shared by saleable units.

The **Accounting Entries** in respect of Normal Loss may be passed as follows :

i) **For Arising Normal Loss :**

    Normal Loss A/c   ... Dr.

        To Process A/c

ii) **For adjustment of the deficiency in the sale of normal loss :**

    Abnormal Gain A/c   ... Dr.

        To Normal Loss A/c

iii) **For sale of scrap, if any :**

    Cash/Bank A/c   ... Dr.

        To Normal Loss A/c

Abnormal Loss

Meaning :

Where the loss is caused by unexpected or abnormal conditions and if it is beyond limit, it is called "**Abnormal Loss**" or unplanned loss. In other words, any wastage arising in excess of the normal wastage is known as "**Abnormal Wastage**". It arises due to abnormal causes or unforseen factors. Use of defective materials, carelessness, fire, machine breakdown, power failure, strike etc. may give rise to abnormal process losses. Abnormal loss is avoidable. It can be controlled by the management by taking proper care. Units of Abnormal Loss is calculated as follows :

Units Introduced (entered)	......
Less : Normal Loss in units	(–) ......
∴ **Normal Output**	......
Less : Actual Output	(–) ......
∴ **Units of Abnormal Loss**	......

(Normal Output = Units Entered – Normal Loss in units)

Thus, in short, the difference between the normal output and the actual output is termed as abnormal loss.

Accounting Treatment :

Accounting procedure for Abnormal Loss is different. Abnormal loss i.e. wastage is valued at the end at which the good units would be valued if there were only normal loss i.e. wastage. The amount of abnormal loss is credited to a process concerned. A separate Abnormal Loss Account is opened and the scrap value, if any is credited to Abnormal Loss Account and the balance on it ultimately transferred to Costing Profit and Loss Account. The value of Abnormal Loss is calculated as under :

$$\text{Value of Abnormal Loss or Wastage} = \frac{\text{Normal Cost of Normal Output}}{\text{Normal Output}} \times \text{Units of Abnormal Loss}$$

[where, i) Normal Cost = Total Process Cost – Value of normal loss, if any

ii) Normal Output = Units entered – Normal Loss in units

The Accounting Entries in respect of Abnormal Loss may be passed as follows :

i) For the value of Abnormal Loss :

  Abnormal Loss A/c   ... Dr.
    To Concerned Process A/c

ii) If any amount is received from sale of scrap :

  Cash/Bank A/c   ... Dr.
    To Abnormal Loss A/c

iii) For Closing Abnormal Loss A/c

  Costing Profit and Loss A/c   ... Dr.
    To Abnormal Loss A/c

The distinction between Normal Loss and Abnormal Loss can be shown as follows :

Normal Loss	Abnormal Loss
i) Normal loss represents the loss under normal conditions.	i) Abnormal loss represents the loss which is unexpected or under abnormal conditions.
ii) Normal loss is unavoidable.	ii) Abnormal loss is avoidable.

Normal Loss	Abnormal Loss
iii) Normal loss is often caused by the factors like evaporation, chemical change, withdrawals for test or sampling unavoidable spoilage, etc.	iii) Abnormal loss arises due to abnormal causes or unforeseen factors such as use of defective materials, carelessness, fire, machine breakdown, power failure, strike-lockouts, etc.
iv) Normal loss can be estimated in advance on the basis of past experience or technical specification.	iv) Abnormal loss cannot be estimated in advance.
v) The normal process cost is borne by the good units produced. In other words it is shared by saleable units.	v) The abnormal process loss is valued at the end at which the good units would be valued if there were only normal loss.
vi) The normal process cost is calculated as follows: $$= \frac{\text{Total Process Cost} (-) \text{Value of Normal Loss}}{\text{Goods Units Produced}}$$	vi) The abnormal process cost is calculated as follows: $$= \frac{\text{Normal Cost of Normal Output}}{\text{Normal Output}} \times \text{Units of Abnormal Loss}$$

Abnormal Gain

Meaning:

The normal loss is an estimated figure. The actual loss may be more or less than the normal loss. If the actual loss is more than the normal loss, it is treated as **Abnormal Loss**. But if the actual loss is less than the normal loss, it is known as **Abnormal Gain or Abnormal Effectives**. The abnormal gain is calculated in a similar manner as an abnormal loss. Units of Abnormal Gain is to be calculated as under:

	Actual Output	....
Less:	Normal Output	(−) ....
	∴ Units of Abnormal Gain	....

(Normal Output = Units Entered − Normal Loss in Units)

Accounting Treatment:

Like Abnormal loss, **Abnormal Gain** also does not affect the cost of normal output as this is also valued in the same manner as abnormal loss. The process account is **debited** with the quantity and value of Abnormal Gain and Abnormal Gain Account is credited. Finally, the Process account is credited with the quantity and value of normal scrap, but the actual quantity is less, the difference is credited to Normal Loss Account by debiting the Abnormal Gain Account.

Finally, the balance to the credit of Abnormal Gain Account is transferred to Costing Profit and Loss Account as Abnormal Gain. The value of Abnormal Gain is calculated as follows:

$$\text{Value of Abnormal Gain} = \frac{\text{Total Process Cost} (-) \text{Value of Normal Wastage}}{\text{Normal Units Produced}} \times \text{Units of Abnormal Gain}$$

The Accounting Entries in respect of Abnormal Gain may be passed as follows:

i) **For the value of Abnormal Gain:**

   Concerned Process A/c   ... Dr.

   To Abnormal Gain

ii) **For adjustment of scrap value of Abnormal Gain:**

   Abnormal Gain A/c   ... Dr.

   To Normal Loss A/c

iii) **For Closing Abnormal Gain Account:**

   Abnormal Gain A/c   ... Dr.

   To Costing Profit and Loss A/c

The distinction between **Abnormal Loss and Abnormal Gain** can be shown as follows:

	Abnormal Loss		Abnormal Gain
i)	If the actual loss is **more** than the normal loss, it is treated as abnormal loss.	i)	If the actual loss is **less** than the normal loss, it is treated as abnormal gain.
ii)	Abnormal loss does not affect the cost of normal output.	ii)	Abnormal gain also does not affect the cost of normal output.
iii)	The amount of abnormal loss is **credited** to the process concerned.	iii)	The amount of abnormal gain is **debited** to the process concerned.
iv)	The balance of abnormal loss account is transferred to the **debit** of Costing Profit and Loss Account.	iv)	The balance of abnormal gain account is transferred to the **credit** of Costing Profit and Loss Account.
v)	Value of abnormal loss is calculated as follows: $= \dfrac{\text{Normal Cost of Normal Output}}{\text{Normal Output}} (\times) \text{Units of Abnormal Loss}$	v)	The value of abnormal gain is calculated as follows: $= \dfrac{\text{Total Process Cost} (-) \text{Value of Normal Loss}}{\text{Normal Units Produced}}$ $(\times) \text{Units of Abnormal Gain}$

ILLUSTRATIONS

ILLUSTRATION 1

In the course of a manufacture relating to Asmita Ltd.; Akola a particular product passes through three distinct processes viz. A, B and C. During a monthly period 1,000 units are produced with which the following additional information is available.

Particulars		Process A	Process B	Process C
Direct Materials	₹	2,000	1,000	1,000
Direct Labour	₹	1,500	700	800
Direct Expenses	₹	300	100	100

Indirect expenses amounted to ₹ 4,500 and they are to be apportioned to the processes on the basis of Direct Labour.

Prepare Process Account showing the total cost and cost per unit at each process.

SOLUTION

In the books of Asmita Ltd.; Akola

Dr.   Process 'A' Account   (Units Produced : 1,000)   Cr.

Particulars	Total Cost ₹	Cost per Unit ₹	Particulars	Total Cost ₹	Cost per Unit ₹
To Direct Materials	2,000	2.00	By Process 'B' A/c *	6,050	6.05
To Direct Labour	1,500	1.50			
To Direct Expenses	300	0.30			
To Indirect Expenses	2,250	2.25			
(₹ 4,500 × 15/30)					
	6,050	6.05		6,050	6.05

Dr.   Process 'B' Account   (Units Produced : 1,000)   Cr.

Particulars	Total Cost ₹	Cost per Unit ₹	Particulars	Total Cost ₹	Cost per Unit ₹
To Process 'A' A/c	6,050	6.05	By Process 'C' A/c *	8,900	8.90
To Direct Materials	1,000	1.00			
To Direct Labour	700	0.70			
To Direct Expenses	100	0.10			
To Indirect Expenses	1,050	1.05			
(₹ 4,500 × 7/30)					
	8,900	8.90		8,900	8.90

Dr.   Process 'C' Account   (Units Produced : 1,000)   Cr.

Particulars	Total Cost ₹	Cost per Unit ₹	Particulars	Total Cost ₹	Cost per Unit ₹
To Process 'B' A/c	8,900	8.90	By Finished Stock A/c *	12,000	12.00
To Direct Materials	1,000	1.00			
To Direct Labour	800	0.80			
To Direct Expenses	100	0.10			
To Indirect Expenses	1,200	1.20			
(₹ 4,500 × 8/30)					
	12,000	12.00		12,000	12.00

ILLUSTRATION 2

The product of Bright Ltd., Baroda passes through two processes viz. A and B. It is ascertained that in each process 10% of the total weight is lost and 20% is scrap. The realisation from scrap amounts to ₹ 160 per ton and ₹ 400 per ton from Process 'A' and Process 'B' respectively. The cost figures relating to processes are as follows :

Particulars		Process A	Process B
Materials Consumed	Tons	2,000	140
Cost of Materials per ton	₹	250	400
Direct Wages	₹	36,000	24,000
Chargeable Expenses	₹	11,000	12,960

Prepare Process Account showing the cost per ton of output in each process.

SOLUTION

In the books of Bright Ltd. Baroda

Dr.   Process 'A' Account   Cr.

Particulars	Quantity Tons.	Amount ₹	Particulars	Quantity Tons.	Amount ₹
To Materials Consumed (2,000 Tons. × ₹ 250)	2,000	5,00,000	By Loss in Weight (10% of 2,000 Tons.)	200	–
To Direct Wages		36,000	By Scrap	400	64,000
To Chargeable Expenses		11,000	(20% of 2,000 Tons.) (₹ 160 × 400 Tons.)		
			By Process 'B' A/c * (@ ₹ 345 per ton)	1,400	4,83,000
	2,000	5,47,000		2,000	5,47,000

Dr.   Process 'B' Account   Cr.

Particulars	Quantity Tons.	Amount ₹	Particulars	Quantity Tons.	Amount ₹
To Process 'A' A/c	1,400	4,83,000	By Loss in Weight (10% of 1,540 Tons.)	154	–
To Materials Consumed (140 Tons. × ₹ 400)	140	56,000	By Scrap (20% of 1,540 Tons.) (₹ 400 × 308 Tons.)	308	1,23,200
To Direct Wages		24,000			
To Chargeable Expenses		12,960	By Finished Stock A/c * (@ ₹ 420 per ton)	1,078	4,52,760
	1,540	5,75,960		1,540	5,75,960

Working Notes :

i) Calculation of cost per ton of output :

$$= \frac{\text{Total Production Cost}}{\text{Actual Output}}$$

- Process 'A' Account :

$$= \frac{₹\,4,83,000}{\text{Tons. }1,400}$$

$$= ₹\,345 \text{ per ton}$$

- Process 'B' Account :

$$= \frac{₹\,4,52,760}{\text{Tons. }1,078}$$

$$= ₹\,420 \text{ per ton}$$

ILLUSTRATION 3

Cansas Ltd., Chennai produces a patent material used in building construction in three consecutive grades viz. soft, medium, and hard.

Particulars		Process 'A'	Process 'B'	Process 'C'
Raw Materials used	Tons	1,000	–	–
Cost per ton	₹	200	–	–
Manufacturing Wages	₹	87,500	39,500	10,710
Weight Lost (% of input of the process)	%	5%	10%	20
Scrap	Tons	50	30	51
Value of scrap per ton	₹	50	50	50
Selling price per ton	₹	350	500	800

Management overheads and selling on cost were ₹ 8,500 and ₹ 10,740 respectively. 2/3rd of the output of Process 'A' and 1/2 of the output of Process 'B' are passed on to the next process and the balances are sold. The entire output of Process 'C' is sold. Approximation should be made wherever necessary.

Prepare Process 'A' Account, Process 'B' Account, Process 'C' Account separately. Also prepare a statement showing profit or loss.

SOLUTION

Working Notes:

i) Calculation of cost of production per ton of output:

$$= \frac{\text{Total Cost} - \text{Scrap Value}}{\text{Units Introduced} - \text{Units Lost}}$$

Process 'A' Account $= \dfrac{₹ 2,87,500 - ₹ 2,500}{\text{Tons. } 1,000 - \text{Tons. } 100}$

$= \dfrac{₹ 2,85,000}{900 \text{ Tons.}}$

$= ₹ 316.667$

Process 'B' Account $= \dfrac{₹ 2,29,500 - ₹ 1,500}{\text{Tons. } 600 - \text{Tons. } 90}$

$= \dfrac{₹ 2,28,000}{510 \text{ Tons.}}$

$= ₹ 447.058$

In the books of Cansas Ltd., Chennai

Dr.   **Process 'A' Account**   **Cr.**

Particulars	Quantity Tons.	Amount ₹	Particulars	Quantity Tons.	Amount ₹
To Raw Materials (1,000 Tons. × ₹ 200)	1,000	2,00,000	By Loss in Weight (5% of 1,000 Tons.)	50	–
To Manufacturing Wages		87,500	By Scrap (50 Tons. × ₹ 50)	50	2,500
To Costing Profit and Loss A/c * (Balancing figure i.e. Profit in Process 'A' A/c)		10,000	By Sales 1/3 of output i.e. 900 Tons.) (300 TONS. × ₹ 350)	300	1,05,000
			By Process 'B' A/c * (²/₃) of output i.e. 900 Tons.) (600 Tons. × ₹ 316.667)	600	1,90,000
	1,000	**2,97,500**		**1,000**	**2,97,500**

Basics of Cost Accounting   4.59   Methods of Costing

Dr.   Process 'B' Account   Cr.

Particulars	Quantity Tons.	Amount ₹	Particulars	Quantity Tons.	Amount ₹
To Process 'A' A/c	600	1,90,000	By Loss in Weight	60	–
To Manufacturing Wages		39,500	(10% of 600 Tons.)		
To Costing Profit and Loss A/c *		13,500	By Scrap	30	1,500
(Balancing figure i.e. Profit in			(30 Tons. × ₹ 50)		
Process 'B' A/c)			By Sales	255	1,27,500
			(¹/₂ of output i.e. 510 Tons.)		
			(255 Tons. × ₹ 500)		
			By Process 'C' A/c *	255	1,14,000
			(¹/₂) of output i.e. 510 Tons.)		
			(255 Tons. × ₹ 447.058)		
	600	2,43,000		600	2,43,000

Dr.   Process 'C' Account   Cr.

Particulars	Quantity Tons.	Amount ₹	Particulars	Quantity Tons.	Amount ₹
To Process 'B' A/c	255	1,14,000	By Loss in Weight	51	–
To Manufacturing Wages		10,710	(20% of 255 Tons.)		
To Costing Profit and Loss A/c *		240	By Scrap	51	2,550
(Balancing figure i.e. Profit in			(51 Tons. × ₹ 50)		
Process 'C' A/c)			By Sales *	153	1,22,400
			(entire output)		
			(153 Tons. × ₹ 800)		
	255	1,24,950		255	1,24,950

Statement showing Profit or Loss for the period ended .....

Particulars		Amount ₹	Amount ₹
Total Profits earned at Processes :			23,740
i) Profits at Process 'A' Account		10,000	
ii) Profits at Process 'B' Account		13,500	
iii) Profits at Process 'C' Account	(+)	240	
Less : Total Expenses incurred			19,240
i) Management Overheads		8,500	
ii) Selling on Cost	(+)	10,740	(–)
∴ Net Profit			4,500

ILLUSTRATION 4

The Doxy Ltd., Durgapur produced three types of chemicals during the month of August, 2015 by three consecutive processes. In each process 2% of the total weight put in is lost and 10% is scrap. In Process 'I' and Process 'II" the scrap realises ₹ 100 a ton and from Process 'III' ₹ 20 a ton.

Particulars		Process 'I'	Process 'II'	Process 'III'
Materials Used	Tons	1,000	140	1,348
Raw Materials consumed	₹	1,20,000	28,000	2,83,620
Manufacturing Wages	₹	20,500	18,520	15,000
General Overheads	₹	10,300	7,240	3,100
The product of three processes are dealt with as follows :				
Passed to next process	%	75	50	–
Sent to warehouse for sale	%	25	50	100

Prepare Process Cost Accounts showing cost per ton of each process.

Basics of Cost Accounting 4.60 Methods of Costing

SOLUTION

In the books of Doxy Ltd., Durgapur

Dr.   Process 'I' Account   Cr.

Particulars	Rate per Ton ₹	Quantity Tons.	Amount ₹	Particulars	Rate per Ton ₹	Quantity Tons.	Amount ₹
To Raw Materials Consumed		1,000	1,20,000	By Loss in Weight		20	–
To Manufacturing Wages			20,500	(2% of 1,000 Tons.)			
To General Overheads			10,300	By Scrap	100	100	10,000
				(10% of 1,000 Tons.)			
				(100 Tons. × ₹ 100)			
				By Transfer to Warehouse	160	220	35,200
				(25% of 880 Tons.)			
				By Process 'II' A/c *	160	660	1,05,600
				(75% of 880 Tons.)			
			1,000	1,50,800		1,000	1,50,800

Dr.   Process 'II' Account   Cr.

Particulars	Rate per Ton ₹	Quantity Tons.	Amount ₹	Particulars	Rate per Ton ₹	Quantity Tons.	Amount ₹
To Process 'I' A/c	160	660	1,05,600	By Loss in Weight		16	–
To Raw Materials Consumed		140	28,000	(2% of 800 Tons.)			
To Manufacturing Wages			18,520	By Scrap	100	80	8,000
To General Overheads			7,240	(10% of 800 Tons.)			
				By Transfer to Warehouse	215	352	75,680
				(50% of 704 Tons.)			
				By Process 'III' A/c *	215	352	75,680
				(50% of 704 Tons.)			
		800	1,59,360			800	1,59,360

Dr.   Process 'III' Account   Cr.

Particulars	Rate per Ton ₹	Quantity Tons.	Amount ₹	Particulars	Rate per Ton ₹	Quantity Tons.	Amount ₹
To Process 'II' A/c	215	352	75,680	By Loss in Weight	–	34	–
To Raw Materials Consumed		1,348	2,83,620	(2% of 1,700 Tons.)			
To Manufacturing Wages			15,000	By Scrap	20	170	3,400
To General Overheads			3,100	(10% of 1,700 Tons.)			
				By Transfer to Warehouse	250	1,496	3,74,000
				(100% of 1,496 Tons.)			
		1,700	3,77,400			1,700	3,77,400

Working Notes :

i) Calculation of cost per ton in Process 'I' Account :

If 880 tones = ₹ 1,40,800

∴ 1 ton = ?

$$= \frac{1 \times ₹ 1,40,800}{880 \text{ Tons.}}$$

= ₹ 160 per ton

ii) Calculation of cost per ton in Process 'II' Account :

If 704 Tons. = ₹ 1,51,360

∴ 1 ton = ?

$$= \frac{1 \times ₹ 1,51,360}{704 \text{ Tons.}}$$

= ₹ 215 per ton

Basics of Cost Accounting   4.61   Methods of Costing

iii) Calculation of cost per ton in Process 'III' Account :

If 1,496 Tons. = ₹ 3,74,000

∴   1 ton = ?

$$= \frac{1 \times ₹\, 3,74,000}{1,496 \text{ Tons.}}$$

= ₹ 250 per ton

ILLUSTRATION 5

The Elpro Chemicals Ltd., Edalabad manufacture and sell their chemical product by consecutive processes. The products of these processes are dealt with as under :

		Process 1	Process 2	Process 3
Transferred to next process	%	$66\,^2/_3$	60	–
Transferred to warehouse for sale	%	$33\,^1/_3$	40	100
Raw Materials	Tons.	1,400	160	1,260
Raw Materials-rate per ton	₹	10	16	17
Wages and Other Expenses	₹	5,152	3,140	8,928

In each process 4% of the total weight put in is lost and 6% is scrap which from Process I realises at ₹ 3 per ton, from Process 2 at ₹ 5 per ton and from Process 3 at ₹ 6 per ton.

Prepare Process Cost Account showing cost per ton of each process.

SOLUTION

In the books of Elpro Chemicals Ltd., Edalabad

Dr.   Process '1' Account   Cr.

Particulars	Rate per Ton ₹	Quantity Tons.	Amount ₹	Particulars	Rate per Ton ₹	Quantity Tons.	Amount ₹
To Raw Materials	10	1,400	14,000	By Loss in Weight	–	56	–
To Wages and Other Expenses			5,152	(4% of 1,400 Tons.)			
				By Scrap	3	84	252
				(6% of 1,400 Tons.)			
				(84 TONS. × ₹ 3)			
				By Transfer to Warehouse	15	420	6,300
				($33\,^1/_3$% of 1,260 Tons.)			
				By Process 2 A/c *	15	840	12,600
				($66\,^2/_3$ % of 1,260 Tons.)			
		1,400	19,152			1,400	19,152

Dr.   Process '2' Account   Cr.

Particulars	Rate per Ton ₹	Quantity Tons.	Amount ₹	Particulars	Rate per Ton ₹	Quantity Tons.	Amount ₹
To Process '1' A/c	15	840	12,600	By Loss in Weight	–	40	–
To Raw Materials	16	160	2,560	(4% of 1,800 Tons.)			
To Wages and Other Expenses			3,140	By Scrap	5	60	300
				(60 Tons. × ₹ 5)			
				(i.e. 6% of 1000 Tons. × ₹ 5)			
				By Transfer to Warehouse	20	360	7,200
				(40% of 900 Tons.)			
				By Process '3' A/c *	20	540	10,800
				(60% of 900 Tons.)			
		1,000	18,300			1,000	18,300

Process '3' Account

Dr.								Cr.
Particulars	Rate per Ton ₹	Quantity Tons.	Amount ₹	Particulars	Rate per Ton ₹	Quantity Tons.	Amount ₹
To Process 2 A/c	20	540	10,800	By Loss in Weight (4% of 1,800 Tons.)	–	72	–
To Raw Materials	17	1,260	21,420	By Scrap (6% of 1,800 Tons.)	6	108	648
To Wages and Other Expenses			8,928	By Transfer to Warehouse (100% of 1,620 Tons.)	25	1,620	40,500
		1,800	41,148			1,800	41,148

Working Notes :

i) Calculation of cost per ton in Process '1' Account :

If 1,260 Tons. = ₹ 18,900

∴ 1 ton = ?

$$= \frac{1 \times ₹\, 18,900}{1,260 \text{ Tons.}}$$

= ₹ 15 per ton

ii) Calculation of cost per ton in Process 2 Account :

If 900 Tons. = ₹ 18,000

∴ 1 ton = ?

$$= \frac{1 \times ₹\, 18,000}{900 \text{ Tons.}}$$

= ₹ 20 per ton

iii) Calculation of cost per ton in Process 3 Account :

If 1,620 Tons. = ₹ 40,500

∴ 1 ton = ?

$$= \frac{1 \times ₹\, 40,500}{1,620 \text{ Tons.}}$$

= ₹ 25 per ton

ILLUSTRATION 6

A product in Femina Ltd., Fattepur passes through two distinct processes A and B. From the following information you are required to prepare Process 'A' Account, Process 'B' Account, Abnormal Loss Account and Abnormal Gain Account.

Particulars		Process 'A'	Process 'B'
Materials (introduced 20,000 units in Process 'A')	₹	30,000	3,000
Labour	₹	10,000	12,000
Overheads	₹	7,000	9,850
Normal Loss	₹	10%	4%
Scrap value of Normal Loss	₹	1 per unit	2 per unit
Output	Units	17,500	17,000

There is no stock or work in progress in any process.

Basics of Cost Accounting — Methods of Costing

SOLUTION

In the books of Femina Ltd., Fattepur

Dr. Process 'A' Account Cr.

Particulars	Quantity Units	Amount ₹	Particulars	Quantity Units	Amount ₹
To Materials	20,000	30,000	By Normal Loss	2,000	2,000
To Labour		10,000	(10% of 20,000 units)		
To Overheads		7,000	(2,000 units × ₹ 1)		
			By Abnormal Loss *	500	1,250
			(Balancing Figure)		
			By Process 'B' A/c	17,500	43,750
	20,000	47,000		20,000	47,000

Dr. Process 'B' Account Cr.

Particulars	Quantity Units	Amount ₹	Particulars	Quantity Units	Amount ₹
To Process 'A' A/c	17,500	43,750	By Normal Loss	700	1,400
To Materials		3,000	(4% of 17,500 units)		
To Labour		12,000	(700 units × ₹ 2)		
To Overheads		9,850	By Finished Stock A/c	17,000	68,000
To Abnormal Gain *	200	800			
(Balancing Figure)					
	17,700	69,400		17,700	69,400

Dr. Abnormal Loss Account Cr.

Particulars	Quantity Units	Amount ₹	Particulars	Quantity Units	Amount ₹
To Process 'A' A/c	500	1,250	By Bank	500	500
			(500 units × ₹ 1)		
			By Costing Profit and Loss A/c *		
			(Balancing Figure)	–	750
	500	1,250		500	1,250

Dr. Abnormal Gain Account Cr.

Particulars	Quantity Units	Amount ₹	Particulars	Quantity Units	Amount ₹
To Normal Loss	200	400	By Process 'B' A/c	200	800
(200 units × ₹ 2)					
To Costing Profit and Loss A/c *					
(Balancing Figure)	–	400			
	200	800		200	800

Working Notes :

i) Calculation of cost of Abnormal Loss in Process 'A' Account :

$$\text{Dr.} - \text{Cr.} = \text{Balance}$$

Quantity : Units 20,000 – 2,000 Units = 18,000 Units : Normal Output
Amount : ₹ 47,000 – ₹ 2,000 = ₹ 45,000 : Normal Cost

If 18,000 Units = ₹ 45,000
∴ 500 Units = ?

$$= \frac{500 \text{ units} \times ₹ 45,000}{18,000 \text{ units}}$$

= ₹ 1,250

ii) Calculation of cost of Abnormal Gain in Process 'B' Account :

$$\text{Dr.} - \text{Cr.} = \text{Balance}$$

Quantity : 17,500 Units – 700 Units = 16,800 units : Normal Output
Amount : ₹ 68,600 – ₹ 1,400 = ₹ 67,200 : Normal Cost

If 16,800 Units = ₹ 67,200
∴ 200 Units = ?
= (200 units × ₹ 67,200) / 16,800 units
= ₹ 800

ILLUSTRATION 7

The product of Glaxo India Ltd., Goregaon passes through two processes A and B and then to finished stock. It is ascertained that in each process normally 5% of the total weight is lost and 10% is scrap which from process A and B realises ₹ 80 per ton and ₹ 200 per ton respectively. The following are the figures relating to both the process.

Particulars		Process 'A'	Process 'B'
Materials	Tons	1,000	70
Cost of materials per ton	₹	125	200
Wages	₹	28,000	10,000
Manufacturing Expenses	₹	8,000	5,250
Output	Tons	830	780

Prepare Process Cost Account showing cost per ton of each process. There was no stock or work-in-progress in any process.

SOLUTION

In the books of Glaxo India Ltd., Goregaon

Dr. Process 'A' Account Cr.

Particulars	Quantity Tons.	Amount ₹	Particulars	Quantity Tons.	Amount ₹
To Cost of Materials	1,000	1,25,000	By Loss in Weight	50	–
(1,000 Tons. × ₹ 125)			(5% of 1,000 Tons.)		
To Wages		28,000	By Normal Scrap	100	8,000
To Manufacturing			(10% of 1,000 Tons.)		
Expenses		8,000	(100 Tons. × ₹ 80)		
			By Abnormal Loss *	20	3,600
			(Balancing Figure)		
			By Process 'B' A/c	830	1,49,400
	1,000	1,61,000		1,000	1,61,000

Dr. Process 'B' Account Cr.

Particulars	Quantity Tons.	Amount ₹	Particulars	Quantity Tons.	Amount ₹
To Process 'A' A/c	830	1,49,400	By Loss in Weight	45	–
To Cost of Materials	70	14,000	(5% of 900 Tons.)		
(70 Tons. × ₹ 200)			By Normal Scrap	90	18,000
To Wages		10,000	(10% of 900 Tons.)		
To Manufacturing			(90 Tons. × ₹ 200)		
Expenses		5,250			
To Abnormal Gain *	15	3,150	By Finished Stock A/c	780	1,63,800
(Balancing Figure)					
	915	1,81,800		915	1,81,800

Basics of Cost Accounting   4.65   Methods of Costing

Dr.   Abnormal Loss Account   Cr.

Particulars	Quantity Tons.	Amount ₹	Particulars	Quantity Tons.	Amount ₹
To Process 'A' A/c	20	3,600	By Bank (20 Tons. × ₹ 80)	20	1,600
			By Costing Profit and Loss A/c * (Balancing Figure)	–	2,000
	20	3,600		20	3,600

Dr.   Abnormal Gain Account   Cr.

Particulars	Quantity Tons.	Amount ₹	Particulars	Quantity Tons.	Amount ₹
To Normal Loss (15 Tons. × ₹ 200)	15	3,000	By Process 'B' A/c	15	3,150
To Costing Profit and Loss A/c * (Balancing Figure)	–	150			
	15	3,150		15	3,150

Working Notes :

i) Calculation of cost of Abnormal Loss in Process 'A' Account :

$$\text{Dr.} - \text{Cr.} = \text{Balance}$$

Quantity : 1,000 Tons. – 150 Tons. = 850 Tons. : Normal Output

Amount : ₹ 1,61,000 – ₹ 8,000 = ₹ 1,53,000 : Normal Cost

If 850 Tons. = ₹ 1,53,000

∴ 20 Tons. = ?

$$= \frac{20 \text{ Tons.} \times ₹ 1,53,000}{850 \text{ Tons.}}$$

= ₹ 3,600

ii) Calculation of cost of Abnormal Gain in Process 'B' Account :

$$\text{Dr.} - \text{Cr.} = \text{Balance}$$

Quantity : 900 Tons. – 135 Tons. = 765 Tons. : Normal Output

Amount : ₹ 1,78,650 – ₹ 18,000 = ₹ 1,60,650 : Normal Cost

If 765 Tons. = ₹ 1,60,650

∴ 15 Tons. = ?

$$= \frac{15 \text{ Tons} \times ₹ 1,60,650}{765 \text{ Tons.}}$$

= ₹ 3,150

iii) Calculation of cost per ton in Process 'A' Account :

If 830 Tons. = ₹ 1,49,400

∴ 1 Tonne = ?

$$= \frac{1 \text{ Ton} \times ₹ 1,49,400}{830 \text{ tons.}}$$

= ₹ 180 per ton

iv) Calculation of cost per ton in Process 'B' Account :
   If 780 Tons. = ₹ 1,63,800
   ∴   1 Ton = ?
          = $\frac{1 \text{ Ton.} \times ₹ 1,63,800}{780 \text{ Tons.}}$
          = ₹ 210 per ton

ILLUSTRATION 8

A product 'Bee' produced in Himani Ltd.; Himmatpur passes through three processes A, B and C. 10,000 units were issued to Process 'A' in the beginning at cost of ₹ 10 per unit.

Prepare Process Account assuming that there was no opening or closing stock. The following information is made available.

Particulars		Process 'A'	Process 'B'	Process 'C'
Sundry Materials	₹	10,000	15,000	5,000
Wages	₹	50,000	80,000	65,000
Direct Expenses	₹	15,300	18,100	30,828
Normal Scrap	%	3	5	8
Value of Scrap per unit	₹	2.50	5.00	8.50
Actual Output	Units	9,500	9,100	8,100

SOLUTION

In the books of Himani Ltd.; Himmatpur

Dr.   Process 'A' Account   Cr.

Particulars	Quantity Units	Amount ₹	Particulars	Quantity Units	Amount ₹
To Cost of Units Issued (10,000 units × ₹ 10)	10,000	1,00,000	By Normal Scrap (3% of 10,000 units) (300 units × ₹ 2.50)	300	750
To Sundry Materials		10,000			
To Wages		50,000	By Abnormal Loss * (Balancing Figure)	200	3,599
To Direct Expenses		15,300	By Process 'B' A/c	9,500	1,70,951
	10,000	1,75,300		10,000	1,75,300

Dr.   Process 'B' Account   Cr.

Particulars	Quantity Units	Amount ₹	Particulars	Quantity Units	Amount ₹
To Process 'A' A/c	9,500	1,70,951	By Normal Scrap (5% of 9,500 units) (475 units × ₹ 5)	475	2,375
To Sundry Materials		15,000			
To Wages		80,000			
To Direct Expenses		18,100			
To Abnormal Gain * (Balancing Figure)	75	2,341	By Process 'C' A/c	9,100	2,84,017
	9,575	2,86,392		9,575	2,86,392

Dr.   Process 'C' Account   Cr.

Particulars	Quantity Units	Amount ₹	Particulars	Quantity Units	Amount ₹
To Process 'B' A/c	9,100	2,84,017	By Normal Scrap (8% of 9,100 units) (728 units × ₹ 8.50)	728	6,188
To Sundry Materials		5,000			
To Wages		65,000			
To Direct Expenses		30,828	By Abnormal Loss * (Balancing Figure)	272	12,302
			By Finished Stock A/c	8,100	3,66,355
	9,100	3,84,845		9,100	3,84,845

Abnormal Loss Account

Dr.					Cr.
Particulars	Quantity Units	Amount ₹	Particulars	Quantity Units	Amount ₹
To Process 'A' A/c	200	3,599	By Bank (200 units × ₹ 2.50)	200	500
			By Costing Profit and Loss A/c * (Balancing figure)	–	3,099
	200	3,599		200	3,599

Abnormal Gain Account

Dr.					Cr.
Particulars	Quantity units	Amount ₹	Particulars	Quantity units	Amount ₹
To Normal Loss (75 units × ₹ 5)	75	375	By Process 'B' A/c	75	2,341
To Costing Profit and Loss A/c * (Balancing Figure)	–	1,966			
	75	2,341		75	2,341

Abnormal Loss Account

Dr.					Cr.
Particulars	Quantity units	Amount ₹	Particulars	Quantity units	Amount ₹
To Process 'C' A/c	272	12,302	By Bank (272 units × ₹ 8.50)	272	2,312
			By Costing Profit and Loss A/c * (Balancing Figure)	–	9,990
	272	12,302		272	12,302

Working Notes :

i) **Calculation of cost of Abnormal Loss in Process 'A' Account :**

　　　　　　　　Dr.　　–　　Cr.　=　Balance

Quantity :　10,000 Units – 300 Units　=　9,700 Units　: Normal Outuput

Amount :　　₹ 1,75,300 – ₹ 750　=　₹ 1,74,550　: Normal Cost

　　　If 9,700 Units　=　₹ 1,74,550

∴　　　　200 Units　=　?

$$= \frac{200 \text{ units} \times ₹ 1,74,550}{9,700 \text{ units}}$$

　　　　=　₹ 3,599

ii) **Calculation of cost of Abnormal Gain in Process 'B' Account :**

　　　　　　　　Dr.　　–　　Cr.　=　Balance

Quantity :　9,500 Units – 475 Units　=　9,025 Units　: Normal Output

Amount :　　₹ 2,84,051 – ₹ 2,375　=　₹ 2,81,676　: Normal Cost

　　　If 9,025 Units　=　₹ 2,81,676

∴　　　　75 Units　=　?

$$= \frac{75 \text{ units} \times ₹ 2,81,676}{9,025 \text{ units}}$$

　　　　=　₹ 2,341

iii) Calculation of cost of Abnormal Loss in Process 'C' Account :

                    Dr.   –   Cr.   =   Balance

Quantity :   9,100 Units – 728 Units = 8,372 Units   : Normal Output

Amount :   ₹ 3,84,845 – ₹ 6,188 = ₹ 3,78,657   : Normal Cost

       If 8,372 Units = ₹ 3,78,657

∴   272 Units =   ?

                     = $\dfrac{272 \text{ units} \times ₹\,3,78,657}{8,372 \text{ units}}$

                     = ₹ 12,302

ILLUSTRATION 9

The finished product of Indiana Ltd.; Igatpuri has to pass through three process 1, 2 and 3. During August 2015 data relating to this product was as shown below :

Particulars		Process 1	Process 2	Process 3	Total
Basic Raw Materials (10,000 Units)	₹	6,000	–	–	6,000
Direct Materials added	₹	8,500	9,500	5,500	23,500
Direct Wages	₹	4,000	6,000	12,000	22,000
Direct Expenses	₹	1,200	930	1,340	3,470
Production Overheads	₹	–	–	–	16,500
(absorbed as a percentage of direct wages)					
Output	units	9,200	8,700	7,900	–
Normal Loss	%	10	5	10	–
Scrap Value of Normal Loss per unit	₹	0.20	0.50	1.00	–

There was no stock at the beginning or at the end of any process. You are required to prepare -

i) Process '1' Account, ii) Process '2' Account iii) Process '3' Account iv) Abnormal Loss Account and v) Abnormal Gain Account.

SOLUTION

In the books of Indiana Ltd.; Igatpuri

Dr.   Process '1' Account   Cr.

Particulars	Quantity Units	Amount ₹	Particulars	Quantity Units	Amount ₹
To Cost of Basic Raw Materials	10,000	6,000	By Normal Loss (10% of 10,000 units) (1,000 units × Re. 0.20)	1,000	200
To Direct Materials		8,500			
To Direct Wages		4,000			
To Direct Expenses		1,200			
To Production Overheads (₹ 16,500 × 2/11)		3,000			
To Abnormal Gain * (Balancing Figure)	200	500	By Process '2' A/c	9,200	23,000
	10,200	23,200		10,200	23,200

Dr.   Process '2' Account   Cr.

Particulars	Quantity Units	Amount ₹	Particulars	Quantity Units	Amount ₹
To Process 'A' A/c	9,200	23,000	By Normal Loss (5% of 9,200 units) (460 units × ₹ 0.50)	460	230
To Direct Materials		9,500			
To Direct Wages		6,000			
To Direct Expenses		930	By Abnormal Loss * (Balancing Figure)	40	200
To Production Overheads (₹ 16,500 × 3/11)		4,500	By Process '3' A/c	8,700	43,500
	9,200	43,930		9,200	43,930

Process '3' Account

Dr. Particulars	Quantity Units	Amount ₹	Cr. Particulars	Quantity Units	Amount ₹
To Process '2' A/c	8,700	43,500	By Normal Loss	870	870
To Direct Materials		5,500	(10% of 8,700 units)		
To Direct Wages		12,000	(870 units × ₹ 1)		
To Direct Expenses		1,340			
To Production Overheads		9,000			
(₹ 16,500 × 6/11)					
To Abnormal Gain *	70	630			
(Balancing Figure)			By Finished Stock A/c	7,900	71,100
	8,770	71,970		8,770	71,970

Abnormal Gain Account

Dr. Particulars	Quantity Units	Amount ₹	Cr. Particulars	Quantity Units	Amount ₹
To Normal Loss	200	40	By Process '1' A/c	200	500
(200 units × ₹ 0.20)					
To Costing Profit and					
Loss A/c	–	460			
(Balancing Figure)					
	200	500		200	500

Abnormal Loss Account

Dr. Particulars	Quantity Units	Amount ₹	Cr. Particulars	Quantity Units	Amount ₹
To Process '2' A/c	40	200	By Bank	40	20
			(40 units × ₹ 0.50)		
			By Costing Profit		
			and Loss A/c *	–	180
			(Balancing Figure)		
	40	200		40	200

Abnormal Gain Account

Dr. Particulars	Quantity units	Amount ₹	Cr. Particulars	Quantity units	Amount ₹
To Normal Loss	70	70	By Process '3' A/c	70	630
(70 units × ₹ 1)					
To Costing Profit and					
Loss A/c *	–	560			
(Balancing Figure)					
	70	630		70	630

Working Notes:

i) Calculation of cost of Abnormal Gain in Process '1' Account:

$$\text{Dr.} - \text{Cr.} = \text{Balance}$$

Quantity: 10,000 Units – 1,000 Units = 9,000 Units : Normal Output

Amount: ₹ 22,700 – ₹ 200 = ₹ 22,500 : Normal Cost

If 9,000 Units = ₹ 22,500

∴ 200 Units = ?

$$= \frac{200 \text{ units} \times ₹ 22,500}{9,000 \text{ units}}$$

$$= ₹ 500$$

Basics of Cost Accounting — Methods of Costing

ii) **Calculation of cost of Abnormal Loss in Process '2' Account:**

	Dr.	–	Cr.	=	Balance	
Quantity:	9,200 Units	–	460 Units	=	8,740 Units	: Normal Output
Amount:	₹ 43,930	–	₹ 230	=	₹ 43,700	: Normal Cost

If 8,740 Units = ₹ 43,700

∴ 40 Units = ?

$$= \frac{40 \text{ units} \times ₹ 43,700}{8,740 \text{ units}}$$

= ₹ 200

iii) **Calculation of cost of Abnormal Gain in Process '3' Account:**

	Dr.	–	Cr.	=	Balance	
Quantity:	8,700 Units	–	870 Units	=	7,830 Units	: Normal Output
Amount:	₹ 71,340	–	₹ 870	=	₹ 70,470	: Normal Cost

If 7,830 Units = ₹ 70,470

∴ 70 Units = ?

$$= \frac{70 \text{ units} \times ₹ 70,470}{7,830 \text{ units}}$$

= ₹ 630

ILLUSTRATION 10

Product X is obtained after it passes through three distinct processes arranged in Jonson Ltd., Jaipur. You are required to prepare Process Account from the following information.

Particulars	Total ₹	Process I ₹	Process II ₹	Process III ₹
Materials	15,084	5,200	3,960	5,924
Direct Wages	18,000	4,000	6,000	8,000
Production Overheads	18,000	–	–	–
Actual Output (units)		950	840	750
Normal Loss (%)		5	10	15
Value of Scrap per unit (₹)		4	8	10

1,000 units @ ₹ 6 per unit were introduced in Process 'I' Account. Production Overheads to be distributed as 100% of Direct Wages.

SOLUTION
In the books of Jonson Ltd., Jaipur

Process 'I' Account

Dr. Particulars	Quantity Units	Amount ₹	Cr. Particulars	Quantity Units	Amount ₹
To Cost of Units Introduced (1,000 units × ₹ 6)	1,000	6,000	By Normal Loss (5% of 1,000 units) (50 units × ₹ 4)	50	200
To Materials		5,200			
To Direct Wages		4,000			
To Production Overheads (₹ 4,000 × 100%)		4,000	By Process 'II' A/c	950	19,000
	1,000	19,200		1,000	19,200

Process 'II' Account

Dr. Particulars	Quantity Units	Amount ₹	Cr. Particulars	Quantity Units	Amount ₹
To Process 'I' A/c	950	19,000	By Normal Loss (10% of 950 units) (95 units × ₹ 8)	95	760
To Materials		3,960			
To Direct Wages		6,000	By Abnormal Loss * (Balancing Figure)	15	600
To Production Overheads (₹ 6,000 × 100%)		6,000	By Process 'III' A/c	840	33,600
	950	34,960		950	34,960

Basics of Cost Accounting 4.71 Methods of Costing

Dr.   Process 'III' Account   Cr.

Particulars	Quantity Units	Amount ₹	Particulars	Quantity Units	Amount ₹
To Process 'II' A/c	840	33,600	By Normal Loss	126	1,260
To Materials		5,924	(15% of 840 units)		
To Direct Wages		8,000	(126 units × ₹ 10)		
To Production Overheads		8,000			
(₹ 8,000 × 100%)					
To Abnormal Gain *	36	2,736			
(Balancing Figure)			By Finished Stock A/c	750	57,000
	876	58,260		876	58,260

Dr.   Abnormal Loss Account   Cr.

Particulars	Quantity Units	Amount ₹	Particulars	Quantity Units	Amount ₹
To Process 'II' A/c	15	600	By Bank	15	120
			(15 units × ₹ 8)		
			By Costing Profit		
			and Loss A/c *	–	480
			(Balancing Figure)		
	15	600		15	600

Dr.   Abnormal Gain Account   Cr.

Particulars	Quantity units	Amount ₹	Particulars	Quantity units	Amount ₹
To Normal Loss	36	360	By Process 'III' A/c	36	2,736
(36 units × ₹ 10)					
To Costing Profit and					
Loss A/c *	–	2,376			
(Balancing Figure)					
	36	2,736		36	2,736

Working Notes :

i) **Calculation of cost of Abnormal Loss in Process 'II' Account :**

                    Dr.   –   Cr.   = Balance

    Quantity :   950 Units – 95 Units = 855 Units   : Normal Output

    Amount :   ₹ 34,960 – ₹ 760   = ₹ 34,200 : Normal Cost

        If 855 Units = ₹ 34,200

  ∴   15 Units = ?

$$= \frac{15 \text{ units} \times ₹ 34,200}{855 \text{ units}}$$

            = ₹ 600

ii) **Calculation of cost of Abnormal Gain in Process 'III' Account :**

                    Dr.   –   Cr.   = Balance

    Quantity :   840 Units – 126 Units = 714 Units   : Normal Output

    Amount :   ₹ 55,524 – ₹ 1,260 = ₹ 54,264 : Normal Cost

        If 714 Units = ₹ 54,264

  ∴   36 Units = ?

$$= \frac{36 \text{ units} \times ₹ 54,264}{714 \text{ units}}$$

            = ₹ 2,736

ILLUSTRATION 11

In Koton Queen Ltd., Kalyan, the product passes through two processes A and B. A loss of 5% is allowed in Process A and 2% in Process 'B', nothing being realised by disposal of wastage. During April 2015, 10,000 units of materials costing ₹ 6 per unit were introduced in Process 'A'. The other costs are as follows :

Particulars		Process 'A'	Process 'B'
Materials	₹	–	6,140
Labour	₹	10,000	6,000
Overheads	₹	6,000	4,600

The output was 9,300 units from Process 'A'. 9,200 units were produced by Process 'B' which were transferred to the finished stock. 8,000 units of the finished product was sold at ₹ 15 per unit, the selling and distribution expenses were ₹ 2 per unit. Prepare, i) Process Account, ii) Statement of Profit or Loss for the month of April 2015, assuming that there were no opening stocks of any type.

SOLUTION

In the books of Koton Queen Ltd., Kalyan

Dr.   Process 'A' Account   Cr.

Particulars	Quantity Units	Amount ₹	Particulars	Quantity Units	Amount ₹
To Cost of Materials Introduced (10,000 units × ₹ 6)	10,000	60,000	By Normal Loss (5% of 10,000 units)	500	–
To Labour		10,000	By Abnormal Loss * (Balancing Figure)	200	1,600
To Overheads		6,000	By Process 'B' A/c	9,300	74,400
	10,000	76,000		10,000	76,000

Dr.   Process 'B' Account   Cr.

Particulars	Quantity Units	Amount ₹	Particulars	Quantity Units	Amount ₹
To Process 'A' A/c	9,300	74,400	By Normal Loss (2% of 9,300 units)	186	–
To Materials		6,140			
To Labour		6,000			
To Overheads		4,600			
To Abnormal Gain * (Balancing Figure)	86	860	By Finished Stock A/c (i.e. @ ₹ 10 per unit)	9,200	92,000
	9,386	92,000		9,386	92,000

Dr.   Abnormal Loss Account   Cr.

Particulars	Quantity Units	Amount ₹	Particulars	Quantity Units	Amount ₹
To Process 'A' A/c	200	1,600	By Bank (200 units × NIL)	200	–
			By Costing Profit and Loss A/c * (Balancing Figure)	–	1,600
	200	1,600		200	1,600

Abnormal Gain Account

Dr.   Cr.

Particulars	Quantity Units	Amount ₹	Particulars	Quantity Units	Amount ₹
To Normal Loss (86 units × NIL)	86	–	By Process 'B' A/c	86	860
To Costing Profit and Loss A/c * (Balancing Figure)	–	860			
	86	860		86	860

Working Notes:

i) **Calculation of cost of Abnormal Loss in Process 'A' Account:**

          Dr.   –   Cr.   =   Balance

Quantity: 10,000 Units – 500 Units = 9,500 Units : Normal Output

Amount: ₹ 76,000 – NIL = ₹ 76,000 : Normal Cost

     If 9,500 Units = ₹ 76,000

∴   200 Units = ?

$$= \frac{200 \text{ units} \times ₹76,000}{9,500 \text{ units}}$$

= ₹ 1,600

ii) **Calculation of cost of Abnormal Gain in Process 'B' Account:**

          Dr.   –   Cr.   =   Balance

Quantity: 9,300 Units – 186 Units = 9,114 Units : Normal Output

Amount: ₹ 91,140 – NIL = ₹ 91,140 : Normal Cost

     If 9,114 Units = ₹ 91,140

∴   86 Units = ?

$$= \frac{86 \text{ units} \times ₹91,140}{9,114 \text{ units}}$$

= ₹ 860

In the books of Koton Queen Ltd., Kalyan
Statement showing Profit or Loss for the month ended 30th April, 2015

Particulars	Amount ₹	Amount ₹
Sale of Finished product (8,000 Units × ₹ 15)		1,20,000
Less: (1) Production Cost of Finished Product (8,000 Units × ₹ 10)	80,000	
(2) Selling and Distribution Expenses (8,000 Units × ₹ 2)	16,000	
(3) Balance of Loss from Costing Profit and Loss A/c	740	
$\left(\begin{array}{c} \text{Abnormal Loss} - \text{Abnormal Gain} = \text{Balance of Loss} \\ ₹1,600 \quad\quad\quad ₹860 \quad\quad\quad ₹740 \end{array} \right)$ (+)		
∴ Net Profit	(–)	96,740
(Subject to Net Profit adjustment of Abnormal Loss Account and Abnormal Gain Account)		23,260

QUESTIONS FOR SELF-STUDY

I. Theory Questions:

i) What is 'Process Costing'? State the important features of 'Process Costing'.

ii) Define the term 'Process Costing'. Name the industries where Process Costing can be applied suitably.

iii) What is 'Normal Loss'? How do you treat normal process loss in process costing?

iv) What is 'Abnormal Loss'? Explain briefly how it should be treated in cost accounts.

v) What is 'Abnormal Gain'? How do you treat abnormal gain in process costing?

vi) What is 'Process Cost'? State the features of process costing.

vii) State the important differences between and the similarities in Job Costing and Process Costing.

viii) What is 'Abnormal Loss'? Explain the possible causes and accounting treatment of Abnormal Loss.

ix) "Job Costing is more accurate than Process Costing". Comment.

x) Write short notes on:
a) Process Costing, b) Features of Process Costing, c) Normal Loss, d) Abnormal Loss, e) Abnormal Gain, f) Accounting treatment of Abnormal Loss and Gain g) Joint Products, h) By-Products.

xi) Distinguish between:
a) Job Costing and Process Costing, b) Normal Loss and Abnormal Loss, c) Abnormal Loss and Abnormal Gain.

II. Practical Problems:

i) An article passed through three processes. From the figures shown the cost of each of the three processes during the month of January 2015. Prepare Process Account.

Particulars		Process I	Process II	Process III
Materials Used	₹	1,500	5,000	2,000
Labour	₹	8,000	20,000	6,000
Direct expenses	₹	2,600	7,200	2,500

The indirect expenses amounting to ₹ 1,500 may be apportioned on the basis of wages. The number of articles produced during the month are 240.

ii) A product passes through two distinct processes A and B and then to finished stock. The output of A passes direct to B and that of B to finished stock. From the following information you are required to prepare the process accounts.

Particulars		Process A	Process B
Materials Consumed	₹	12,000	6,000
Direct Labour	₹	14,000	8,000
Manufacturing Expenses	₹	4,000	4,000
Output	Units	9,400	8,300
Input in Process A	Units	10,000	–
Input in Process A	Value in ₹	10,000	–
Normal Wastage	(% of input)	5%	10%
Value of normal wastage	(per 100 units)	₹ 8	₹ 10

No opening or closing stock is held in process.

iii) A product passes through three processes X, Y and Z before its completion. From past experience it is realised that wastage is incurred in each process as under :

X – 2%, Y – 5% and Z – 10% of the units introduced in the process.

Scrap value : X ₹ 10 for 100 units

Y ₹ 15 for 150 units

Z ₹ 40 for 100 units

Other details are :

Particulars		X	Y	Z
Materials	₹	6,000	3,000	1,500
Direct Wages	₹	9,000	6,000	4,500
Manufacturing Expenses	₹	1,500	1,500	2,200

30,000 units are issued to Process 'X' at a cost of ₹ 15,000. The output of Process 'X' – 29,200 units, 'Y' – 28,200 units and 'Z' – 24,000 units.

Show the Process Accounts.

iv) A product passes through three processes to completion in January 2015, the cost of production were given as below :

Particulars		Process I	Process II	Process III
Direct Materials	₹	2,000	3,020	2,462
Wages	₹	3,500	4,226	5,000
Production Overheads	₹	1,500	2,000	2,500

1000 units were issued to Process I at ₹ 5 each

Particulars		I	II	III
Normal Loss	%	10%	5%	10%
Wastages Realised	per unit	₹ 3	₹ 5	₹ 6
Actual production	units	920	870	800

Prepare the necessary process accounts.

v) The product 'X' is obtained after it is produced through three distinct processes. The following cost information is available for the operation :

Particulars		Total	Process I	Process II	Process III
Materials	₹	5,625	2,600	2,000	1,025
Direct Wages	₹	7,330	3,500	4,226	5,000
Production Overheads	₹	7,330	–	–	–

500 units at ₹ 4 per unit were introduced in Process I. Production overheads are absorbed at 100% of direct wages. The actual output and normal loss of the respective processes are :

Particulars	Output Units	Normal Loss on Input %	Value of Scrap per unit ₹
Process I	450	10%	2
Process II	340	20%	4
Process III	270	25%	5

There is no stock of work-in-progress in any process.

Show the three process accounts and abnormal loss and abnormal gain account.

vi) In a manufacturing concern the output of 'A' Process is transferred to 'B' Process. It has been the experience that normal wastage in Process A is 5% and in case of B 10% of the units entering the process. The scrap value of normal wastage ₹ 50 per hundred units in Process A and ₹ 80 per hundred units in Process B.

Particulars	Process A	Process B
Materials	10,000	6,000
Wages	8,000	4,000
Manufacturing Expenses	2,000	2,000

In Process A and thousand units were entered at a cost of ₹ 5,000. The output of Process A is 900 units and Process B 750 units.

Prepare Process 'A' Account and Process 'B' Account.

4.3 SERVICE COSTING

4.3.1 Meaning

Service Costing is a method of costing to ascertain the cost of providing or operating a service. The cost of providing a service is termed as "Operating Cost". Operating Costing which is also known as **"Service Costing"** is defined by **I.C.M.A.**, as, *"that form of operation which applies where standardised services are provided either by an undertaking or by a service cost centre within an undertaking"*. This method may be used where service is not completely standardised but where it is convenient to regard it as such, and to calculate average cost per period in relation to the standardised list of measurement. Thus, it is the cost of producing and maintaining a service.

Operating Costing should not be confused with Operation Costing. Operating Costing is applied to determine the cost of providing a service whereas Operation Costing is a refinement and more detailed application of Process Costing.

A manufacturing process may sometimes be sub-divided into a number of parts, each of which is known as an Operation. Operating Costing is the determination of the cost of each operation (which is a part of a process).

4.3.2 Features

The important features of **Service Costing** are as follows :
i) A uniform service is rendered to the customers.
ii) Many processes and stages are involved in converting the basic materials and facilities to the ultimate service rendered. These processes and operations are standardised repetitive and continuous.
iii) Usually large plants are involved and the concerns are either large monopolistic units or public utility undertakings.
iv) The distinction between direct and indirect cost is largely unnecessary. The costs and expenses are traced to the individual plants or facilities which render the services. The cost of plant, transport vehicles and facilities is distributed to the volume of services rendered on a pro-rata basis.

v) The distinction between fixed cost and variable cost is extremely important as the economies of state of operations considerably affect the unit cost of the services.
vi) Optimum efficiency is considered by factors related to usage and idle capacity cost. This initially affects the pricing system of such services.
vii) Costs are usually computed periodwise. However, under special circumstances costs are computed orderwise in the case of utilisation of vehicles, use of road-roller etc.
viii) No difficulty arised in respect of valuation of work-in-progress or closing stock as compared to other industries.
ix) This method requires a more detailed, but simpler statistical data for proper costing.
x) Selection of cost unit is difficult in Operating Costing.

Objectives :

The important **objectives of Operating Costing** are as follows :
i) To calculate the cost of uniform service rendered to the customers.
ii) To ascertain cost of all services produced within an undertaking viz. internal and external services.
iii) To keep the operating cost at the optimum level.
iv) To make a comparative analysis of operating cost incurred for different periods.
v) To make proper evaluation of different alternatives available.
vi) To determine whether to produce a service or buy it from outside.
vii) To ascertain whether the cost incurred on maintenance is excessively incurred or not.

4.3.3 Application

Service Costing is applied to those organisations which render service externally (i.e. to public at large) or internally (i.e. to various departments of the same organisation). Some examples of services rendered to outsiders are electricity supply, water supply, gas supply, lodging and boarding and so on. While services such as repairs and maintenance, purchasing and storage, internal transport etc. constitute services rendered internally. There is a point of difference in respect of accounting of services rendered. Whereas the objective of accounting external service is to know the total cost of manufacturing and profit on provision of such service, the object of internal service is to facilitate apportionment of service department cost to various other departments.

Service Costing is applied to the following undertakings :
i) Transport undertakings such as Roadways, Railways, Tramways and Airways.
ii) Municipal services such as supply of water, street light etc.
iii) Steam and Electricity Undertakings.
iv) Hotels covering lodging and boarding.
v) Hospitals.
vi) Educational Institutions.
vii) Public Libraries.
viii) Service departments in big factories.
ix) Cinemas.
x) Distribution of gas, air compressor, air conditioning.
xi) Sports and Recreational clubs.
xii) Services such as supply cranes, road-roller, water pumping, fire extinguishers etc.

4.3.4 Cost Unit : Simple and Composite

A basic problem in Service Costing is the adoption of the suitable cost units. A cost unit should be one which is related to the service rendered. Selection of cost unit depends upon the nature of business. Each undertaking is free to determine the cost unit most appropriate for its own purpose. However, a common cost unit by similar undertakings facilitates valuable cost comparisons. Selection of suitable cost unit depends on :
i) Management's need and requirement.
ii) Efforts involved in ascertainment of costs.
iii) Practice followed by other similar concerns.
iv) Practical use of the data for effective cost control.

Generally, the following are the two types of cost units :

i) **Simple Cost Unit :**

These are the units of measurements of cost that measure a single characteristics, the examples of which are as follows :

Undertaking	Cost Unit
• Transport	• Per km or Per passenger or Per tonne
• School or College	• Per student
• Hospital	• PER Bed
• Canteen	• Cup of tea sold/Meals served
• Electricity undertakings	• KWH
• Water supply	• A Gallon
• Gas supply	• Cubic Metre of Gas
• Boiler Home	• Quantity of Steam raised (kg.)
• Cinemas	• A seat per show

ii) **Composite Cost Unit :**

These are the units of measurement of cost that measure two characteristics simultaneously, the examples of which are as follows :

Undertaking	Cost Unit
• Transport	• Per passenger km. or Per tonne
• Hospital	• Per bed per day
• Cinemas	• Per seat per show
• Electricity	• Per killowatt hour
• Canteen	• Per meal/Per cup of tea sold

Compilation of Costs :

In Operating Costing, costs are classified and compiled as follows :

i) **Fixed Costs (Standing charges) :**

These are constant costs and are incurred irrespective of the extent of service rendered. These include Garage Rent, Insurance, Road licence, Depreciation, Interest on capital, General supervision, Vehicle tax, Salary of Operating Manager, Establishment expenses of the work-shop and office, Wages of drivers and cleaners (if it is fixed on period basis) etc.

ii) **Maintenance Costs :**

These are semi-variable in nature and include spare parts, repairs and maintenance, tyres and tubes, overheads, paintings etc.

iii) **Operating and Running Costs :**

These are variable in nature and include cost of petrol and diesel, lubricating oil, grease, wages of drivers, conductors and cleaners (if payment is according to distance or trips), transit insurance, allowances to staff etc.

Determination of the cost per unit of service :

To ascertain cost per unit of service, it is necessary to divide total cost by the number of units of service.

4.3.5 Preparation of Cost Sheet for Transport Service

In Transport undertaking, costing consists of the determination of the operating cost of each vehicle and the application of the cost, thus, determined to find out the cost per unit of service rendered by a vehicle. Transport includes Air, Water, Road, Railways and Motors. Motor transport includes private cars and carriers for owners, buses, taxies, carrier's lorries, etc.

Purposes :

Determination of Operating Costs for each vehicle serves the following important purposes :
i)   Determining the price at which a vehicle should be hired out.
ii) Cost of running own vehicles may be compared with hired or other forms of transport.
iii) Comparison between owned transport and hired transport to decide whether it is economical to go in for a hired one.
iv) Determining the basis for charging departments using the service.
v)   Control of operating and running costs and avoidance of waste of fuel and other consumable material.
vi) Suitable information is obtained for efficient routing of vehicles.
vii) Cost of idle vehicles and lost running time are easily obtained.
viii) The operational efficiency of transport services can be judged by utilisation ratio.
ix) Determining the basis for quotations and fixing of rates.
x)   Comparison between the cost of maintaining of one group of vehicles with another group.
xi) For deciding at what price the use of vehicle can be charged.

Classification of Costs under Transport Costing :

The operating costs of a transport undertaking composed of various items are classified under the following three categories :

i) **Standing Charges :**
   Standing charges represent expenses which have to be incurred whether the vehicle operates or not. The vehicle may be idle, but even then its expenses have to be met. These are more or less fixed in nature in a transport company. The typical items of standing charges are : Road licence fees, insurance premium, interest on capital, garage rent, depreciation, general supervision, vehicle tax, salary of operating manager, establishment costs of workshop and head office, wages of drivers, conductors and cleaners etc.

ii) **Maintenance Charges :**
    These expenses are incurred on the repairs and maintenance of vehicles as to keep them in proper condition. They are semi-variable in nature and include the cost of tyres and tubes, repairs and maintenance, spares and accessories, overheads, painting etc.

iii) **Operating and Running Charges :**
     These are just the opposite of standing charges. These expenses are incurred on the actual running of vehicles. These vary from day-to-day and come to zero when the vehicles are off the road. These are variable in nature and include the cost of petrol and diesel, lubricating oil, grease, wages of drivers, conductors and attendants etc. (if payment is related to distance run or trips made or when drivers and cleaners are specially deployed to man specific vehicles, operating and running costs may be easily allocated to each vehicle).

Collection of Cost :

Cost accumulation procedure in operating costing is the same as in Job Order Costing. Each vehicle is given a distinct number and all the basic documents bear the assigned numbers. For cost ascertainment and cost control a separate Log Book is maintained for each vehicle. The Log Book gives performance statistics of each vehicle the details shown in the log book enable the management to make suitable allocation of vehicles, to avoid unnecessary or duplicate trips and to avoid waste or idle running capacity. It is usually divided into three parts. The first part gives the full description of the vehicle, for e.g., the name, its registration number, date of purchase, cost capacity, insurance policy number, amount of premium, taxes paid, estimated life and scrap value. These details facilitate – collection of fixed charges in respect of the vehicle.

The second part contains details relating to names and address of the driver, conductor, cleaner and mechanic, their salaries and wages, repairs and maintenance charges, garage rent, renewals of tyres, batteries etc. these details facilitates collection of maintenance charges.

The third part of the Log Book contains - particulars of operating expense such as the number of trips made, number of kilometers run, petrol, oil, the ratio of kilometers run per litre of petrol, hours lost due to the vehicle remaining idle, exceptional delays such as loading delays, traffic delays and accidents. Thus, this part gives the essential information for the computation and control of the operating costs.

The daily log sheet contains the same particulars as those in the third part of the log book. It is handed over to the transport manager. A specimen of Daily Log Sheet is given as under.

Daily Log Sheet

Vehicle No. ....
Route No. ....
Name and No. of Driver :
Registration/Licence No. :

Date :
Time of leaving the garage :
Time of returning :
TRIP PARTICULARS

Trip No.	From	To	Tonnes or Packages Collected Out in route	Kilometres	Time Out In	Remarks

Supplies	Worker's Time	Exceptional Delays
Petrol	Driver	Loading and Unloading
Oil	Conductor	Traffic delays
Grease etc.	Cleaner	Accidents
	Mechanic	Others

Daily Log Sheet

Operating Cost Sheet :

It is said that, "a well-designed cost sheet is the heart of transport costing". For collecting and controlling costs, costs are classified and accumulated under the three heads stated as above, suitably analysed and presented periodically in the form of an operating cost sheet. A specimen of Operating Cost Sheet is given as follows.

	Roadways Transport Co., Ltd.		
	Operating Cost Sheet		
Vehicle No.	No. of Trips :	Period :	
Registration No.	Kms. run :	Capacity :	
Route No.	Total weight carried :	No. of Cost units.	
Cost :	Total hours operated :		
Estimated Life :			

	Particulars		Total	Per Unit
A)	**Fixed Costs :**			
	Garage Rent			
	Licences and Taxes			
	Insurance			
	Interest on Capital			
	Supervision Charges			
	Establishment and General Charges	(+)		
	Sub-Total (A)		....	....
B)	**Maintenance Costs :**			
	Tyres and Tubes			
	Repairs and Maintenance			
	Spare Parts and Accessories			
	Overhauling			
	Painting	(+)		
	Sub-Total (B)		....	....
C)	**Operating and Running Costs :**			
	Depreciation			
	Petrol and Diesel			
	Oil and Grease			
	Transit Insurance			
	Wages of Drivers, Cleaners and Conductors	(+)		
	Sub-Total (C)	(+)	....	....
	Grand Total (A + B + C)		....	....
D)	Ton Km/Passenger Km. run			
E)	Cost per ton Km/passenger Km.			

Operating Cost Sheet

ILLUSTRATIONS

ILLUSTRATION 1

From the following data relating to the vehicle, of Ghatge Patil Transport Co., Kolhapur calculate the cost per running kilometre.

	₹
Cost of Vehicle	1,00,000
Road Licence Fees (annual)	5,100
Garage Rent (annual)	4,800
Insurance Charges (annual)	2,100
Supervision and Salary (annual)	12,000
Drivers Wages per hour	2.00
Cost of Diesel per litre	4.00
Repairs and Maintenance per km	2.20
Tyres and Batteries per km	1.80
Kilometres run per litre 20 km	
Kilometres run annually 20,000 km	
Estimated Life of the vehicle 1,00,000 km.	

You are required to charge Interest on Cost of vehicle @ 10% p.a., the vehicle runs 20 km per hour on an average :

SOLUTION

In the books of Ghatge Patil Transport Co., Kolhapur
Statement showing Cost per km.

(Cost unit – per km)

Particulars		Per Year ₹	Per km ₹
A) Standing Charges : (Fixed Charges)			1.70
i) Road Licence Fees		5,100	
ii) Insurance Charges		2,100	
iii) Supervision and Salary		12,000	
iv) Interest on Cost of Vehicle		10,000	
v) Garage Rent	(+)	4,800	
∴ Total Standing Charges		34,000	
B) Maintenance Charges : (Semi-Variable charges)			
i) Repairs and Maintenance			2.20
ii) Tyres and Batteries			1.80
C) Running Charges : (Variable charges)			
i) Depreciation			1.00
ii) Drivers Wages			0.10
iii) Cost of Diesel	(+)		0.20
∴ Cost per km			7.00

Working Notes :

i) Depreciation : $= \dfrac{\text{Cost of Vehicle}}{\text{Estimated Life}} = \dfrac{₹\,1,00,000}{\text{Km. }1,00,000} = ₹\,1$

ii) Drivers Wages : $= \dfrac{₹\,2}{20\text{ km}} = 10\text{ Ps.}$

Basics of Cost Accounting 4.83 Methods of Costing

iii) Cost of Diesel : $= \dfrac{₹\,4}{km\,20} = 20\,Ps.$

iv) Interest on Cost of Vehicle : = 10% of ₹ 1,00,000
 = ₹ 10,000

v) Standing Charges : $= \dfrac{₹\,34,000}{km\,20,000} = ₹\,1.70$

ILLUSTRATION 2

From the following data, calculate the cost per running mile of Road Lines Transport Co., Raipur.

Particulars	Vehicle I	Vehicle II
Mileage run (annual)	15,000	6,000
Cost of Vehicle	₹ 2,50,000	₹ 1,50,000
Road Licence (annual)	₹ 7,500	₹ 7,500
Annual Insurance	₹ 7,000	₹ 4,000
Annual Garage Rent	₹ 7,250	₹ 5,420
Supervision and Salaries (annual)	₹ 24,000	₹ 24,000
Driver's Wages per hour	₹ 30	₹ 30
Cost of fuel per litre	₹ 20	₹ 20
Miles run per litre	20 miles	15 miles
Repairs and Maintenance per mile	₹ 1.65	₹ 2
Tyre Allocation per mile	₹ 0.80	₹ 0.60
Estimated Life of vehicles	1,00,000 miles	75,000 miles

Charge interest @ 15% p.a. on the cost of vehicles. The vehicle run 20 miles per hour on an average.

SOLUTION

In the books of Road Lines Transport Co., Raipur
Statement showing Cost per mile (Cost unit – per mile)

Particulars	Vehicle – I		Vehicle – II	
	Per Year ₹	Per Mile ₹	Per Year ₹	Per Mile ₹
A) Standing Charges : (Fixed Charges)		5.55		10.57
i) Road licence	7,500		7,500	
ii) Insurance	7,000		4,000	
iii) Supervision and Salaries	24,000		24,000	
iv) Interest on Cost of Vehicles	37,500		22,500	
v) Garage Rent (+)	7,250	(+)	5,420	
∴ Total Standing Charges	83,250		63,420	
B) Maintenance Charges (Semi-variable charges)				
i) Repairs and Maintenance		1.65		2.00
ii) Tyre Allocation		0.80		0.60
C) Running Charges : (Variable Charges)				
i) Depreciation		2.50		2.00
ii) Drivers wages		1.50		1.50
iii) Cost of fuel (+)		1.00	(+)	1.33
∴ **Cost per mile**		**13.00**		**18.00**

Working Notes:

		I	II
i)	Depreciation:	$= \dfrac{₹\,2,50,000}{M\,1,00,000}$	$= \dfrac{₹\,1,50,000}{M\,75,000}$
		= ₹ 2.50	= ₹ 2
ii)	Driver's Wages:	I	II
		$= \dfrac{₹\,30}{M\,20}$	$= \dfrac{₹\,30}{M\,20}$
		= ₹ 1.50	= ₹ 1.50
iii)	Cost of Fuel:	I	II
		$= \dfrac{₹\,20}{M\,20}$	$= \dfrac{₹\,20}{M\,15}$
		= ₹ 1	= ₹ 1.33

iv) Interest on Cost of vehicle:
   I – 15% – ₹ 2,50,000 = ₹ 37,500
   II – 15% – ₹ 1,50,000 = ₹ 22,500

v) Standing Charges:

	I.	II.
	$= \dfrac{₹\,83,250}{M\,15,000}$	$= \dfrac{₹\,63,420}{M\,6,000}$
	= ₹ 5.55	= ₹ 10.57

ILLUSTRATION 3

From the following information relating to Royal Transport Co., Raigad, calculate the cost per running km.

Wages to Drivers per month	₹		500
Cost of Diesel per litre	₹		1.50
Cost of Motor Oil per litre	₹		10.00
Annual Cleaning and Servicing	₹		2,460
Insurance Charges per year	₹		4,000
Yearly Road Tax	₹		6,400
Repairs and Maintenance for twelve months	₹		1,200
Cost of Tyre, Tubes etc. per year	₹		1,800
Diesel km. per litre	km.		4
Motor km. per litre	km.		50
Cost of Vehicle	₹		1,30,000
Estimate Life			5 years
Residual Value of Vehicle	₹		30,000
Interest on Cost of Vehicle			7% p.a.
Estimated annual run	km.		36,000

SOLUTION

Working Notes:

i) Driver's Wages:

$$= \dfrac{₹\,500 \times 12\ \text{months}}{\text{km. }36,000} = ₹\,0.17$$

ii) Cost of Diesel:

$$= \dfrac{₹\,1.50}{\text{km. }4} = ₹\,0.38$$

iii) **Cost of Motor Oil :**

$$= \frac{₹10}{km.\ 50} = ₹0.20$$

iv) **Repairs and Maintenance :**

$$= \frac{₹1,200}{km.\ 36,000} = ₹0.03$$

v) **Cost of Tyre, Tubes etc. :**

$$= \frac{₹1,800}{km.\ 36,000} = ₹0.05$$

vi) **Interest on Cost of Vehicle :**

$$= 7\% \text{ of } ₹1,30,000 = ₹9,100$$

vii) **Depreciation :**

$$= \frac{\text{Cost of Vehicle} - \text{Residual value of Vehicle}}{\text{Estimated life of Vehicle}}$$

$$= \frac{₹1,30,000 - ₹30,000}{5 \text{ years}} = ₹20,000$$

$$= \frac{₹20,000}{km.\ 36,000}$$

$$= ₹0.56$$

viii) **Standing Charges :**

$$= \frac{₹21,960}{km.\ 36,000} = ₹0.61$$

In the books of Royal Transport Co., Raigad
Statement Showing Cost per running Km.

	Particulars		Per Year ₹	Per Km ₹
A)	**Standing Charges :** (Fixed Charges)			0.61
	i) Cleaning and Servicing		2,460	
	ii) Insurance Charges		4,000	
	iii) Road Tax		6,400	
	iv) Interest on Cost of Vehicle	(+)	9,100	
	∴ Total Standing Charges		21,960	
B)	**Maintenance Charges :** (Semi-Variable Charges)			
	i) Repairs and Maintenance			0.03
	ii) Cost of Tyre, Tubes etc.			0.05
C)	**Running Charges :** (Variable Charges)			
	i) Drivers Wages			0.17
	ii) Cost of Diesel			0.38
	iii) Cost of Motor Oil			0.20
	iv) Depreciation		(+)	0.56
	∴ **Cost per km**			**2.00**

ILLUSTRATION 4

Varun Transport Co., Pune, owns a fleet of taxis and the following information is available from their records.

Number of Taxis	10
Cost of each Taxi	₹ 20,000

Monthly Salary to the Staff –

    i) Manager – ₹ 3,000

    ii) Accountant – ₹ 2,500

    iii) Cleaner – ₹ 2,000

    iv) Mechanic – ₹ 1,500

Garage Rent per month	₹ 1,000
Monthly Insurance Premium	₹ 84
Yearly Taxes	₹ 600 per taxi
Monthly Salary to Driver per taxi	₹ 200
Annual Repairs per taxi	₹ 1,000

Total life of a taxi is about 2,00,000 km. A taxi runs in all 3,000 km. in a month, of which 30% it runs empty. Petrol consumption is one litre for 10 km. @ ₹ 21.80 per litre. Oil and other sundries are ₹ 5 per 100 km.

Calculate the cost of running a taxi per km.

SOLUTION

Working Notes :

i) Calculation of effective kms run per month :

The taxi runs 30% empty which means its effective run is only 70% and hence, all costs must be calculated taking into consideration its effective run i.e. 70% of 3,000 km i.e. 2,100 km.

	Kms.
Monthly running of a taxi-km	3,000
Less : 30% empty i.e. 30% of 3,000 km	(–) 900
∴ Actual monthly run-km	2,100

ii) Depreciation :

$$= \frac{\text{Cost of Taxi}}{\text{Estimated Life of a Taxi}}$$

$$= \frac{₹ 20,000}{\text{km. } 2,00,000} = \text{Re. } 0.10$$

$$= \frac{₹ 0.10 \times 3,000 \text{ km}}{2,100 \text{ km.}}$$

$$= \text{Re. } 0.14$$

iii) Salary of Manager :

$$= \frac{₹ 3,000}{10 \text{ Taxis}}$$

$$= ₹ 300$$

In the books of Varun Transport Co., Pune
Statement showing Cost of running a taxi per km.
(Cost Unit – per Km.)

Particulars	Per Month ₹	Per Km. ₹
A) Standing Charges : (Fixed Charges)		0.54
i) Manager's Salary	300	
ii) Accountant's Salary	250	
iii) Cleaner's Salary	200	
iv) Mechanic's Salary	150	
v) Insurance Premium	84	
vi) Taxes	50	
vii) Garage Rent	100	
∴ Total Standing Charges	1134	
B) Maintenance Charges : (Semi-Variable Charges)		
i) Repairs		0.04
C) Running Charges : (Variable Charges)		
i) Depreciation		0.14
ii) Driver's Salary		0.10
iii) Petrol Consumption		3.11
iv) Oil and Other Sundries	(+)	0.07
∴ Cost per km		4.00

iv) **Salary of Accountant :**
$$= \frac{₹2,500}{10 \text{ Taxies}}$$
= ₹ 250

v) **Salary of Cleaner :**
$$= \frac{₹2,000}{10 \text{ Taxis}}$$
= ₹ 200

vi) **Salary of Mechanic :**
$$= \frac{₹1,500}{10 \text{ Taxis}}$$
= ₹ 150

vii) **Garage Rent :**
$$= \frac{₹1,000}{10 \text{ Taxis}}$$
= ₹ 100

viii) **Taxes :**
$$= \frac{₹600}{12 \text{ Months}}$$
= ₹ 50

ix) **Driver's Salary :**
$$= \frac{₹200}{2,100 \text{ km.}}$$
= ₹ 0.10

x) **Repairs :**

$$= \frac{₹1,000}{12 \text{ Months}}$$

$$= ₹83.33$$

$$= \frac{₹83.33}{2,100 \text{ km.}}$$

$$= ₹0.04$$

xi) **Petrol Consumption :**

$$= \frac{₹21.80}{10 \text{ km.}}$$

$$= ₹2.18$$

$$= \frac{₹2.18 \times 3,000 \text{ km}}{2,100 \text{ km.}}$$

$$= ₹3.11$$

xii) **Oil and Other Sundries :**

$$= \frac{₹5}{100 \text{ km.}}$$

$$= ₹0.05$$

$$= \frac{₹0.05 \times 3,000 \text{ km}}{2,100 \text{ km.}}$$

$$= ₹0.07$$

xiii) **Standing Charges :**

$$= \frac{₹1,134}{2,100 \text{ km}}$$

$$= ₹0.54$$

ILLUSTRATION 5

From the following data relating to two passengers vehicles named Ganga and Yamuna, of Saibaba Transport Co., Sangli, you are required to calculate the cost per running km.

Particulars	Ganga ₹	Yamuna ₹
Cost of Vehicle	1,00,000	60,000
Annual Road Licence	3,000	3,000
Insurance Per Annum	2,800	1,600
Yearly Garage Rent	2,400	2,000
Supervision and Salaries for twelve months	5,200	2,325
Driver's Wages per running hour	6	6
Cost of Petrol per litre	3.50	3.50
Repairs and Maintenance per km.	3.30	3.30
Cost of Tyre and Tubes per km.	3.59	4.10
	kms.	kms.
Estimate Life	1,60,000	1,20,000
km. per litre of petrol	10	12
Annual km. run	24,000	9,000

Charge interest @ 10% p.a. on cost of vehicles and vehicle runs 40 km. per hour on an average.

Basics of Cost Accounting — 4.89 — Methods of Costing

SOLUTION

Working Notes:

	Ganga	Yamuna
i) Depreciation: $= \dfrac{\text{Cost of Vehicle}}{\text{Estimated Life of Vehicle}}$	$= \dfrac{₹1,00,000}{\text{km. }1,60,000}$ = ₹0.63	$= \dfrac{₹60,000}{\text{km. }1,20,000}$ = ₹0.50
ii) Driver's Wages:	$= \dfrac{₹6}{40 \text{ km.}}$ = ₹0.15	$= \dfrac{₹6}{40 \text{ km.}}$ = ₹0.15
iii) Cost of Petrol:	$= \dfrac{₹3.50}{\text{km. }10}$ = ₹0.35	$= \dfrac{₹3.50}{\text{km. }12}$ = ₹0.29
iv) Interest on Cost of Vehicle:	= 10% of ₹1,00,000 = ₹10,000	= 10% of ₹60,000 = ₹6,000
v) Standing Charges:	$= \dfrac{₹23,400}{\text{km. }24,000}$ = ₹0.98	$= \dfrac{₹14,925}{\text{km. }9,000}$ = ₹1.66

In the books of Saibaba Transport Co., Sangli
Statement showing Cost per running km.

(Cost unit – per km)

Particulars	Ganga Per Year ₹	Ganga Per km. ₹	Yamuna Per Year ₹	Yamuna Per km. ₹
A) Standing Charges: (Fixed Charges)		0.98		1.66
i) Road Licence	3,000		3,000	
ii) Insurance	2,800		1,600	
iii) Supervision and Salaries	5,200		2,325	
iv) Interest on Cost of Vehicle	10,000		6,000	
v) Garage Rent (+)	2,400	(+)	2,000	
∴ Total Standing Charges	23,400		14,925	
B) Maintenance Charges: (Semi-Variable Charges)				
i) Repairs and Maintenance		3.30		3.30
ii) Cost of Tyre and Tubes		3.59		4.10
C) Running Charges: (Variable Charges)				
i) Depreciation		0.63		0.50
ii) Driver's Wages		0.15		0.15
iii) Cost of Petrol (+)		0.35	(+)	0.29
∴ Cost per km		9.00		10.00

ILLUSTRATION 6

Prasanna Transport Co., Pimpri, supplies you the following information in respect of a truck of 5 tonne capacity.

	₹
Cost of Truck	90,000
Estimated Life 10 years	
Diesel, Oil etc. per trip per day	15
Monthly Repairs and Maintenance	500
Drivers Wages per month	500
Cleaners Wages per month	250
Yearly Insurance	4,800
Annual Tax	2,400
General Supervision Charges p.a.	4,800

The truck carries goods to and from city covering a distance to the extent of 50 km. each way. On outward trip, freight is available to the extent of full capacity and on return trip 20% of capacity. Assuming that the truck runs on an average 25 days in a month workout:
(i) Operating Cost per ton km. and
(ii) The rate per ton trip that the company should charge if a profit of 50% on freight is to be earned.

SOLUTION

Working Notes:

i) **Calculation of ton km. per month:**
   = (km. for outward trip × capacity) + (km for return trip × capacity) × Number of working days
   = (50 km. × 5 ton i.e. full capacity) + (50 km. × 1 ton i.e. 20% capacity) × 25 days
   = (250 km. + 50 km.) × 25 days
   = 300 km. × 25 days
   = 7,500 ton km.

ii) **Depreciation:**
   = $\dfrac{\text{Cost of Truck}}{\text{Estimated Life of Truck}}$
   = $\dfrac{₹90,000}{10 \text{ years}}$
   = $\dfrac{₹9,000}{12 \text{ Months}}$
   = $\dfrac{₹750}{7,500 \text{ ton km}}$
   = ₹0.10

iii) **Diesel, Oil etc.:**
   ₹15 × 2 Trips
   = ₹30 per day × 25 days
   = ₹750
   = $\dfrac{₹750}{7,500 \text{ ton km.}}$
   = ₹0.10

iv) **Repairs and Maintenance:**
   = $\dfrac{₹500}{7,500 \text{ ton km.}}$
   = ₹0.07

v) **Driver's Wages:**
   = $\dfrac{₹500}{7,500 \text{ ton km.}}$
   = ₹0.07

vi) Cleaner's Wages :
$$= \frac{₹\ 250}{7,500\ ton\ km.}$$
$$= ₹\ 0.03$$

vii) Insurance :
$$= \frac{₹\ 4,800}{12\ Months}$$
$$= ₹\ 400$$

viii) Tax :
$$= \frac{₹\ 2,400}{12\ Months}$$
$$= ₹\ 200$$

ix) General Supervision Charges :
$$= \frac{₹\ 4,800}{12\ Months}$$
$$= ₹\ 400$$

x) Standing Charges :
$$= \frac{₹\ 1,000}{7,500\ ton\ km.}$$
$$= ₹\ 0.13$$

xi) Calculation of profits per ton km. @ 50% of Freight :

Freight = Operating Cost + Profit
100 = 50 + 50
If 50 O.C. = 50 Profit
∴ Re. 0.50 O.C. = ?
$$= \frac{0.50 \times 50}{50}$$
$$= ₹\ 0.50$$

In the books of Prasanna Transport Co., Pimpri
Statement showing Operating Cost and Freight per ton km.

(Cost unit – per ton km.)

Particulars		Per Month ₹	Per ton km. ₹
A) Standing Charges : (Fixed Charges)			0.13
i) Insurance		400	
ii) Tax		200	
iii) General Supervision Charges (+)		400	
∴ Total Standing Charges		1,000	
B) Maintenance Charges : (Semi-Variable Charges)			
i) Repairs and Maintenance			0.07
C) Running Charges : (Variable Charges)			
i) Diesel, Oil etc.			0.10
ii) Driver's Wages			0.07
iii) Cleaners Wages			0.03
iv) Depreciation		(+)	0.10
Operating Cost per ton km.	(1)		0.50
Add : Profits			
(50% of Freight per ton km.)	(2)	(+)	0.50
Freight per ton km.	(3)		**1.00**

QUESTIONS FOR SELF STUDY

I. Theory Questions :
i) Define 'Service Costing'. Give the name of industries where it can be applied.
ii) What is Service Costing ? Explain the features of Service Costing.
iii) What is Costing ? How costs are compiled in Transport Costing ?
iv) What is Costing ? What purposes are served in determination of the operating costs for each vehicle ?
v) What is Service Costing ? Prepare a proforma of operating cost sheet in Transport costing.
vi) Write short notes on :
a) Transport costing, b) Features of Service costing, c) Cost unit
vii) Distinguish between :
(a) Job Costing and Contract Costing, (b) Work Certified and Work Uncertified, (c) Escalation Clause and De-escalation Clause, (d) Job Costing and Process Costing, (e) Normal Loss and Abnormal Loss. (f) Abnormal Loss and Abnormal Gain.

II. Practical Problems

i). The following is the cost information from the books of Adarsh Transport Co., Ambegaon.

No. of taxies	10
Cost of each taxi	₹ 20,000
Salary of Manager	₹ 600 p.m.
Salary of Accountant	₹ 500 p.m.
Salary of Cleaner	₹ 200 p.m.
Salary of Mechanic	₹ 400 p.m.
Garage Rent	₹ 600 p.m.
Insurance Premium	5% p.a.
Annual Tax	₹ 600 Per taxi
Driver's Salary	₹ 200 Per taxi
Annual Repairs	₹ 1,000 Per taxi

Total life of taxi is 2,00,000 kms. A taxi runs in all 3,000 kms. in a month of which 30% it runs empty. Petrol consumption is one litre for 10 kms. @ ₹ 4.80 per litre. Oil and other sundries are ₹ 5 per 100 kms.

Calculate the cost of running a taxi per km.

ii) Bansilal Transport Co., Bandra, is running 4 buses between two towns which are 50 miles apart, seating capacity of each bus is 40 passengers. The following particulars were obtained from their books for the month of April, 2008.

Wages of drivers and conductors	₹ 2,400
Office and Staff Salaries	₹ 1,000
Diesel and other oils	₹ 4,000
Repairs and Maintenance	₹ 800
Taxes and Insurance	₹ 1,600
Depreciation	₹ 2,600
Interest	₹ 2,000

Actual passengers carried were 75% of the seating capacity. All the four buses run on all the days of the month. Each bus made one round trip per day. Find out the cost per passenger mile.

iii) From the following data, calculate the cost per mile of a vehicle of Charminar Transport Co., New Delhi.

	₹
Cost of vehicle	1,00,000
Garage Rent per year	4,800
Insurance charges per year	1,600
Road tax per year	2,000
Driver's wages per month	805
Cost of petrol per litre	5.60
Tyre maintenance per mile	0.80
Estimated life of vehicle	1,50,000 miles
Miles per litre of Petrol	5
Estimated annual mileage	10,000

iv) From the following data, you are required to ascertain the cost of running the lorry per tonne-mile of Durga Transport Co., Dombivili.

Total tonnage carried in a week 30 tonnes and total mileage carried in a week was 600 miles. Details of above are as follows :

Days	Miles	Tonnes
Monday	120	6
Tuesday	125	5
Wednesday	110	4
Thursday	100	5.5
Friday	80	4.5
Saturday	65	5.0
	600	30.00

The expenses for the week were as follows :

Driver's salary ₹ 200 per month,

Cleaner's salary ₹ 100 per month,

Petrol, Oil etc. 30 paise per mile,

Repairs and Maintenance ₹ 300 per month,

Depreciation ₹ 4,800 per annum,

Other expenses ₹ 200 per month.

(There are four weeks in a month).

v) M/s Eagle Transport Ltd., Edalabad, charges ₹ 60 per tonne for a 5 tonne lorry from Edalabad to Jalgaon. The charge for return trip is ₹ 56 per tonne.

In the month of July 2015, WBX 4889 made ten outward journey's with full load-out of which 3 tonnes were unloaded at Pachora twice in the month. It returned once without any load from Burdwan.

The details of expenses are as follows :

Annual fixed charges	₹ 19,000
Annual maintenance charges	₹ 9,600
Monthly operating charges	₹ 12.2
Additional data available are :	
Distance from Edalabad to Pachora	30 kms.
Distance from Pachora to Jalgaon	45 kms.

WBX 4889 carried a load of 8 tonnes, 5 times in the month while returning from Jalgaon but was once caught by the police and fined ₹ 1,000.

You are required to calculate the cost per ton km. and also the profit in the month of July 2015, assuming that no concession is made for delivery at the intermediate stages.

vi) Harekrishna owns a luxury bus which runs from Bengaluru to Chittor and back for 10 days in a month. The distance from Bangalore to Chittor is 200 kms. The bus completes the trip from Bangalore to Chittor and back on the same day. The bus goes another 10 days in a month towards Mysore. The distance from Bangalore to Mysore is 130 kms. The trip is also completed on the same day. For the rest 4 days its operation in a month it runs in the local city. The daily distance covered in the local city is 70 kms. Calculate the rate that Harekrishna should charge per passenger, when he wants to earn a profit of 25% of his takings. The other information is given below :

	₹
Cost of the bus	1,50,000
Depreciation rate	15% per annum
Salary of driver	500 per annum
Salary of conductor	500 per annum
Salary to part time accountant	250 per annum
Insurance	1,800 per annum
Diesel consumption 6 km per litre	1.50 per litre
Token tax	800 per annum
Lubricant oil	20 per 100 km.
Repairs and maintenance	1,000 per month
Permit fee	560 per month
Normal capacity	50 persons

The bus uses generally 90% of the capacity when it goes to Chittor and 80% when it goes to Mysore. It is always full when it runs within the city. The passenger it 25% of the next takings.

vii) Mr. Milkha Singh has started transport business with a fleet of 10 taxis. The various expenses incurred by him are given below :

			₹
a)	Cost of each taxi		75,000
b)	Salary of office staff		1,500 per month
c)	Salary of general staff		2,000 per month
d)	Rent of garage		1,000 per month
e)	Driver's salary (per taxi)		400 per month
f)	Road tax and Repairs (per taxi)		2,160 per annum
g)	Insurance premium		at 4% of cost p.a.

The life of a taxi is ₹ 3,00,000 km. and at the end of which it is estimated to be sold at ₹ 15,000. A taxi runs on an average 4,000 km. per month of which 20% it runs empty. Petrol consumption is 9 km. per litre of petrol costing ₹ 6.30 per litre. Oil and other sundry expenses amount to ₹ 10 per 100 km.

Calculate the effective cost of running a taxi per km. If the hire charge rate is ₹ 1.80 per kilometre, find out the profit Mr. Milkha Singh may expect to make in the first year of operation.

viii) From the following data, calculate the cost per mile of vehicle :

	₹
Value of vehicle	25,000
Garage rent per year	1,200
Insurance charges per year	400
Road tax per year	500
Driver's wages per month	400
Cost of petrol per litre	1.40
Tyre maintenance per mile	0.20
Estimated life :	1,50,000 miles
Miles per litre of Petrol:	5
Estimated annual mileage :	10,000

ix) Modern Transport Co., Mumbai, is running two buses between two places – 100 kms. apart. Seating Capacity of each bus is 50 passengers. The following particulars are taken from their books for a month of December, 2014.

	₹
Wages of drivers, conductors and cleaners	3,000
Salary of supervisory and office staff	1,500
Diesel, oil etc.	6,000
Repairs and maintenance	1,500
Taxation and insurance	2,000
Depreciation	3,000
Interest and other charges	2,500

Actual passengers travelled were 80% of the capacity. The buses ran on all the days. Each bus made a to and fro trip. Find out the cost per passenger kilometre.

x) Surya Transport Co., Sangli, owns a fleet of 10 trucks each costing ₹ 60,000. The company has employed one manager to whom it pays ₹ 450 p.m., an accountant who gets ₹ 250 p.m., and a peon who gets ₹ 100 p.m. The company has got it's trucks insured @ 2% per annum. The annual total tax is ₹ 1,200 per truck. The other expenses were as follows :

Driver's salary	₹ 200 per month
Cleaner's salary	₹ 80 per month
Mechanic's salary	₹ 300 per month
Repairs and maintenance	₹ 1,200 per year for one truck
Diesel consumption	3 kms. per litre at ₹ 0.90 per litre

The estimated life of the truck is 5 years.

Other information :

Distance travelled by each truck, per day 200 kms.

Normal loading capacity 100 quintals

Wastage in loading capacity 10%

Percentage of truck laid up for repair 5%

Effective days in a month 25

Calculate :

a) Cost per quintal km.

b) Cost per km. of running a truck.

Unit ... 5

COST AUDIT

5.1 Meaning, Definitions, Objectives and Scope of Cost Audit
    5.1.1 Meaning
    5.1.2 Definitions
    5.1.3 Objectives of Cost Audit
    5.1.4 Scope of Cost Audit
5.2 Advantages of Cost Audit
5.3 Difference between Financial Audit and Cost Audit
5.4 Types of Cost Audit
* Questions for Self-Study

5.1 MEANING, DEFINITIONS, OBJECTIVES AND SCOPE OF COST AUDIT

Cost Audit, in real terms is an audit of actual performance. As an audit implies audit of financial records, a cost audit means audit of cost records. A cost audit, therefore, includes verification of correctness of the cost accounts, cost statements, cost reports, cost data and costing techniques used and ultimately checking these data to see that they adhere to cost accounting principles, plans, procedures and objectives. Therefore, "Efficiency Audit" and "Propriety Audit" are the two important phases of Cost Audit.

5.1.1 Meaning

The concept of costing is stated to have originated from engineers. But putting the costing information in a formal set of records amounts to 'Cost Accounting'. Cost audit presupposes the existence of cost accounts. **Cost Accounting** is *a process of accounting by which relevant data are collected, classified, analysed and interpreted with a view to present current and/or prospective costs of selected centre for costing. A system of cost accounting embraces identification, ascertaining, allocation, apportionment and or assignment of cost data to respective centres.*

The policies of our Government are directed towards economic growth with social justice. In this context, it is always necessary to examine whether the operation of industrial ventures is contributing to the goal of the society and does not in any way harm the society. For this purpose, quantitative data should be generated and should be authenticated to verify the fact. A mere Balance-Sheet or Profit and Loss Account cannot provide any information regarding the operations of the industry with reference to its contribution to the social goal. **'Cost Audit'**, however, provides valuable information for assessment of the operations with reference to the needs of the society and their fulfillment.

5.1.2 Definitions

The term Cost Audit has been defined by different experts and professional institutes in the manner stated below.

i) **Smith and Day :**
"It means the detailed checking of costing system, technique and accounts to verify their correctness and to ensure adherence to the objectives of accounting".

ii) **The Institute of Cost and Works Accountants of India :**
"It is the verification of the correctness of cost accounts and adherence to the cost accounting principles, plans and procedures".

iii) **The Institute of Cost and Works Accountants of London :**
"The verification of the correctness of cost accounts and adherence to the cost accounting plans".

iv) **Montgomery :**
"It is an examination of the records and methods employed in determining the cost of goods manufactured and sold, with two fold purpose of verifying the accuracy of the costs obtained and criticising, the methods whereby they are developed".

Thus, Cost Audit is a systematic and accurate recording of detailed transactions and operations of manufacturing, constructing, extracting, transporting, supplying etc. so as to show the actual cost of each individual piece of work, service or separate process comprised in the operation of the business. In short, **Cost Audit** may be defined as a detailed checking of cost records and verifying the correctness and propriety of those recorded value and adherence to the principles of cost accountancy.

Reasons for Introducing 'Cost Audit' :

The various important reasons that may prompt to introduce cost audit besides the provisions of the Act may be summed up as follows :

i) An authentic cost data is available from the cost audit report reflecting increases in costs which can be compared with increases in prices to assess the extent, if any, to which society has been over-charged. This important aspect of cost audit has been commended by the high powered committee on simplification of company law - (known as Sachar Committee) in para 8.21 of its report stated that *"We are of the opinion that maintenance of Cost Accounting Record in certain types of industries and their Continuous Audit by an appropriate Cost Auditor will not be a step in the direction of consumer protection but will also be advantageous to the company itself"*.

ii) The cost audit may be introduced in case of industries of national importance like steel, cement, vanaspati, infant milk food etc. where prices become high due to high cost of production.

iii) In the area of both direct and indirect taxes, cost audit has got a useful role to play which is still to be appreciated. In respect of corporate taxation, the extent of profit declared by the company is very much influenced by the methods of inventory valuation. The cost auditor is expected to analyse the cost structure and its built-up and he certifies the inventory figures at cost price. Where the assessment of tax relates to a cost of product, an audit for cost of products may be called for by the Government.

iv) A substantial amount of the Government revenue goes out towards export subsidies on account of exporter losing money in export trade. A look at the cost audit report would show whether the export business is losing or gaining. Information about each product is available in this regard in cost audit reports whereas it would not be available from the audited financial statements.

v) The introduction of cost audit becomes essential in case of manufacturing units which run at a loss.

vi) The Government may pass an order for cost audit against those companies where frauds are suspected.

vii) The auditor has to offer his comments on the activities of the company which can include the comments on social benefits and social obligations also. Since there is no limitation regarding the area for comments, social aspects can be dealt with by the cost auditor.

viii) Where the manufacturing process used by the company is harmful to the society in any way, to judge this, useful information is available only from cost audit report dealing with the 'process of manufacture' which would not be available from any other audit reports.

ix) The unhealthy working conditions of some units or products are revealed from the study of inter-firm-comparison, may be probed through introduction of cost audit.

x) Before making payment for contracted job on cost plus profit basis, the correctness of cost may be verified through introduction of cost audit.

xi) The cost audit report contains the information about the employment situation as well as comments on incentive schemes, if any, for labour. This information enables one to verify the extent of employment in the company and the extent of industrial peace by comparing the man-days available with the man-days actually performed, alongwith the analysis of the man-days lost.

xii) It can be established that no other audit besides cost audit is so well designed to bring out the efficiency aspect of operations of a manufacturing unit.

xiii) The government may order for cost audit in cases of industries which seek tariff protection from the government. The government takes its decision whether to grant protection, on the basis of the report of cost structure of those companies.

xiv) The cost auditor is expected to comment on :
    a) The consumption of power and fuel in total as well as per unit of output;
    b) The budgetary control system and internal audit systems, if any prevailing in the organisation;
    c) Various matters like rectification of imbalances in production facilities, fuller utilisation of installed capacities, cost of production, increased productivity, limiting factors causing production bottle-necks and improved inventory policies, etc.

Thus cost audit has all the potential both efficiency and social audit. It is upto industry and the Government to introduce this potential.

5.1.3 Objectives of Cost Audit

The **Objectives of Cost Audit** are two-fold and are indicated as stated below in Figure 5.1 as follows :

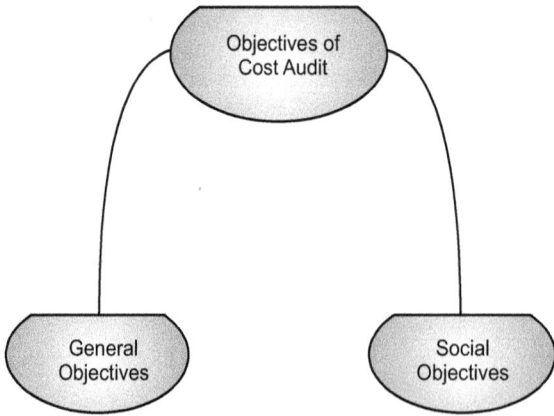

Fig. 5.1 : Objectives of Cost Audit

A) General Objectives :

The following are the general objectives of Cost Audit :

i) To verify the arithmetical accuracy of Cost Accountancy entries in the books of accounts.

ii) To find out whether cost accounts have been properly maintained according to the principles of costing employed in the industry concerned.

iii) To detect the errors of principles of cost accountancy.

iv) To detect the frauds that are made in Cost Records, which might have been committed intentionally or otherwise.

v) To verify the total cost of each product, process and job for seeing that they are accurately ascertained.

vi) To help management by pinpointing either deficiency of inefficiencies in the use of man, machine and material.

vii) To find out whether the cost accounting procedures prescribed by the company have been adhered or not.

viii) To verify the adequacy of the books of account and records relating to cost.

ix) To find out whether each item of expenditure involved into the relevant components of the goods manufactured or produced has been properly incurred or not.

x) To value accurately the value of work in progress and closing stock.

xi) To advice the management for the adoption of alternative course of action by preparing cost plan.

xii) To see whether the chargeable expenses as recorded by the cost accountant of the manufacturer are correct or not.

xiii) To verify that the cost statements are properly drawn up as per the records and that they represent a true and fair view of the cost of production and marketing.

xiv) To see whether the company is adequately managed.

xv) To report to appropriate authority as to the state of cost affairs of the company.

B) Social Objectives :

Cost audit provides valuable information for assessment of the operations with reference to the needs of the society and their fulfillment. To protect the interest of the contributors, to stop capital erosion, production of quality goods at a minimised price, to control the inflationary trend, to provide authentic data for the assessment of direct and indirect taxes, and to help for the improvement of the standard of common people etc. are the examples of the social objects of cost audit. These objectives can be achieved in the following manner.

i) Application in Agricultural Sector :

The agricultural productivity may be improved if the cost accounting and cost audit is applied in agricultural field on a wide basis. The introduction of cost accounting system and its audit in agricultural industry may call for availability of agricultural produces at a lower price which may ultimately increase the standard of living of common man of the society.

ii) A step in the direction of Consumer Protection :

Our society is constantly reeling under the pressure of inflation. Increase in prices are justified by the industry under the pretext of increases in costs. If increase in prices are only to the extent of increase in costs, then the extent of profits should not be increase. However, we find that profit levels are also increasing which obviously means that increase in prices are more than the increase in costs. Alternatively, reduction in costs are not passed on to customers. It is only in the cost audit report which reflect increase in costs which can be compared with increase in prices to assess the extent, if any, to which society has been overcharged. This objective will be more clear by the following observations of *the Institute of Cost and Works Accountants of India (ICWAI)* "*Cost Audit aims at increasing the added value through increased profitability per unit of input or resources. This added value can be shared by all the participants and certainty part of the benefit may reasonably be expected to be passed down to the consumer by way of reduced prices*".

iii) Increasing Productivity :

The cost audit has much role to play in increasing productivity by efficient management of man, material and efficient utilisation of installed capacities of the industries. Ultimately this may bring about an important of existing economic conditions of the common people.

iv) Creation of Cost-Awareness in Business Houses :

The cost auditor can do a lot of creating cost-awareness in connection with the utilisation of available financial resources in a systematic manner, controlling waste, verifying the cost sheet and finally control of material and men.

v) Creation of New Employment Opportunity :

Preparing cost plan in a systematic manner for untapped natural resources. The cost audit may benefit the society for new employment opportunity. It can be possible, if wastage of resources can be minimised and if the new fund created out of proper utilisation of material and men, these efforts can call for new investment opportunity and ultimately creates for new employment opportunity.

vi) Fixation of Price and Price Control :

The increasing rise in prices caused by monopolistic attitude may be controlled by an order of the government to conduct cost audit for those items. For example :

In 1984, the Monopolies and Restrictive Trade Practices Act (MRTP) has been ammended to define 'Monopolistic Trade Practice'. According to this amendment, any unreasonable increase in profit, price or cost, of any product will be considered as 'Monopolistic Trade Practice' which is not in the interest of the consumer. It is obvious that the cost audit report is the only potential document to reflect such increases on a regular basis.

If the cost structure is properly studied and prices are fixed accordingly it may benefited to the society in respect of quality and pocket.

vii) Tapping the Uneconomic Product Line :

The cost audit can also provide the society by identifying uneconomic product and thus help the entrepreneur by switch over of those cost to productive line of operation. This may indicate better position of working capital and production of quality items at a minimised price.

viii) Protection Against Evasion of Tax :

Payment of proper tax to the Government falls under the category of social obligation of the business. To meet demands for financing growth plans, taxation is the main source for fund-rising. It may some time happen that the unscrupulous management evade the payment of taxes through the adoption of certain technique that may result least profit and thereby misappropriates fund. Ultimately this results loss on national welfare and national development. Under such circumstances the cost audit has much important role to play in showing correct valuation of inventory and in eliminating artificial cost in the computation of cost of production. **It affects the reported profit of the business**. For example : Recognising the significance of the cost auditor's report the income tax department, while prescribing the annextures to be annexed to the income tax returns of the company insists on a copy of the cost audit report if such an audit is conducted. This provision is further reinforced by an *amendment of Section 139 (a) of the Income Tax Act, 1961 by the Finance Act, 1985*. As per the amendment, the Income Tax return submitted by a company will be considered as defective in case it is not accompanied by a copy of the cost audit report when such an audit has been conducted.

ix) Better Utilisation of Alternative Resources :

Generally contributors interests are safeguarded through proper rate of return of their investments. But it was found that the shareholders' interest does not end when a good dividend is earned by their undertaking. The question would naturally arise as to whether it was not possible to earn better profit with the same resources or alternative channeling of the existing resources by better management. Here, the adoption of cost audit system may be of greater benefit in this regard. A good control system is an instrument for achieving management objectives.

x) Promoting Export and Earning Foreign Exchange :

It has been proved that 'the success of export promotion depends mainly on production of quantity and quality goods. So if the products are competitive in respect of both quality and price, then it would be possible to stand in the foreign market. Thus, it appears that the cost audit has much role to play in promoting export and earning foreign exchange by its efficient application of suitable methods of analysis. For example :

Particulars of export sales and profitability from export sales, after taking into account expenses of exports, are also available in the cost audit report. The cost audit report giving the profitability or otherwise of exports for the company.

The using of marginal costing technique may call for more profitable line of operation and may also help either to continue or discontinue the uneconomic line of operation.

In this way, Cost Audit protects the interest of the society.

The existence of Cost Accounts assume **importance** for two reasons viz. :

i) The structure of cost accounts involves cost analysis of the extent and so tends to bring to light any errors existing in the original material or the analysis thereto.

ii) It is only the light of cost accounts that is reliable valuation of manufacturing of cost, or work-in- progress, can be arrived at for the purpose of the preparation of Balance Sheet.

Hence, the **basic objectives of cost audit** can be summarised as follows :

i) To verify the arithmetical accuracy of cost accountancy entries in the books of accounts.

ii) To find out whether the cost accounts have been properly maintained according to the principles of costing employed in the industry concerned.

iii) To verify that the cost statements are properly drawn up as per the records and that they represent a true and fair view of the cost of production and marketing.

iv) To find out whether each item of expenditure involved into the relevant components of the goods *manufactured or produced* has been properly incurred or not.

v) To find out whether the *cost accounting procedures* prescribed by the management have been adhered or not.

vi) To detect any error or fraud which might have been committed intentionally or otherwise.

vii) Cost Auditors are required to see whether the chargeable expenses as recorded by the cost accountant of the manufacturer are correct or not.

viii) To assist in reducing the amount of detail checking by the external auditor where the internal Cost Audit system is in opposition.

5.1.4 Scope of Cost Audit

The **Scope of 'Cost Audit'** varies widely and depends on the purpose of an audit, the condition of different process of manufacturing adopted by the industry and the procedures of auditing done previously by the client's staffs. The performance of cost audit work depends on the discretionary power on this part of the auditor, hence it is basically constructive in its conception and objective in its approach. It has but one purpose, that of helping the business houses/enterprises to better the position in manufacturing process. The net result is the diagnosis of the present state of performance of the business with attention focused on what needs improvement and with clear-cut recommendations. The scope of cost audit work depends on the process of manufacturing and the data/information maintained by the company. Sufficient examinations of the books of Accounts/Records together with supporting vouchers and relevant papers/documents should be made by the auditor to ensure their reliability and authenticity. In the case of a big manufacturing industry which maintains a well trained cost accounting and internal checking staff, the audit work may require comparatively little time and may involve a minimum of detail work.

The Companies Act, 1956, in India envisages the following kinds of Cost Audit in the normal functioning of a company.

i) Cost Audit.

ii) Cost Audit under Section 233 B of the Companies Act 1956.

iii) Cost Audit ordered by the Management for those years in which an order under Section 233 B of the Companies Act 1956, is not issued by the Government.

iv) Social audit being an independent assessment as to whether, and what extent, the activities of the enterprise are beneficial and contribute to the society at large.

Cost audit results in a report by the cost auditor which *'inter-alia'* contains an independent opinion as to whether :

i) The cost records as prescribed by the law have been maintained or not;

ii) The cost statements give a true and fair view of the cost of production, processing and marketing of the product under Audit.

In addition, the auditor should also provide information regarding various matters as specified in the format of annexures to the cost audit report. Thus, cost audit is product-oriented with reference to each company but limited to the particular industrial activity for which the audit is ordered to be carried out. The prerequisite for cost audit is that the company should be engaged in the manufacture of the product for which cost accounting record rules have been prescribed. Cost Audit is not necessary a regular annual exercise as it is to be carried out only in case of the government orders a company to get cost audit done. It is however, open to a company to get a cost audit carried out voluntarily in which case the report need not be submitted to the Government.

Thus, in short, Cost Audit is concerned with auditing of Allocation and Apportionment of expenses under natural heads to determine the cost of functions, products and services, as the case may be, with reference to a particular product or service. So it is obvious that the aspect of rendering satisfactions to all factors of the society interested in the affairs of the business may be included within the scope of cost audit function.

5.2 ADVANTAGES OF COST AUDIT

Cost Audit appears that it not only serves the management of the company and the shareholders but it serves the customers as well as the nation also. The Figure 5.2 shows the graphical presentation of **Advantages of Cost Audit.**

Fig. 5.2 : Advantages of Cost Audit

a) **To the Management :**
   i) It provides reliable cost data for managerial decisions.
   ii) It helps the management in finding out the correct cost of production.
   iii) It helps the management to regulate production.
   iv) It helps in obtaining licences for either expansion or diversification of the various product-lines of the business.
   v) It is a basis in evaluating the internal-divisional performance.
   vi) It acts as an effective managerial tool for the detection of errors, frauds, inconsistencies and irregularities so that reliable and smooth functioning of the system is continued.
   vii) It reduces the cost of production, through plugging loopholes relating to wastage of material, labour and overheads.
   viii) It can increase the productivity by pin-pointing the weak area of cost of production.
   ix) It can fix the responsibility of an individual wherever irregularities or wastage is found. The inefficiencies of the personnels working in the cost department, may be revealed.
   x) It can measure the profitability of the organisation.
   xi) It helps in comparing actual results with budgeted by means of various analysis and points out the areas where management action is more essential.
   xii) It exercises moral influence on employees which keeps them efficient and alert.
   xiii) It ensures that the cost accounts have been maintained in accordance with the principles of costing employed in the industry concerned.
   xiv) It can ensures accurate determination of profit for tax purposes.
   xv) It can stop the capital erosion by constant watch on the better plant utilisation, discontinuing uneconomic product-lines and elimination of wastage.

b) **To the Shareholders :**
   i) The cost audit enables shareholders to determine whether or not they are getting a fair return on their investments. It reflects the managerial skill and efficiency or inefficiency of those who are at the helm of the affairs of the company i.e. Board of Directors, General Manager and other senior officials.
   ii) It ensures a true picture of company's state of affairs. It reveals factual information by comparing resources and their proper utilisation. It enables the shareholder whether the plant and equipments are properly utilised or not by adopting several methods and techniques.
   iii) It ensures that proper records are maintained as to purchases, utilisation of materials and the expenses incurred on various items. It also makes sure that the industrial unit has been working accurately, economically and efficiently.

c) **To the Society :**
   i) It can bring about an overall improvement of the community by drawing up plans and programmes relating to cost for the part of the natural resources which are still unutilised.

ii) It indicates the true cost of production. From this the consumer may aware, whether the market price of the article is fair or not. It means the cost audit try to save the consumer from the exploitation.

iii) It improves the efficiency of industrial units and thereby assists in economic growth of the nation.

iv) Since price-increase by the industry is not allowed without justification as to increase in cost of production, consumers can maintain their standard of living.

v) It can control different elements of cost viz. materials, labours and overheads, which help to the society at large.

vi) It serves an important task in holding the price-line and serves the interest of the society. (means whether factors of the society).

d) To the Government :

i) It helps the Government in fixing and regulating prices, tariff protection.

ii) It facilitates settlement of trade disputes of the companies.

iii) Cost Statements may be helpful to authorities in levying tax or duty on the cost of finished products.

iv) It enables the Government to ascertain the cost of work under "cost plus percentage contract", if it is done by the proper examination of cost record.

v) It can also reveal the fraudulent intentions of the management.

vi) It helps the Government to take necessary steps to improve the efficiency of sick industrial units.

vii) It provides factual information to the Government for fixing up ceiling prices of the various commodities and to curb profiteering by the manufacturing concerns.

viii) It also helps in ascertaining whether any particular industry should be given any subsidy in order to develop that industry.

xi) It forms a basis for assessment of income tax.

x) It can also check some extent the high inflationary trend.

xi) It helps in promoting export.

xii) It helps to have better inter-firm comparison.

Disadvantages of Cost Audit :

Infact, Cost Audit should have no limitation of its own. If there be any intimation, it does not relate to the objectives for which it has been introduced. Sometime, it may arise due to its limited scope of application in the related fields of operation. However, it is found to be criticised on the following ground only.

i) It involves maximum amount of cost for the jobs which can be done by the internal auditor.

ii) It becomes very difficult to quantify responsibility of the accountants, chartered accountant and cost accountant, in case of the company which goes into liquidation.

iii) The cost audit reports are not published regularly for the protection of the interest of the shareholders.

iv) It has been superimposed on the financial audit.

v) It deters the progress of the organisation by interfering the work of the organisation by talking about efficiency and propriety.

vi) The Cost Audit staffs in actual practice do not perform any important function except gossiping.

vii) Cost Auditors are not always above frauds, errors and misappropriation and manipulation.

5.3 DIFFERENCE BETWEEN FINANCIAL AUDIT AND COST AUDIT

It is very difficult to make a **distinction between Financial Audit and Cost Audit** from the practical point of view. In **Cost Audit** as well as in **Financial Audit**, the auditor is ultimately concerned with financial aspect of every business transaction. However, following points are considered as *distinction between the two audits*.

	Financial Audit		Cost Audit
i)	It is compulsory under the Companies Act.	i)	It is not compulsory except in case of companies carrying on manufacturing or mining business.
ii)	It objects are to find out whether the accounts of the company have been properly maintained.	ii)	It objects are to find out whether the expenditure involved have been wisely incurred or not.
iii)	Whether the Profit and Loss Account and Balance Sheet represent a true and fair view of the State of affairs of the Company	iii)	To find out the cost of manufacture of each units of goods.
iv)	In this audit, the auditor does not go into the details of the cost records, which can be made to manipulate the facts.	iv)	The Cost Auditor's duty is not only to bring to light the errors of omission and commission but also to detect manipulation in the cost accounts.
v)	In case of *closing stock* the auditor has to see whether it has been properly valued or not.	v)	Cost Auditor has to see whether the stock is excessive or *inadequate* for the needs of the factory.
vi)	The *field* of Audit is limited.	vi)	The *field* of Audit is wider.
vii)	The Auditor has to see whether the ledger entries and castings are arithmatically corrected.	vii)	The Auditor (cost) has to take into aspect of the cost accounts.
viii)	The Financial Auditor is not concerned whether *raw materials* are issued according to the programme or not.	viii)	A Cost Audit has to see to this aspect of the cost accounts.
ix)	The auditor examines the financial aspect of the accounts.	ix)	It is concerned with the cost aspect of accounts.

	Financial Audit		Cost Audit
x)	It is concerned to serve the interest of *shareholders*.	x)	Cost Audit is concerned to serve the interest of *management*.
xi)	The Auditor sends the report to the management.	xi)	The report is sent to the company Board and to the Company.
xii)	The role of the Financial Auditor is in the office.	xii)	Cost Auditor is in the factory.

Cost Investigation and Cost Audit :

Cost Investigation refers to a systematic and detailed investigation of cost records of an undertaking with a specific purpose. **Cost Audit** is a system of audit of cost records which involves checking up the arithmetical accuracy of the books of cost accounts and verifying whether the principles laid down has been followed correctly or not. Cost Investigations totally differs from the cost audit. The important **differences between Cost Investigation and Cost Audit** are summarised as follows :

	Cost Investigation		Cost Audit
i)	It is a systematic and detailed investigation of cost records.	i)	It is the verification of the correctness of cost accounts and of the adherence to the cost accounting plan.
ii)	It is a specific exercise conducted with a specific purpose to investigate the matters relating to cost records.	ii)	It is a recurring exercise of examination of the costing books and records undertaken to certify their arithmetical accuracy and principles of cost accounting.
iii)	The scope of cost examination is very much narrow and specific.	iii)	The scope of cost verification is very much broad and general.
iv)	Cost investigators are interested in conclusive evidence of cost records.	iv)	Cost auditors are interested in persuasive evidence of cost records.
v)	Cost investigators are not bound by any accounting conventions and policies.	v)	Cost auditors are bound by accounting conventions and policies.
vi)	The Central Government may appoint the cost investigators to examine in detail the cost records of a company.	vi)	It is introduced by the Government of India for the review examination and appraisal of the accounting records.
vii)	After the achievement of the specific objective, the cost investigation is completed.	vii)	Cost audit is a continuous process carried out generally on yearly basis.
viii)	Generally, a well-experienced and professional cost accountant is appointed as a cost investigator.	viii)	A cost accountant within the meaning of Cost and Works Accountant Act, 1959 is appointed as a Cost Auditor.

5.4 TYPES OF COST AUDIT

The various **types of Cost Audit** generally depends upon the circumstances and the officating persons who take the actual initiative for conducting such a cost audit. The usual types of Cost Audit undertaken for a company on behalf of the following :

1) **Cost Audit on behalf of the Management :**

The principal object of cost audit is to ensure that the cost data placed before the management are verified and reliable and will assist in decision-making. The objectives of Cost Audit on behalf of the Management are as follows :

   i) Establishing accuracy of the costing data.

   ii) Ascertaining abnormal losses/gains along with the relevant causes and the person responsible.

   iii) Determination of the cost per unit of production.

   iv) Establishing suitable overhead absorption rates to mnimise over/under recovery of expenses.

   v) Fixation of the selling price and any additional charges.

   vi) Obtaining audit observations and suggestions of the cost auditor.

ii) **Cost Audit on behalf of a Customer :**

In case of cost plus contracts, the buyer or contractee may insist on a cost audit to satisfy himself about the correct ascertainment of cost. Sometimes, the agreement between the two parties may contain a stipulation in this regard.

iii) **Cost Audit on behalf of Government :**

The Government, when approached for subsidies or cash assistance, may require to be satisfied about the genuineness of the cost of production or the efficiency of the company. The Government, at its own may also initiate cost audit, in public interest to establish the fair price of any product.

iv) **Cost Audit by Trade Association :**

Sometimes, trade association may take the responsibility of fair pricing of the products manufactured by the member units or where there is a pooling or contribution arrangement between the members. For this, they may require the accuracy of costing data checked and may seek full information on the costing system, level of efficiency, utilisation of capacity, etc.

v) **Statutory Cost Audit :**

Section 22B of the Companies Act provides for statutory cost audit. This is ordered by the Government whenever it feels necessary to do so. Cost audit is ordered from year to year. The company concerned is required to maintain statutory cost audit is usually prescribed industrywise, it is possible that the company might be manufacturing or selling two or more products but, only one product might come under the purview of cost audit.

QUESTIONS FOR SELF-STUDY

I. **Theory Questions:**

i) What is Cost Audit? State the objectives of Cost Audit.

ii) Define 'Cost Audit'. Explain the scope and objectives of Cost Audit.

iii) What do you understand by the term 'Cost Audit'? Explain the advantages of Cost Audit.

iv) "Cost Audit is necessity and not a luxury and is viewed as a barometer to measure the operational performance, the effectiveness of utilisation and working results". Discuss.

v) Explain in brief the objectives and advantages of Cost Audit.

vi) "Cost Audit is more an aid to management than a statutory check of its performance". Explain.

vii) What is Cost Audit? How it differentiates from 'Financial Audit'?

viii) "Cost Audit aims at establishing truth and fairness of cost accounting records". Describe.

ix) What is Cost Audit? Enumerate the types of Cost Audit.

x) Write short notes on:
   a) Objectives of Cost Audit
   b) Scope of Cost Audit
   c) Advantages of Cost Audit
   d) Types of Cost Audit

xi) Differentiate between:
   a) Cost Audit on behalf of Management and Cost Audit on behalf of Government
   b) Cost Audit and Financial Audit.

***

GLOSSARY
(BASIC COST ACCOUNTING TERMS WITH SIMPLIFIED EXPLANATIONS)

- **Composite Cost Unit :** It is a unit which measures two characteristics simultaneously. For e.g., per tonne-mile, per passenger-kilometre, kilowatt-hour etc.
- **Cost Centre :** It is a location, person or item of equipment for which costs may be ascertained and used for the purpose of control.
- **Cost Unit :** It is a unit of a quantity of product, service or time in relation to which costs may be ascertained or expressed.
- **Fixed Cost :** A cost which accrues in relation to the passage of time and which, within certain output and turnover limits, tends to remain unaffected by the fluctuations in the level of activity (of the output or turnover) for e.g., rent, rates, insurance etc.
- **Impersonal Cost Centre :** It is a cost centre which consists of a location or item of equipment.
- **Operating Cost :** It is the cost incurred in providing a service.
- **Operating Cost Centre :** It is a cost centre which consists of those machines and persons which carry out the same operations.
- **Personal Cost Centre :** It is a cost centre which consists of a person or group of persons.
- **Process Cost Centre :** It is a cost centre which consists of a continuous sequence of operations.
- **Production Cost Centre :** It is a cost centre where actual production takes place for e.g., welding, mechanical, electrical, assembly etc.
- **Semi-variable Cost :** A cost which has an element of fixity and also of variability for e.g., telephone charges, electricity charges etc.
- **Service Cost Centre :** It is a cost centre which renders services to production department for e.g., power generation plant, repair shop, personnel department etc.
- **Simple Cost Unit :** It is a unit which measure one characteristics such as length or volume or area or weight for e.g., per metre, per kilogram etc.
- **Variable Cost :** A cost which in aggregate, tends to vary in the direct proportion with the changes in the volume of production or turnover for e.g., direct material cost, direct labour cost, direct expenses etc.
- **Abnormal Costs :** A cost which is normally incurred at a given level of output in the conditions in which that level of output is normally attained.
- **Abnormal Gain :** It is a result of the excess of actual output over normal output due to excellent climatic conditions for production, exceptionally good material, new equipments, etc.

- **Abnormal Loss :** It is the loss caused by abnormal conditions which is excess of actual loss over normal loss which may arise due to poor quality of raw materials, defects in machines, carelessness on the part of workers, etc.

- **Abnormal Overheads :** These are the overhead costs which are not expected to occur in producing a given output e.g. abnormal idle time, abnormal wastage etc.

- **Absorption of Overheads :** It is the process of charging of overheads of a cost centre to different cots units in such a way that each cost unit bears an appropriate portion of its share of overheads.

- **Actual Overhead Rate :** It is the rate calculated by dividing the actual overhead expenses incurred by the actual quantity or value of selected base for the corresponding period.

- **Administration Costs :** The sum of these costs of general and management, and of secretarial, accounting and administrative services which cannot be directly related to production, marketing, research and development function of the enterprise.

- **Allocation of Overheads :** It is the process of allotment of an entire cost to a particular cost centre or cost unit.

- **Apportionment of Overheads :** It is the process of distribution of overheads to cost centes on an equitable basis.

- **Architect's Certificate :** It is the certificate issued by the contractees architect specifying clearly as to the value of work so far performed.

- **Batch Costing :** It is that form of specific order costing, which applies where similar articles are manufactured in batches either for sale or use, within the undertaking.

- **Capital Costs :** A cost which is intended to benefit in future period.

- **Class-Cost Method :** It is the method of job costing where the costing of goods is done by classes instead of the unit or a piece.

- **Classification of Overheads :** It is the process of grouping of overhead costs on the basis of common characteristics and clear objectives.

- **Codification of Overheads :** It is a method of identifying and describing various overhead expenses in numbers or letters or in a combination of both so that cost data can easily be collected.

- **Contract Costing :** It is that form of specific order costing, which applies where work is undertaken regarding customers special requirements and each order is of long duration.

- **Controllable Costs :** A cost chargeable to a cost centre, which can be influenced by the actions of the person in whom control of the centre is vested.

- **Controllable Overheads :** These are the overhead costs which can be controlled by executive action at the point of their incurrance e.g. advertisement, delivery-van running expenses etc.

- **Cost :** It is the amount of expenditure (actual or notional) incurred on or attributable to a specified thing or activity.

- **Cost Account Numbers :** These are the code numbers given to an item of administration overheads or selling and distribution overheads.

- **Cost Accountancy :** It is the application of costing and cost accounting principles, methods and techniques to the science, art and practice of cost control and the ascertainment of profitability.
- **Cost Accounting :** It is that branch of accounting dealing with the classification, recording, allocation, summarisation and reporting of current and prospective costs.
- **Cost Audit :** It means the detailed checking of costing system, the technique and accounts to verify their correctness and to ensure adherence to the objective of accounting.
- **Cost Audit Manual :** It is a written and formal document giving necessary details regarding the conduct of cost audit.
- **Cost Audit Notes :** It refers to any matter of notes of points noticed which are necessarily to be disclosed in an Annual Reports of Accounts or in Audit Report with a view to presenting a true and fair view of the state of affairs of a company for the knowledge and information of all concerned and interested.
- **Cost Audit Programme :** It is a detailed plan which shows the various phases of audit and the audit checks to be carried out in each phase.
- **Cost Classification :** It is a grouping of cost according to their common characteristics.
- **Cost Investigation :** It is a systematic and detailed investigation into the cost records of an undertaking.
- **Cost Plus Contracts :** It is that type of account, where a contractor is paid with actual cost of direct materials, direct labour, direct factory expenses and a stipulated amount or percentage of cost to cover overheads and profits.
- **Cost Sheet :** It is a statement which shows the details regarding total cost of the job or a product.
- **Costing :** It is the technique and process of ascertaining costs.
- **Daily Log Sheet :** It is the main source document which provides analytical service cost data required for cost ascertainment and cost control.
- **De-escalation Clause :** It is the clause which provides for a decrease in the contract price due to a decrease in the price of inputs, so that the benefit of price decrease is passed on to the contractee.
- **Departmentalisation of Overheads :** It is the process of allocation and apportionment of overheads to different departments or other costs centres.
- **Development Costs :** The cost of process which begins with the implementation of the decision to produce or new or improved methods and ends with the commencement of formal production of that product or by that method.
- **Direct Expenses :** Costs other than materials or wages which are incurred for a specific product or a saleable service.
- **Direct Labour Costs :** The cost of remuneration for employee's efforts and skills applied directly to a product or saleable service.

- **Direct Material Costs :** The cost of materials entering into and becoming constituent element of a product or saleable service.
- **Distribution Costs :** These are the costs incurred for despatching the products which are ready after packing.
- **Efficiency Audit :** The audit which seeks to review the performance of an organisation against the parameters of efficiency.
- **Escalation Clause :** It is the clause which aims at safeguarding the interests of the contractor against unforeseen rise in cost.
- **Expenses :** The cost of services provided to an undertaking.
- **Factory Costs :** These are certain indirect expenses incurred by a concern right from the receipt of an order to the final delivery of goods to the customer, or for storing the finished goods in the godowns.
- **Financial Accounting :** It is concerned with recording, classifying, analysing and summarising financial transactions and preparing financial statements with a view to showing profitability and financial state of the affairs of the business.
- **Financial Audit :** It is the audit of financial books and vouchers which aims at reporting on truth and fairness of income and position statements.
- **Fixed Overheads :** These are the overhead costs which tend to be unaffected by the variations in the volume of output e.g. office rent and taxes, depreciation on factory premises etc.
- **Historical Costs :** The costs which are ascertained after these have been incurred.
- **Indirect Expenses :** The expenses other than direct expenses.
- **Indirect Labour Costs :** The Labour Cost other than Direct Labour Cost.
- **Indirect Material Costs :** The Material Cost other than Direct Material Cost.
- **Job Cost Sheet :** It is a cost statement prepared to analyse and ascertain the actual cost incurred with respect to the individual jobs.
- **Job Costing :** It is that form of specific order costing, which applies where work is undertaken regarding customer's special requirements.
- **Labour Costs :** The sum total of all payments made by the employer to the work-force for performing production activity and the cost to the employer of all benefits granted to the work-force for the same.
- **Maintenance Charges :** These are certain semi-variable expenses which are to be incurred on the maintenance of the vehicles to keep them in proper conditions e.g. repairs and maintenance, painting etc.
- **Management Audit :** It is a comprehensive and complex audit involving appraisal of all round performance of the management of the organisation.
- **Material Costs :** The cost of commodities, other than Fixed Assets, introduced in products or consumed in the operation of an organisation.
- **Methods of Costing :** It indicates a systematic procedure established for ascertaining cost of product, job, process or services by using the principles of costing.

- **Multiple Costing :** It is an application of more than one method of cost ascertainment in respect of the same product.
- **Non-cost Items :** These are certain items of financial nature, which are excluded from the ascertainment of cost.
- **Normal Costs :** A cost which is normally incurred to a given level of output in the condition in which that level of output is normally attained.
- **Normal Loss :** It is the loss of materials under normal conditions, which is unavoidable, as a result normally expected quantity of output is less than the input.
- **Normal Overheads :** These are the overhead costs which are expected to be incurred in producing a given output e.g. catalogues and price-lists, salary and commission to traveling salesmen etc.
- **Notional Profit :** It is the difference between the value of work certified and cost of work certified.
- **Office Overheads :** These are the cost of formulating the policy, directing the organisation and controlling the operations of an undertaking which is not related directly to research, development, production, selling or distribution activity function e.g. printing and stationery, office rent and taxes etc.
- **Operating Costing :** It is that form of operation costing, which applies where standardised services are provided either by an undertaking or by a service cost centre within an undertaking.
- **Operation Costing :** The category of basic costing methods applicable where standardised goods or services result from a sequence of repetitive and more or less continuous operations or process to which costs are charged, before being averaged over the units produced during the period.
- **Output Costing :** It is that form of operation costing where large number of identical units are produced.
- **Over-Absorption of Overheads :** It is the excess of absorbed overheads over actual overheads.
- **Overhead Absorption Rate :** These are the rates determined for the purpose of absorption of overheads.
- **Overheads :** It is the aggregate of indirect material, indirect labour and indirect expenses.
- **Partly Producing Department :** It is one that is normally treated as service department, but sometime they are also required to undertake direct production work.
- **Period Costs :** These are the costs which are associated with a particular accounting period.
- **Pre-determined Costs :** The costs which are ascertained in advance of production on the basis of a specification of all the factors affecting cost.
- **Process Costing :** It is that form of operation costing, which applies where the standardised goods are produced.
- **Process Loss :** It is the difference between the input quantity of raw materials and the output quantity.

- **Product Costs :** These are the costs which are directly associated with the product.
- **Proprietary Audit :** It is the audit of executive action and plans having an impact on the finance and expenditure of the company.
- **Research Costs :** The cost of seeking new or improved products, applications of material or methods.
- **Retention Money :** It is the money which serves as a security with the contractee and also acts as a deterrent against leaving the work incomplete by the contractor.
- **Revenue Costs :** A cost which is incurred to benefit the current period.
- **Running Charges :** These are certain variable operating expenses which are to be incurred on the actual running of the vehicle e.g. petrol and fuel, oil and grease etc.
- **Scrap :** These are the discarded material having some recovery value, which is usually disposed off without further treatment or re-introduced into the production process in place of raw materials.
- **Selling Cost or Selling Overheads :** These are the costs incurred for attracting the potential customers and retaining the existing customers.
- **Source Document :** It is an original record that supports journal entries in an accounting system.
- **Specific Order Costing :** The category of basic costing methods applicable where the work consists of separate contracts, jobs or batches each of which is authorised by a special order or contract.
- **Statutory Cost Audit :** It is a compulsory cost audit ordered by the Government of India under the provisions of Section 233 B of the Indian Companies Act, 1956.
- **Sub-Contract Cost :** These are the cost incurred for a sub-contract, where the contractor has entrusted some special work to some expertise sub-contractor for e.g., electrification, sanitary work, welding, digging, installation of lifts, painting work, etc.
- **Uncontrollable Costs :** A cost chargeable to a cost centre which cannot be influenced by the actions of the person in whom control of the centre is vested.
- **Waste :** These are the discarded substances having no value.
- **Work Certified :** It is the cost of that part of work-in-progress, which is being completed successfully by the contractor and has been approved by the certifier.
- **Work Uncertified :** It is the cost of that part of work-in-progress which is being completed by the contractor, but not approved by the certifier because of the faulty work or the work not according to the specifications.

OBJECTIVE QUESTIONS
TRUE/FALSE STATEMENTS

- State with reasons whether the following statements are True or False :
  1. Financial Accounting has been developed out of the limitations of Cost Accounting.
  2. Cost is an increase in assets or decrease in liabilities made to secure an economic benefit.
  3. Costing is simply the technique and process of ascertaining costs.
  4. Cost Accounting can replace Financial Accounting.
  5. Cost Accounting is concerned with cost ascertainment, cost presentation and cost control.
  6. Cost Accountancy is the application of costing and Cost Accounting principles.
  7. A cost unit is a unit of measurement of efficiency.
  8. A cost centre is a location, person or item of equipment, for which costs may be ascertained and used for the purposes of control.
  9. A service cost centre renders services to production departments.
  10. Per passenger-kilometre is an example of composite cost unit in passenger transport company.
  11. A process cost centre is that which consists of a specific process or a continuous sequence of operations.
  12. 'Cost + Profit = Sales' is the equation of costing.
  13. The classification of costs into fixed costs and variable costs helps the management to take vital decisions.
  14. Prime Costs are identifiable.
  15. Depreciation on Fixed Assets is always a Marginal Cost.
  16. Semi-fixed costs are partly controllable and partly uncontrollable.
  17. Fixed Cost decisions, once implemented are irreversible.
  18. Motive power is an example of administration overheads.
  19. Total Fixed Cost always increases in proportion to output.
  20. Period costs are not assigned to products.
  21. Cost-Sheet is a statement which shows only the indirect components of the total cost.
  22. Works Cost is the difference between Gross Cost and Management Cost.
  23. Hire charges of a special machinery is an example of unproductive expenses.
  24. Clay used in bricks manufacturing is an example of indirect material.
  25. Prime Costs are aggregate of indirect materials, indirect labour and indirect expenses.
  26. The difference between cost of sales and value of sales is known as a loss.
  27. Leather used in shoe making business is an example of indirect material.
  28. Underwriting commission is a non-cost item.
  29. Material Cost is the cost of commodities supplied to an undertaking.
  30. All overheads are costs, but all costs may not be overheads.
  31. Cleaning materials used to maintain the machine in factory workshop is an example of Prime Cost Material.
  32. Carriage on Sales is a Prime Cost expense.
  33. Wages paid to watchman is an item of productive labour.
  34. Selling Overheads are the cost of promoting sales and retaining customers.
  35. Salary paid to computer operator increases direct labour cost in software industries.

36. All variable costs are direct and indirect costs.
37. Per unit fixed cost is always constant.
38. All costs are variable in the long run.
39. All costs are controllable.
40. All costs are relevant for some decisions or the other.
41. Methods of Costing refers to the process of collecting, arranging, processing and presenting costs.
42. Methods of Costing are introduced for controlling the cost.
43. Job Costing is applicable to cases, where the work is done according to customers' specification.
44. Contract Costing is a method used in civil engineering works, plant installations, etc.
45. A clause providing for reduction in the contract price, in case of falling prices to protect the interest of the contractee is termed as Escalation clause.
46. Retention money is the amount paid to the contractor after the satisfactory completion of the work.
47. Each contract is treated as a separate cost unit.
48. Work certified in a subsequent year is always greater than in the preceding year.
49. Cost-plus-contracts are entered into when the cost of contract can be determined in advance.
50. Process Costing is a method of operation costing.
51. In process manufacturing industries, there is a flow of materials from one operation to the next operation.
52. Each process is treated as a separate cost centre.
53. Normal losses are not charged to the product in Process Costing.
54. Excess of actual loss over normal loss is termed as abnormal loss.
55. The loss inherent in the production process is treated as a normal loss.
56. Process Costing is applicable to those industries, where manufacture of product is of uniform standards.
57. Operating Costing is a part of specific order costing.
58. Operating Costing deals with costing of services.
59. Operating Costing method can suitably be applied in transport undertakings.
60. Operating Costing is used for evaluating alternatives.
61. A standard method of costing cannot be used for all types of industries.
62. Job Costing and Contract Costing are the forms of operation costing.
63. Difference between a job and a contract is that of time involved and cost.
64. Most of the costs in case of contracts are direct costs.
65. Work uncertified does not contain a profit element.
66. Cost of additional work is to be recovered from the contractee.
67. Supplementary costs are also termed as 'Overheads'.
68. Abnormal overheads are charged to Production Account.
69. Direct costs can not be conveniently identified with a particular cost unit.
70. Overhead costs changes in proportion to changes in output.
71. All overheads are the costs, but all costs are not the overheads.
72. Behavioural classification of overheads is highly helpful to the management for the efficient working of the production shop.
73. Increase in overhead costs due to higher level of mechanisation result in reducing the labour cost.
74. Secondary packing costs are treated as prime cost.
75. Rigid overheads are generally uncontrollable.

76. Fixed overheads are influenced by policy decisions of top management, hence they are termed as Policy costs.
77. Office overheads are controllable at lower level of management.
78. Marginal costs are always fixed in total.
79. Depreciation on plant and machinery changes only with a change in capacity.
80. Per unit semi-fixed overheads decline with decrease in output.
81. Lubricants are the indirect materials which can be ascertained from stores requisitions.
82. Certain direct costs of very small value though identifiable with specific cost units may be treated as overhead costs.
83. Some cost may be direct in one situation and indirect in other situation.
84. If no payment of rent of owned premises by the owner, the notional rent may be charged as overhead.
85. The overheads incurred for procuring, promoting and effecting sales are termed as distribution overheads.
86. Fixed, variable and semi variable overheads is the classification of overheads as per variability.
87. Cost of power used by a specific department can be better controllable by the shop supervisor.
88. Due to improvement of technology, overheads are becoming more or less equal to direct costs.
89. Fixed overhead cost is a committed cost.
90. Variable overhead is a period cost.
91. Factory rent is a direct cost to the factory as a whole but indirect to the departments.
92. Fixed costs vary with the volume rather than time.
93. Variable overheads vary with the volume of output.
94. Packing cost is usually treated as distribution overhead.
95. After sales service cost is the part of distribution on cost.
96. Cost of unsuccessful research should be charged to costing Profit and Loss Account.
97. An increase in output reduces per unit overhead cost and increases profits at higher rate.
98. Direct costs are also termed as overheads.
99. High overhead cost increases the risk profile of the business.
100. Sales commission is an example of direct overheads.
101. Costs which do not change with change in output upto given capacity, are marginal costs.
102. What is controllable now may not remain controllable in future.
103. Allocation of overheads refers to the process of charging full amount of overheads to a particular cost centre.
104. The code number given to an item of factory overhead is termed as factory order number.
105. The process of assigning service department overheads to production departments is called as secondary distribution.
106. Departmentalisation overheads is the process of assigning overheads to various departments.
107. Secondary distribution of overheads is impossible after completion of primary distribution.
108. Codification of overheads facilitates appropriate accounting and systematic analysis of indirect costs.
109. Absorption of overheads is nothing but charging of overheads to cost units.
110. Office overheads are recovered as a percentage of prime cost materials.
111. Apportionment is nothing but charging of overheads to cost centres.
112. When actual overheads are in excess of absorbed overheads, it is a case of over absorption.
113. When absorbed overheads are in excess of actual overheads, it is the case of under absorption.

Basics of Cost Accounting T.4 Objective Questions

114. Allocation of cost is always direct.
115. Under or over absorption due to cyclical fluctuations is generally carried over to the next year.
116. All overheads are fixed costs.
117. The overhead rate should be simple to understand and easy to operate.
118. Cost Audit is applicable only to those companies whose products are covered by cost accounting record rules.
119. A cost auditor will have the right to receive remuneration for the work done for the company.
120. If the cost audit is compulsorily conducted, the entire community stands to gain in terms of better quality of the products at reasonable prices.
121. The work of cost auditor and financial auditor are partially interrelated.
122. The field of cost audit is very limited.
123. Cost Audit is concerned to serve the interest of shareholders.
124. The main object of cost audit is to ensure that the cost data presented to the management are verified and reliable, which will assist in decision-making.
125. Cost Audit has an important role to play in promoting export and earning foreign exchange.

ANSWERS

True :

3, 5, 6, 8, 9, 10, 11, 12, 13, 14, 16, 17, 20, 22, 26, 28, 29, 30, 34, 35, 36, 38, 40, 41, 43, 44, 46, 47, 48 50, 51, 52, 54, 55, 56, 58, 59, 60, 61, 63, 64, 65, 66, 67, 71, 72, 73, 75, 76, 79, 81, 82, 83, 84, 86, 88, 89, 91, 93, 94, 96, 97, 99, 100, 102, 103, 105, 106, 108, 109, 111, 114, 115, 117, 118, 119, 120, 121, 124, 125.

False :

1 - Cost Accounting has been developed out of the limitations of Financial Accounting 2 - A decrease in assets or an increase in liabilities, 4 - Both are necessary, 7 - A unit of measurement of cost, 15 - can be a Fixed Cost, 18 - Factory Overheads, 19 - Total Variable Cost, 21 - Shows direct and indirect components of the Total Cost, 23 - Productive expenses, 24 - Direct Material, 25 - are aggregate of direct materials, direct labour and direct expenses, 27 - Direct Material, 31 - Indirect Material, 32 - Distribution overhead, 33 - unproductive labour, 37 - always variable, 39 - are not controllable, 42 - for ascertaining the cost, 45 - De-escalation clause, 49 - Cannot be determined in advance, 53 - are charged to the product, 57 – operation costing, 62 - forms a specific order costing, 68. are changed to costing Profit and Loss Account, 69. indirect costs, 70. direct costs, 74. overhead costs, 77. uncontrollable, 78. variable in total, 80. decline with increase in output, 85. selling overheads, 87. departmental manager, 90. product cost, 92. vary with time rather than volume, 95. selling on cost, 98. indirect costs, 101. fixed costs, 104. standing order number, 107. possible, 110. percentage of works cost. 112. under absorption, 113. over absorption, 116. fixed or variable costs, 122. is much wider, 123. interest of management.

FILL IN THE BLANKS

1. The amount of expenditure incurred on a given thing is terms as ....
2. Costing is the technique and process of .... costs.
3. Cost Accounting is based on .... system.
4. Cost Accounting helps in .... appraisal.
5. .... is the application of costing and cost accounting principles, methods and techniques.
6. Cost Accounting focusses on .... and not on ....
7. Cost Accounting is a system of .... and not a postmortem examination.
8. The basic object of cost accounting is to ....
9. Need for cost accounting arises because of limitations of .... accounting.
10. Larger the number of alternative techniques of production, greater is the need for ....
11. Cost Accounting begins where .... ends.
12. Both financial accounting and cost accounting are basically the branches of ....
13. Financial Accounting generally discloses the profitability of the .... organisation.
14. Financial Accounting record .... costs, whereas Cost Accounting record .... costs.
15. The main function of financial accounting is .... reporting.
16. The basic needs of the majority of the users of accounting information can be satisfied by .... accounting.
17. .... is the price paid for something.
18. Opportunity cost means the .... made for not utilising the other alternatives.
19. Cost Accounting is concerned with .... of cost.
20. Cost .... includes costing and cost accounting.
21. .... Accounting shows only the overall performance of the business.
22. Cost Accounting has become an essential .... of management.
23. Cost Accounting helps the management in .... making.
24. Cost unit is a unit of measurement of ....
25. Cost unit should be neither too .... nor too ....
26. In cement industries, the cost unit is per ....
27. .... refers to an outflow of resources without any commensurate benefit.
28. .... cost centre is that which consists of a location or item of equipment.
29. Direct cost is .... to cost unit or cost centre, whereas indirect cost is ....
30. A cost unit for measuring products is mostly .... cost unit.

31. Cost unit is a .... unit of a product or service or time in relation to which costs are ascertained.
32. In passenger transport company, per passenger is a .... cost unit.
33. In goods transport company, per tonne per kilometer is a .... cost unit.
34. A cost .... is a sub unit of the organisation for which costs may be collected separately for cost ascertainment and cost control.
35. .... cost units are mostly applicable in case of services rendered.
36. Repair shop is an example of .... cost centre.
37. .... costs remain constant with changes in volume of output.
38. .... costs benefit the current period only, whereas .... costs benefit more than one particular period.
39. .... is a statement which provides for the assembly of the detailed cost of a cost centre or a cost unit.
40. .... is the physical or mental effort expended in production.
41. Abnormal costs are charged to ....
42. .... costs are based on recorded facts.
43. Pre-determined cost ascertained on scientific basis becomes .... cost.
44. .... costs are the costs directly associated with the product.
45. Primary packing charges is an example of direct .... cost.
46. The marginal cost per unit of product remains ....
47. Direct expenses are also known as .... expenses.
48. .... cost is the cost of seeking new or improved products, applications of material or methods.
49. The sum total of .... cost, production and administration overheads is known as cost of production.
50. Direct cost plus variable overheads is known as .... cost.
51. If profits are 20% of value of turnover and the cost of turnover is ₹ 80,000, the profits will be ....
52. Prime cost and overhead cost makes the .... cost.
53. Milk used in dairy products is the example of .... materials.
54. It is more appropriate to treat threads in dress making businesses as .... materials.
55. Lubricants used in factory workshop is the example of .... materials.
56. Direct materials form the part of .... products.
57. .... cost is the cost of remuneration of the employees of an undertaking.
58. Wages paid for factory supervision is the example of .... labour.
59. Expenses which can be identified with and allocated to cost centres and cost units are termed as ....
60. Royalty payable in mining business is to be treated as ....
61. .... costs are the operating expenses of a business enterprise.

62. The costs incurred in promoting sales and retaining customers is treated as ....
63. Carriage on purchases is the part of direct .... cost.
64. Bad debts recovery is a .... cost item.
65. The .... of cost of a product are material, labour and expenses.
66. .... is the physical or mental effort expended in production.
67. Fixed cost can be controlled mostly by .... level management.
68. All costs are .... in the long run.
69. Electricity charges is the most suitable example of .... cost.
70. .... costs are objective in nature.
71. Product costs are .... costs because they form a part of value of inventories of finished stock.
72. .... costs are non-inventoriable costs, as they are not included in the value of finished stocks.
73. Revenue costs are incurred for maintaining .... capacity of the business.
74. .... is a document which provides for the assembly of the estimated detailed cost in respect of a cost centre or cost unit.
75. Underwriting commission should not be incorporated in the cost sheets because these are expenses of .... nature.
76. Overheads are the .... costs of a business enterprise which can not be traced directly to a particular unit of output.
77. The aggregate of indirect material cost, indirect wages and indirect expenses is termed as ....
78. Wages of store-keeper is an example of .... overheads.
79. .... overheads are related to the periods, hence they are termed as period costs.
80. .... classification of overheads, is the grouping of overheads with reference to the major activity of an organisation.
81. Variable overheads .... in direct proportion to the volume of output.
82. Normal bad debts is an example of .... overheads.
83. An increase in efficiency .... per unit overhead cost.
84. Generally items of manufacturing overheads are to be apportioned to various departments on the basis of .... hours.
85. Training expenses would be abnormally .... in case of high labour turnover.
86. Normal rent of shop supervisor is to be charged as ....
87. Technical directors travelling expenses form a part of .... overheads.
88. .... means the allotment of whole items of cost to cost centres or cost units.
89. .... is the allotment of proportionate items of cost to cost centres or cost units.
90. In telephone charges, telephone rent is .... whereas charges for telephone calls are ....

91. The overhead .... is the process of charging of overheads to cost units on an estimated basis.
92. Under absorption of overheads signifies .... financial profit compared with cost profit.
93. .... absorption of overheads signifies higher financial profit compared with cost profit.
94. When actual overheads are ₹ 21,500 and overhead absorbed are ₹ 20,600, there is .... absorption of ₹ 900.
95. The .... absorption of machine overheads would indicate the extent to which the machines have been idle.
96. If under absorption of overheads arises due to defective planning, it may be transferred to ....
97. Under absorption of overhead results in .... statement of cost.
98. Absorption of overhead takes place only after the .... and apportionment of overheads.
99. Contract costing is a variant of .... costing.
100. The contracts undertaken are always completed from the .... premises.
101. The difference between the value of work certified and the cost of work certified is known as ....
102. In contract accounting, the total loss if any, is transferred to .... account.
103. Under .... the value of contract is determined by adding a fixed margin of profit to the total cost of contract.
104. Under the .... clause the contract price is increased for a given increase in the prices of inputs.
105. Materials issued to the sub-contractor free of charge, should be charged to .... account.
106. A contract is generally of a .... duration.
107. Escalation clause is generally included in case of .... contract agreement.
108. Cost-plus-contracts are undertaken for production of .... products.
109. Work certified is always valued at contract .... whereas work uncertified is always valued at ....
110. Work certified in a .... year is always higher than in the .... year.
111. Work certified in a subsequent year is always .... than that in the preceding year.
112. Cost plus contract is mainly used in ....
113. In contract costing, usually work .... should form the basis of profit computation.
114. The .... certificate forms the basis of release of payments to the contractor.
115. Retention money serves as a .... with the contractee.
116. An escalation clause usually relates to the change in prices of ....

117. When the completion of the contract is less than 50%, profit to be credited to profit and loss account will be equal to ....
118. When cash ratio is ...., retention money is 13%.
119. A bigger job is referred to as a ....
120. In a particular building construction company the estimated profit is ₹ 90,000 and the contract is almost two-third complete. If the cash ratio is 90%, the profit to be transferred to profit and loss account is ₹ ....
121. Process costing represents one extreme of .... costing.
122. In process costing, as the product passes from one process to another, the .... cost of previous process is transferred to the next process.
123. In oil and petroleum refineries, ... costing may be adopted more suitably.
124. The .... is a material residue from certain manufacturing operations that has relatively minor value.
125. In process industries there is a continuous flow of .... from one operation to the next operation.
126. Make or buy decisions are involved before and after different ....
127. In process industries materials move down the production line in a .... stream.
128. In process costing each process is treated as a separate ....
129. In process industries the output is generally for ....
130. All normal losses in process costing are charges directly to the ....
131. Cost per unit remains .... in case of abnormal loss as well as abnormal gain.
132. .... loss is what which arises under efficient operating conditions.
133. Abnormal gain may be the result due to the errors in ....
134. Generally normal loss is ....
135. Balance in abnormal loss account is transferred to .... account.
136. Normal wastage is credited to process account and debited to .... account.
137. If the actual loss is .... than normal loss, it is termed as abnormal loss.
138. Process costing is .... suitable for industries manufacturing colour television.
139. The cost finding method is more simple and less expensive in .... costing than that of .... costing.
140. In process costing the output of one process becomes the .... of another process.
141. The cost of abnormal gain is computed on the basis of .... production.
142. Operating cost is the cost incurred for providing ....
143. Under service costing, the examples of standing charges are .... and ....
144. In transport undertakings a vehicle .... is maintained for each vehicle to record summary of trips made by the vehicles during a specific period.
145. An example of composite cost unit in transport costing ....
146. Per kilometer is an example of .... cost unit used in transport undertakings.
147. In service cost sheet costs are generally classified into ....

148. If the profits are 50% of operating cost, it is .... of invoice price.
149. .... costing involves the method of ascertainment of cost of services.
150. Service costing is also called as ....
151. Services rendered by transport undertakings to the public are .... products.
152. Number of passenger kilometers = Number of passengers (x) ....
153. The total cost of carrying 73 tons of weight over a distance of 100 kilometers amounted to ₹ 36,500, therefore the cost per ton-kilometer will be ....
154. Generally in service costing mostly the costs are .... in nature.
155. In service costing division is an ....
156. Transport cost-sheet provides sufficient information to judge the .... of the vehicles.
157. The working capital requirements are comparatively .... in those industries where service costing system is implemented.
158. Operating costing system is more suitable to .... organisation rather than .... organisations.
159. Service costing method clearly indicates the change in the cost structure due to change in the .... level.
160. A cost auditor has to attach several .... to the cost audit reports.
161. If the cost auditor fails to submit the cost audit report in time, he is punishable with ....
162. A .... is liable to his clients, third parties and also to the central Government.
163. The cost audit report is to be sent to the company ....
164. The appointment of a .... is for every audit and audit period.
165. The three wings of integrated audit are financial audit, management audit and .... audit.
166. Cost Audit is concerned with the verification of the correctness of .... accounts.
167. Performance audit is generally conducted to determine the performance against .... standard.
168. The cost audit of a company engaged in processing activity is ....
169. The .... auditor can be a cost accountant or a chartered accountant.
170. The basic purpose of cost audit is to establish accuracy of .... accounts.

ANSWERS

1. cost, 2. ascertaining, 3. double entry, 4. performance, 5. Cost Accountancy, 6. cost-revenues, 7. foresight, 8. control the costs, 9. financial, 10. costing, 11. costing, 12. accounting, 13. entire, 14. historical-projected, 15. external, 16. Financial, 17. Cost, 18. sacrifice, 19. recording, 20. accountancy, 21. Financial, 22. tool, 23. decision, 24. cost, 25. big-small, 26. tonne, 27. Loss, 28. Impersonal, 29. allocated-apportioned, 30. single, 31. quantitative, 32. single, 33. composite, 34. centre, 35. Composite, 36. service, 37. Fixed, 38. Revenue-capital, 39. Cost sheet, 40. labour,

41. costing profit and loss, 42. Historical, 43. standard, 44. Direct, 45. material, 46. fixed, 47. chargeable, 48. Research, 49. prime cost, 50. marginal, 51. ₹ 20,000, 52. total, 53. direct, 54. indirect, 55. indirect, 56. finished, 57. Labour, 58. indirect, 59. direct, 60. direct expense, 61. Overhead, 62. selling, 63. material, 64. non, 65. elements, 66. Labour, 67. top, 68. variable, 69. semi-variable, 70. Historical, 71. inventoriable, 72. Period, 73. earning, 74. Cost sheet, 75. financial, 76. operating, 77. overheads, 78. factory, 79. Fixed, 80. Functional, 81. changes, 82. selling, 83. reduces, 84. machine/labour, 85. high, 86. factory overheads, 87. works, 88. Allocation, 89. Apportionment, 90. fixed/variable, 91. absorption, 92. labour, 93. over, 94. under, 95. under, 96. costing profit and loss account, 97. under, 98. allocation, 99. job, 100. contractors, 101. notional profit, 102. costing profit and loss, 103. cost plus contract, 104. escalation, 105. contract, 106. long, 107. fixed price, 108. highly specialised, 109. price-cost, 110. subsequent-preceding, 111. higher, 112. government, 113. certified, 114. architects, 115. security, 116. inputs, 117. $1/3 \times \text{Notional Profit} \times \frac{\text{Cash Received}}{\text{Work Certified}}$, 118. 87%, 119. contract, 120. ₹ 54,000, 121. product, 122. accumulated 123. process, 124. scrap, 125. material, 126. processes, 127. continuous, 128. cost centre, 129. stock, 130. product, 131. same, 132. Normal, 133. estimate, 134. unavoidable, 135. costing profit and loss, 136. normal wastage, 137. greater, 138. not, 139. process-job, 140. input, 141. normal, 142. services, 143. insurance-taxes, 144. log book, 145. per passenger per kilometer, 146. simple, 147. standing charges, maintenance charges and running charges, 148. 33 1/3%,149. Service, 150. operating, 151. intangible, 152. number of kilometers, 153. ₹ 5, 154. fixed, 155. operation, 156. efficiency, 157. small, 158. service-manufacturing, 159. operating, 160. annexure, 161. fines, 162. cost auditor, 163. law board, 164. cost auditor, 165. cost, 166. cost, 167. pre-determined, 168. compulsory, 169. Cost, 170. tax.

***

BIBLIOGRAPHY

1. Advanced Cost Accountancy by S. P. Jain and Narong.

2. Cost Accounting by S. N. Maheshwari.

3. Cost Accounting by Ratnam.

4. Practice in Advanced Costing and Management Accounting by Prof. Subhash Jagtap.

5. Cost Accounting - Bhatta HSM, Himalaya Publication.

6. Cost Accounting - Prabhu Dev. Himalaya Publication.

7. Advanced Cost Accounting - Made Gowda, Himalaya Publication.

8. Cost Accounting Principles and Practice by M. N. Arora.

***

OCTOBER 2014

B.B.A. (Semester - II)
Basics of Cost Accounting
(New 2013 Pattern)

Time: 3 Hours   Max. Marks: 80

Instructions to the candidates:
1. All questions are compulsory.
2. Figures to the right indicate full marks.
3. Use of calculator is allowed.

1. (a) Fill in the blanks (Any Five) :   [5]
   - (i) Prime Cost + Factory Overheads
   - (ii) Cost Audit is the part of ......
   - (iii) Administration Costs are mostly ......
   - (iv) ...... is also known as service costing.
   - (v) At B.E.P. Fixed Cost is equal to ......
   - (vi) Cost Accounting system is evolved from ......

   (b) State which are the following statements are true or false (Any Five):   [5]
   - (i) Cotton waste used in Factory workshop is the example of Indirect Material.
   - (ii) In case of job costing, each Job is considered to be a distinct cost unit.
   - (iii) Profit on every contract is computed only when the contract is complete.
   - (iv) Normal and abnormal losses do not co-exist in process costing.
   - (v) Operating costing is the method of ascertaining cost of service rendered by a service organisation.
   - (vi) Cost Accounting is historic in nature.

2. Explain advantages of cost accounting.   [15]

OR

Define cost accounting? Explain limitations of cost accounting.

3. Write short notes (Any Three):   [15]
   - (a) Cost Center   (b) Elements of Cost
   - (c) Limitations of Job Costing   (d) Abnormal gain
   - (e) Work in Progress.

4. The Amul Products Ltd. produced 1000 completed units of products A during the month ended 31st March 1999 and the following Figures were available for the year. [16]

Particulars	₹
Opening stock 31-3-1999 (200 units)	36,000
Closing stock on 31-3-1999 (400 units)	72,000
Opening stock of Raw Materials	6,000
Purchase of Raw Materials	34,000
Sale of Scrap	2,000
Rent, Rates (Factory)	4,800
(Office)	4,400
Depreciation of Plant	400
Bad Debts	800
Advertising	4,800
Agent's Commission	6,000
Delivery Van Expenses	1,200
Salesman's Salary	4,000
Sales	2,08,000
Advance Income Tax	24,000
Direct Wages	48,000
Indirect Wages	1,200
Power	18,000
Carriage Inward	1,200
Closing stock of Raw Materials	5,200
Direct Expenses	24,000
Lighting (Factory)	1,600
(Office)	2,000
Insurance (Factory)	1,200
(Office)	1,600
Indirect Material	3,200
Repairs of Machinery	800
Supervision (Factory)	5,600
(Office)	2,000
Work in Progress (1-3-1999)	4,800
Work in Progress (31-3-1999)	6,000
Office Salaries	18,400
Sundry Expenses	3,600
Repairs to office buildings	800
Depreciation to buildings	1,200
Carriage Outward	800
Travelling Expenses	2,400
Counting house salaries	2,000
Drawing Office Salaries	2,000

Prepare a Statement of Cost showing
(a) Cost of Material consumed
(b) Prime Cost
(c) Factory Cost
(d) Cost of Production
(e) Cost of goods sold
(f) Cost of Sales
(g) Profit

5. (a) From the following information relating to Mauli Ltd. prepare a cash Budget for half year ended 30-6-2008. [12]

Months 2008	Materials ₹	Selling ₹	Works Overhead	Wages	Office Expenses	Sales
January	25,000	4,000	6,000	10,040	1,500	72,000
February	31,000	5,000	6,300	12,190	1,700	97,000
March	25,500	5,500	6,000	10,620	2,000	86,000
April	30,600	6,700	6,500	25,042	2,200	88,600
May	37,000	8,500	8,000	22,075	2,500	1,02,500
June	38,800	9,000	8,200	23,039	2,500	1,08,700

The Cash Balance on 1-1-2007 is ₹ 2,500. Assume that 50% of the total sales are cash sales. Assets are too acquired in the month of Feb. and April. Hence provision should be made for the payment of ₹ 8,000 and ₹ 25,000 respectively for the same. An application has been made to the bank for the grant of loan of ₹ 30,000 and it is also anticipated that a dividend of ₹ 35,000 will be paid in June. Debtors are allowed one month credits whereas creditors, for goods or overheads, grant months credit. Sales commission 3% on total sales is to be paid in the same month.

(b) From the following find out [12]
(i) P/V Ratio, (ii) Break even point, (iii) MOS.
Total variable cost = 10 per unit
Selling price per unit = ₹ 25.
Fixed cost ₹ 6,000.
Sales ₹ 1,000 units.

OR

(b) From the following data, calculate [12]
(i) Material Cost Variance.
(ii) Material Price Variance.
(iii) Material Usage Variance.
Stock of Raw Material as on 01/06/2012 - nil
Stock of Raw Material as on 30/06/2012 - 2000 units
Standard quantity - 100 units
Standard rate of Material per unit - ₹ 2.50.
Actual quantity purchased - 20000 units.
Total Cost incurred for Material used ₹ 3000.
Production 200 Finished Units.

***

APRIL 2015

B.B.A. (Semester - II)
Basics of Cost Accounting
(New 2013 Pattern)

Time: 3 Hours   Max. Marks: 80

Instructions to the candidates:
1. All questions are compulsory.
2. Figures to the right indicate full marks.
3. Use of calculator is allowed.

Q. 1 (a) Fill in the blanks (Any five): [5]
  (i) The aggregate of Factory Cost and Administration overheads is known as ....
  (ii) ...... is also known as service costing.
  (iii) Carriage outward is an example of ...... overheads.
  (iv) In case of ...... costing, cost is ascertained for each job.
  (v) The prime cost includes all ...... costs.
  (vi) Abnormal losses are charged to ......

(b) State whether following statements are true or false (Any Five): [5]
  (i) Cost Accounting is an expensive system of Accounting.
  (ii) Contract costing is applicable for small jobs of short duration.
  (iii) Cost Audit is compulsory for all companies.
  (iv) Process costing is applicable to service Industry.
  (v) Motive power is an example of Factory overheads.
  (vi) Income Tax paid is not recorded in cost sheet.

Q. 2 Define the term cost Accounting. State the advantages and disadvantages of cost Accounting. [15]

OR

Define the term overheads and explain the steps for distribution of overheads.

Q. 3 Write short notes (Any Three): [15]
  (a) Cost Unit
  (b) Limitations of Financial Accounting
  (c) Contract Costing
  (d) Cost Audit
  (e) Abnormal Loss.

Basics of Cost Accounting   P.2   April 2015

Q. 4 The following information has been obtained from the books of M/S Omprakash Ltd. for the year ended 31-3-2014. [16]

Particulars	₹
Stock on 1-4-13	
– Raw materials	75,000
– Work-in-progress	22,000
– Finished Goods	50,000
Stock on 31-3-14	
– Raw Materials	55,000
– Work-in-progress	27,000
– Finished Goods	45,000
Carriage Outward	18,000
Legal Charges	15,000
Works Repaires	8,000
Bad Debts	3,500
Purchase of raw material	1,85,000
Productive wages	75,000
General Expenses	12,000
Motive Power	32,000
Salesman's Salary	26,000
Printing and stationery	14,000
Royalty	20,000
Sales 6,00,000	
Factory Rent	25,000
Warehouse Rent	30,000
Directors Fees	35,000
Consumable stores	10,000

Prepare cost Sheet and show the following:
(a) Cost of Raw Material consumed
(b) Prime cost
(c) Factory Cost
(d) Cost of production
(e) Total cost
(f) Net Profit

Q. 5 (a) The following are the particulars relating to a contract which has began on 1st January, 2014. [12]

Particulars	₹
Contract price	5,00,000
Machinery purchased	30,000
Materials issued	1,70,600
Wages paid	1,48,750

Basics of Cost Accounting   P.3   April 2015

Direct Expenses	6,330
Cash received	3,51,000
Value of work certified	3,80,000
Outstanding wages	5,380
Work uncertified	19,000
Overheads	8,240
Material returned to stores	1,400
Material at site 31-12-14	3,900
Machinery at site 31-12-14	22,000

Prepare the contract Account and Contractee's Account for the year 2014.

(b) From the following information relating to the vehicle of Om Transport, Pune calculate the cost per running kilometre. [12]

Particulars	₹
Cost of Vehicle	1,50,000
Road License (Annual)	7,500
Insurance (Annual)	4,000
Garage rent (Annual)	5,000
Supervision and salaries (Annual)	12,000
Interest and other charges (Annual)	2,500
Wages to Driver (Annual)	8,000

Cost of petrol per litre ₹ 30 repairs and maintenance per km ₹ 4 kilometre run per litre 150 kms kilometre run annually 6000 kms estimated life of the vehicle 75,000. OR

(b) Product Y is obtained after it passes through three distinct process, you are required to prepare process accounts showing the total cost & cost per unit of each process from the following information

Items	Process		
	I ₹	II ₹	III ₹
Materials	5,200	3,960	5,924
Wages	4,000	6,000	8,000

Production overheads ₹ 18,000 to be apportioned on 100% of wages 1000 units @ ₹ 6 per unit were introduced in process I.

Actual Output	Unit	Normal Loss	Value of Scrap per unit ₹
Process I	950	5%	4
Process II	840	10%	8
Process III	750	15%	10

***

www.ingramcontent.com/pod-product-compliance
Lightning Source LLC
Chambersburg PA
CBHW062133160426
43191CB00013B/2288